SEEING THE UNSEEN

SEEING THE UNSEEN

Revised and Updated

Preparing Yourself for Spiritual Warfare

SEEING THE UNSEEN

JOE BEAM

Our purpose at Howard Publishing is to:

- *Increase faith* in the hearts of growing Christians
- *Inspire holiness* in the lives of believers
- *Instill hope* in the hearts of struggling people everywhere

Because He's coming again!

Printed in the United States of America

Published by Howard Publishing Co., Inc.
3117 North 7th Street, West Monroe, Louisiana 71291-2227

Library of Congress Cataloging-in-Publication Data
Beam, Joe.
Seeing the unseen : preparing yourself for spiritual warfare / Joe Beam.—Rev. and updated.
p. cm.
Includes bibliographical references.
ISBN 1-58229-139-X
1. Spiritual warfare. 2. Devil. I. Title.

BV4509.5 .B43 2000
235'.4—dc21 00-061367

Interior design by Stephanie Denney
Edited by Philis Boultinghouse

For my wife, Alice

If it had not been for her
unquenchable love,
I surely would have lost
my spiritual war.

For though we live in the world, we do not wage war as the world does. The weapons we fight with are not the weapons of the world. On the contrary, they have divine power to demolish strongholds. We demolish arguments and every pretension that sets itself up against the knowledge of God, and we take captive every thought to make it obedient to Christ.

2 Corinthians 10:3–5

CONTENTS

SECTION 4: FORCES AT WORK FOR US

Acknowledgments

Whom do I thank for helping me turn my studies into a book? Certainly, I thank God. After all, every truth in this book came from Him. And I thank the churches who have invited me to present this material across the United States and Canada. They are responsible for prodding me to study this great war in depth. My studies for the first edition of this book began to take organized form when Dan Dozier, a minister for the Madison Church of Christ in Nashville, Tennessee, invited me to present three one-hour lectures to the thousands of Christians who attended the Nashville Jubilee. As the videotapes of those lectures spread across the continent, I received many requests to come share the message in person. Because I was unable to visit all the churches who invited me, several suggested that I write a book on the subject; thus, the first writings for this book began.

I also owe a debt of gratitude to several people who helped make this book a reality.

Gary Myers of Howard Publishing saw the vision of what could be done for God through this book and made the rest of us believe it.

Jonie Craig of Irvine, California, read the early manuscripts of the first edition and became my teacher. Using her great talent, she added her creative touches to my dull words in an effort to teach me how to write.

No, she hasn't finished teaching me, but she has taught me enough that this book is much better than it would have been without her input and help.

Dwight Lawson is a very intelligent young preacher who also happens to be my wife's nephew. He contributed immeasurably to my study of spiritual warfare through his extensive research, his challenging questions, and his openness to reading the Word without prejudice.

Philis Boultinghouse proved to be the editor I hoped she would be. She challenged my statements. She reorganized my material, making points stronger and clearer. She recast sentences to make them more understandable. Utterly unafraid of critiquing my writing, she did her job well and without hesitation. Throughout the process, she also showed me great compassion and patience. She is a true professional who does her job with quality and excellence. I in no way want you to think that she's responsible for anything I've written, but I do want you to know she made what I've said 100-percent better by her editing.

My wife, Alice, and my children, Angela, Joanna, and Kimberly, put as much into both the first and second edition of this book as I did. They avoided me when I wrote, understood when I arrived late for meals, and forgave me for lost nights of fun family activities. My wonderful family made the sacrifice for the same reason I did. We all want lives to be changed by *Seeing the Unseen.*

May God use this book for His glory and our victory.

Introduction

You would think that by now we would know enough about science to eradicate superstitious beliefs, especially beliefs in invisible entities flittering around us. There is no logical reason for believing in such nonsense, unless, of course, there really are unseen beings hovering around us, beyond the reach of current scientific measurement. Remember, it was eons before scientists detected germs, atoms, or molecules, but they existed just the same.

Several years ago, I made a rational study leading me to the decision that God exists, that Jesus is His Son, and that the Bible is a supernatural book that could only come from God. I believe what God says through His Bible, and my occasional human doubts don't erode that conviction.

The Bible clearly teaches the existence of things we cannot see. Several passages in the Scriptures teach that there are invisible beings. Here are two examples: "Now faith is being sure of what we hope for and *certain of what we do not see"* (Hebrews 11:1). Speaking of Jesus, Paul said, "He is the image of the *invisible* God, the firstborn over all creation. For by him all things were created: things in heaven and on earth, *visible and invisible,* whether thrones or powers or rulers or authorities; all things were created by him and for him" (Colossians 1:15–16).

I believe that beings roam the earth today who are altogether spiritual. I mean "spiritual" in the sense that they don't have corporal bodies—the kind of beings Jesus referred to when He said, "A ghost does not have flesh and bones" (Luke 24:39). The koine Greek word translated in the New International Version as "ghost" is the same word translated as "spirit" throughout the New Testament. It refers to beings who exist only as spirits, without physical bodies.

Do such creatures exist? In the passage from Colossians just mentioned, Paul said there are things visible and invisible. Then he immediately said, "whether thrones or powers or rulers or authorities." The verse plainly states that invisible thrones, powers, rulers, and authorities exist. They are in the world today, and they are working powerfully in our daily lives.

WHAT YOU'LL FIND IN THIS BOOK

This book exposes invisible authorities and powers and illustrates how various spiritual forces work against us, within us, and for us. But this book is not a collection of scary stories of exorcisms and wild speculations about Satan and his angels. The unprovable, often unbiblical, misleading speculations on this subject don't help Christians win the spiritual war; they aid and abet Satan. Those believing the wildly sensational are so busy looking for a demon under every bush that they unwittingly expose themselves to the real attacks of satanic forces, which come unseen from seemingly innocent sources and hit them on the blind side. On the other hand, those who reject sensationalism often reject the reality of the spiritual war that sensationalism masks. Rejecting the foolish, they also reject the wise. The devil becomes a cartoon character not to be feared but to be ignored, having no more power or substance than the goblins of children's dreams.

This book gives the Bible a position preeminent to any speculation or opinion. In this book, we will study Scriptures about Satan, angels, demons, the dead, and much more. We will discuss openly the roles of angels, both good and bad, and of the demons working for the most evil angel of all.

In this revised version of *Seeing the Unseen,* you will find new chapters on the subject of demons, reflecting my recent findings, and many other rewritten portions throughout the book. This book will also share the stories of many people—any one of whom may reflect you almost perfectly and give you insight into yourself and your circumstances that will change you forever. No, not stories of supernatural occurrences, but stories of real people facing real life with all its complications and frustrating puzzles. While I will always tell you the true core of each story, many names and other details will be altered. Sometimes I will blend two stories into one when they fit well without damaging either. My purpose in altering these stories is to protect identities and to ensure privacy. I have no right to bring more harm or pain to anyone, including myself, and especially my family. When both first and last names are used, you will know that the names and the stories are not disguised; they are told just as they happened. While it's true that anecdotal evidence proves nothing, the common threads of these lives weave a tapestry of revelation and conviction.

To make this study about spiritual warfare easier, this book is divided into four sections:

- Learning to See the Unseen
- The Forces at Work against Us
- The Forces at Work within Us
- The Forces at Work for Us

Each section is important and each relates to the other. I suggest you start at the beginning and read the chapters in order, making notes in the margins and writing questions that come to mind.

SPIRITUAL WARFARE IS REAL

The real battle of evil is not against ghosts or demonic possession; it is within ourselves. The primary tool of Satan is not possession; it is deception. He deceives us into believing that he is not real.

While each one of us is very much responsible for our own actions, unseen beings do influence us, either for good or for bad. And because their influence is so powerful, it is imperative that we understand who they are and what they do. Only then will we be at a vantage point to accept or reject their subtle, or not-so-subtle, guidance.

Satan *is* real, and there *are* angels around us. If you believe the Bible is true, you must believe in spiritual warfare.

I pray for you an enlightening and profitable reading. May God bless you as you study.

SECTION

1

LEARNING TO SEE THE UNSEEN

SEEING THE UNSEEN

CHAPTER ONE

What Is Spiritual Vision?

Slapping some sense into her wasn't an option, so I just sat there, drenched in frustration. No matter how hard I tried to help her see it, she couldn't believe she was sinning.

"How can you say I shouldn't see him again?" she asked incredulously. "God sent him to me."

"Then why are you here? If there isn't an awareness deep within you that you are doing wrong, why did you come to me about this?" I struggled to pierce her barricade.

"I don't know why I'm here, but I know God sent him to me, and I know that God wants me to be with him."

He was married, an alcoholic, and habitually unemployed. She was lonely and longing. Those filters distorted her clear-sightedness, and all she could see was his handsomeness, his charm, and that he wanted her more than anything or anyone. He appeared at just the right time, saying just the right words, and filling just the right needs. Since she had been praying for precisely those things, she was convinced, without doubt, that God had sent him. When he divorced his wife, they would live happily ever after, praising God for the introduction.

As I listened, I felt it again, that same desire I've felt so many other times. "God, if You ever offer me one gift like You did to Solomon, I know what I want. Give me the ability to lay hands on people to give them supernatural vision. God, I want to be able to make people see the unseen."

If I'd had that gift that day, I would have walked around my desk, placed my hands on Charlotte, and prayed, "God, for the next week open her eyes to the unseen spirit world. Make visible to her every angel, demon, or spirit who comes into her presence. Don't let them hide from her or disguise themselves. Make them plain." Then I would have sent her out to see the "shining knight" who had come to rescue her from her loneliness.

She would have come back.

Terrified.

She would have seen the spirits escorting this man, and she would have fled, screaming for deliverance. Because she was not yet completely corrupt, she would have been repulsed by the sight and nearness of the evil ones leading her into this trap.

But as it was, she did not see. They offered her a lie; she bought it altogether. The lie was leading to a disaster in her life and the lives of everyone who would be touched by their sin.

SPIRITUAL VISION = DISCERNMENT + BIBLE KNOWLEDGE

I didn't have the gift of imparting spiritual vision that day, and God hasn't given it to me since. In fact, no one has it. But He has given His people the *ability to discern good and evil and the ability to understand His Word.* And well used, these two abilities can accomplish the same things as the gift I begged for. God has not left us defenseless against the attack of the evil ones, nor has He allowed them any advantage. He has made sure the vantage is ours. But, tragically, it is an advantage seldom used.

Charlotte didn't use it. She refused to discern good from evil, and she refused to listen to those who did. She refused to see the truth. Her knight kept his sheen until she married him. It lasted less than a year. Now Charlotte is lonely and longing again, but this time, she has an added bitterness that makes it likely she will be lonely forever. Spiritual men are repelled by her malignant aura. Deplorably, the hunters who stalk carnal pleasure aren't repulsed by it at all; they read it well and are drawn to her. Her angry isolation identifies her as an easy prey for seduction.

The evil ones do their job well.

CHOOSE TO SEE

Charlotte could have seen what was happening if she had chosen to. All of us can. God has warned us of every trick, every deception, and every power that stands against us, and He has given us the knowledge to see through the deceptions and to overcome. These spiritual weapons are revealed in the Scriptures, but they are so often neglected that, for many Christians, the weapons are rusty or misused or laid aside where they can't be found.

And that leaves those Christians exposed to terrible spiritual assault.

Without the awareness of which urgings are from evil beings and which nudges are from good beings, you may find yourself in situations without the wisdom you need to make right decisions.

You are the only barrier that cannot be overcome in opening your eyes to the unseen. If you refuse to see it, nothing I write will make any difference. You must open yourself to the truth of God, and you must allow His truth to become part of who you are and how you live. *Just* knowing about spiritual matters doesn't make you a powerful soldier in the spiritual war, and *just* being aware of Satan's attacks won't prevent their success. But victory is possible when you use the weapons God makes available to you. Spiritual war is an active, not passive, process.

WHAT WOULD YOU SEE?

If God opened your eyes to see all the spiritual beings around you for the next week, what would you see?

For example, are you going someplace where God's angels would be out of place, but where Satan's angels feel right at home? Look around when you get there, and think about who's present—both seen and unseen.

Are you planning to do something that neither God nor His angels will benevolently watch? Whatever you do, you will be seen. The question is, what kind of beings will be smiling as they watch your actions? If God's angels aren't happily smiling on you, Satan's angels are malevolently grinning as you carry out your plan.

Be open with yourself. Are you involved in a relationship you know isn't right? Do you have feelings of hatred, jealousy, or resentment toward a fellow human being? Are you an agent of gossip? Is your life guided by greed? Have you been lulled into complacency and inaction?

The next time you sense one of these or any other sin rearing its head in your heart and life, look around you and ask yourself, "What kinds of beings could I see here right now if God opened my eyes? Who's helping me in this?"

Whatever you are doing or planning to do, continually ask yourself, "What would I see if God gave me the gift of seeing the unseen?"

The truth may terrify you.

Or it may give you great peace.

It's time you learn to discern the invisible power of good and evil and to release the greatest power of all—the power of God—to work in you.

Read on if you are ready to see the unseen.

CHAPTER TWO

What Is Satan's Master Strategy for Destruction?

She might have been described as pretty, except that the word is seldom used to portray the dead. I find it unpleasant to be in the presence of the dead, even pretty ones, and all the more so when the dead person is speaking to me.

We were sitting in a restaurant, sipping coffee politely, being ignored by the other patrons who were enjoying living. Though still breathing, her heart beating within her, Jane was as dead as if she were wearing a shroud. She spoke of the child in her womb—the first to have been there in her forty years—without warmth or love, just detachment. Smiling vacantly, looking past me, she told her story in a voice I could have vanquished with a whisper.

"My husband's happy. All these years he's wanted a child, and now I'm pregnant. I don't want to destroy him.... I've decided not to tell him the child isn't his."

Because of the timing of the conception, she was positive the child was her lover's. He wasn't her first lover, but she was as in love with him as she could ever be with anyone, at least as much as with the lovers who had preceded him. Parts of the story were routine. Any counselor could have told it for her, missing few of the details. She had married young, escaping an unhappy childhood home. Not really in love with the man who proposed, but craving deliverance, she convinced herself he was God's blessing and the answer to her prayers, so she said yes.

The first lover had come within a year.

Other lovers followed, but no one, especially her husband, had ever known. The single exception was her closest friend at the time of each affair. Since each liaison had happened while she lived somewhere new, she always had a new best friend with whom to share. Sometimes it was someone from church, sometimes someone from work, depending on where she lived and whom she felt she could trust at the time. Her current best friend was from her church, and it was she who insisted that Jane see me.

I asked Jane about her view of God, Jesus, the church, and many other things we Christians hold dear. Then I asked her about her commitment to her Christianity. How could Jesus be the Lord of her life if she continued to go from one sinful relationship to another? And how could she possibly justify the decision she was unemotionally revealing? She planned to leave her husband and marry her lover, just as soon as he divorced his wife. Finally, in exasperation because she felt no guilt or shame for any of her sins, I asked, "What do you think would happen if this building split open right now and Jesus stood in the sky, ready to pronounce judgment? What do you believe He'd say to you?" In the same lifeless, quiet voice, she replied, "He'd say, 'I understand. It's okay. I just want you to be happy.'"

THE ESSENCE OF SPIRITUAL WAR

Jane's story illustrates what spiritual warfare is all about: *It's a battle of the mind and heart.* God gives light and truth; Satan tries his best to cloud light and truth with darkness and lies. His primary tool is deception, convincing human beings that the lies they believe are the truth—even the truth of God Himself. Some momentarily buy the lies, but in their hearts they want truth. Others live in lies permanently because they can no longer face the truth. The consequences are terrifying. To those in Bible times who desperately wanted to believe the lies glittering with false promises, God gave this terrifying counsel: "They perish because they refused to love the truth and so be saved. For this reason God sends them a powerful delusion so that they will believe the lie and so that all will be condemned who have not believed the truth but have delighted in wickedness" (2 Thessalonians 2:10–12).

Paul uses this verse to apply to a specific lie, but the truthfulness of the principle is universal. If you really want to buy the lies that Satan sells, God will not stop you: He will even speed you on your way.

Before you panic, note that Paul isn't saying that God despairs of and rids Himself of one who still cares about the difference between truth and lies. He's not writing about those who struggle. Destruction only comes to those who don't love truth. There is a difference between those who love truth but are temporarily deluded and those who refuse to love truth at all.

The very essence of spiritual warfare is lies versus truth. Satan and his angels go all out to get you to love their lies more than you love the truth of God. Since they can't *make* you do that, or make you do anything else for that matter, they try to find some way to delude you. They wage war to confuse your mind and capture your heart.

SATAN'S MASTER STRATEGY

Ephesians 4:18–19 reveals Satan's strategy for destruction. Describing the Gentiles who were captured by satanic forces, Paul writes, "They are darkened in their understanding and separated from the life of God because of the ignorance that is in them due to the hardening of their hearts. Having lost all sensitivity, they have given themselves over to sensuality so as to indulge in every kind of impurity, with a continual lust for more."

Follow the logical progression: Darkened understanding leads to a hardened heart; a hardened heart leads to lost sensitivity and an immersion in sensuality. (This is not a "good sensuality" but one that indulges itself in every kind of impurity with a continual lust for more.) Reaching this point, the lie is believed. Having no communion with God, spiritual destruction results.

See the strategy? The steps usually come in the following order:

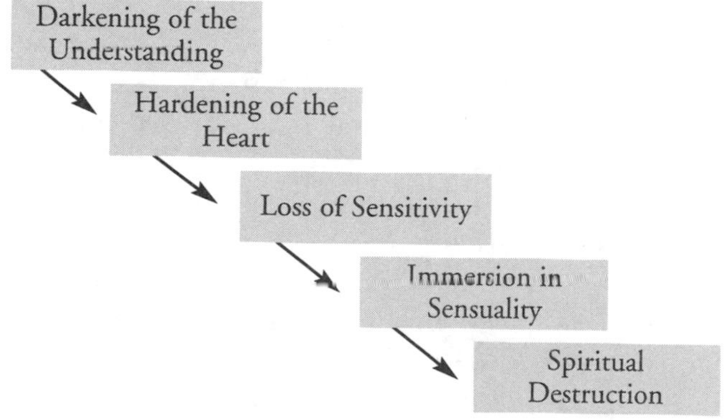

It's a simple strategy, and it's just as effective now as it has been throughout the history of the world. On this master template, Satan overlays varying substrategies to mislead, confuse, deter, manipulate, and deceive, as I will show you throughout this book.

Let's take a closer look at this terrifying master strategy.

1. Darkening of the Understanding

It's easy for us to see that darkness is dangerous. We wouldn't willingly walk down a lonely, dark city street, hugging the alleys and walking in the shadows. We want to be in the brightest available light, where there is safety and protection. If someone calls to us from the shadows, we are not easily persuaded to investigate. Things seen in the darkness are murky, fuzzy, and, on close inspection, quite different than when seen in the bright light of day. We don't trust the darkness; we want the light.

Paul uses the word *darkened* to describe what happens to the understanding. *Understanding* refers to intellectual reasoning. Satan's goal is to confuse the understanding and fog the reasoning. He uses darkness to distort the truth.

Jane is a perfect example of how this strategy works.

Did you discern the lie Jane bought? It's a prevalent lie in the world today—the one that assures us that love (as defined by the lies of Satan) is the texture of life.

Believing the lie was easy for Jane. No one wants to live without love, and it well may be that no one can live without love. But what Jane sought as "love" wasn't love at all. Passion, romance, and all the intensity accompanying those emotions are ecstasy. We savor the experience, but passion and love aren't equal. Passion is one facet of love, but love isn't always a part of passion.

Real love, even in the terms of modern psychology, is comprised of trust, concern, honesty, friendship, and respect. These qualities were the things that Jane really wanted, but she confused sparkle with substance and found it impossible to grasp the glitter. You see, sparkle wasn't the object of Jane's continuing search for the meaning of life. She was searching for the things she didn't get growing up. The tragedy is that those were the very things her husband wanted to give her, but Jane couldn't see. The lie she believed blinded her. She had somehow learned to equate passion with love and was now on a never-ending quest, for no passionate relationship remains intensely passionate forever. Even the added thrill of clandestine meetings with stolen, furtive moments can't keep the emotion at a peak indefinitely. Eventually, every relationship has either to wither and die or to grow into real love, complete with the intangibles of trust, honesty, concern, friendship, and respect.

For Jane, love is passion; she is fruitlessly searching for an unending supply. Satan's lie leads her from one man to another as long as men will have her.

Shadows. That's what they are. Jane could see the truth if she would only turn on the light.

2. Hardening of the Heart

After darkening the understanding, Satan's second step is to harden the heart. The difference in the understanding and the heart is a subtle one. People in the first century didn't use the word *heart* to mean what it means to us today; to them it was not primarily emotion. They used heart more in the sense of discernment. While directly *affecting* the emotions, the heart was not the *seat* of emotion in their way of thinking. Paul warns that confusion of the intellect (darkening of the understanding) destroys the ability to discern what is right, what is best, or even the real consequences of our actions.

Because a hardened heart, according to Paul's definition, leads directly to what we think of today as a hardened heart, we do no damage to the text, and maybe even broaden our understanding, if we think of his warning in both ways. Confused thinking leads to inability to reason (or discern) correctly, and that leads to enslavement to our twisted emotions. Emotions are like that: They take you captive and lead you to abandon logic so you can have what you want at the moment.

Jane is an example of how a confused mind leads to a hardened heart. The word *hardened* in the text refers to the process of becoming petrified. What was once alive has, over time, become hard as rock. The mind and heart of anyone who pursues the wrong path long enough eventually turn into stone.

Along with the other lies, Jane also bought the lie that she could find herself only in the arms and affections of another person. Her identity existed only in the reflection of her lover's eyes. As long as a man could feel romantic love for her and demonstrate it in ways she could deeply feel, she felt worthy and valuable—at peace with herself. When a lover tired of her or began to treat her with less intensity than she needed to sustain her borrowed value, she became confused as to who she really was and why she was in this relationship. Then, in an emotional haze that she mistakenly equated with religious conviction and genuine repentance, she would quit the affair and throw herself headlong into her church. Unable to stand contact with her lover any longer, she would soon convince her husband to transfer to another city, effectively ending the affair. When her beauty and need advertised her availability, the next candidate would appear, and the cycle began again.

Her husband never had a chance. No person can maintain his or her own identity while being essential to the identity of another. Neither her husband nor any lover could do it for long.

Finally, Jane bought the largest lie of all: God would accept anything she did with kind benevolence because, above all else, He wanted her happy. Jane's darkened understanding led to the hardening of her heart. She was totally self-absorbed, and even God couldn't convince her that she was wrong. In her mind, He became part of her sin.

3. Loss of Sensitivity

As Paul wrote in Ephesians 4:19, "Having lost all sensitivity, they have given themselves over to sensuality so as to indulge in every kind of impurity, with a continual lust for more." That's what sin does for you. Accept it into your life, and it will eventually take control. Live in sin long enough for it to harden your heart, and you can no longer feel natural emotions, such as the ability to mourn. Selfless emotions directed toward others are replaced by selfish emotions directed only inward. Sensitive people can cry for others. Though mourning can still occur with a hardened heart, it is not for the person lost, it is for the personal loss felt because the other person is no longer there. That is what sin does to you.

This is not to say that sin is unemotional. But, over time, the intensity of the emotion must increase because the emotion is absorbed and consumed, dying within the sinner.

4. Immersion in Sensuality

Paul describes this immersion in sensuality as an indulgence in every kind of immorality with a continual lust for more. The petrified heart is insatiable, craving more sin, more often, with more selfishness. If the sin is an affair, as it was with Jane, the lover will eventually be unable to sustain the demands. He will feel trapped and depleted and will want deliverance from the vacuum siphoning him from himself. The sin consumes itself as it devours its victims. Needing more but having no source, the sinner is forced to search for, and always finds, new sins that are stronger and more demanding.

Heavy words, aren't they? I simply write from experience—not only my own but also the experiences of those who share their stories with me.

5. Spiritual Destruction

While studying clinical psychology in graduate school several years ago, I ran across a photo in one of my textbooks of a young heroin addict that perfectly illustrated sin's addictive power. To satisfy his need, he had collapsed every vein in his arms, then his legs, and finally, through the course of depleting all other available spots, he had found the last. He lay in a doorway, dead, the hypodermic needle still in his tongue. It was an unpleasant yet graphic picture, showing the end of every addictive sin.

Not only are alcohol and drugs addictive; all sin is addictive. That same self-destructive behavior exists in all who allow the devil to deceive them to the point of having petrified hearts—no matter which route of temptation and sin they take. The end is spiritual destruction.

CHRISTIANS AREN'T IMMUNE

How could anyone ever go that far? Who would choose to believe a lie leading to ultimate destruction? If you don't arm yourself against the devil's schemes, you could be overcome by his attacks.

If you are a Christian, you may read the preceding paragraph with smug denial. After all, don't you have security as a believer? Yes. There is ample security in Christ for those who love and commit themselves to Him. Security in Christ, however, does not mean that evil has no access to us. The tempter brings alluring attacks against each child of God. He watches, looking for ways to destroy our faith and our relationship with Jesus, or, at the very least, our productivity. If he cannot lure us into forfeiting our souls, he devises intricate schemes to cripple us spiritually, making us useless in God's army.

From the master template in Ephesians 4, you see that evil forces will try to confuse your understanding. If they cause you to question truth, they have a much greater chance of corrupting your reasoning and hardening your heart. They then move you toward self-absorption so that you view everything from the context of your desires rather than what is right before God. Eventually, they corrupt you so you no longer care for anything but your own self-indulgence.

How do these beings cause you to question truth? There are hundreds of ways. I'll give you a few examples.

Some scientists ridicule the Bible, and many, even in the church, allow that ridicule to make them distrust the Scriptures. Some psychologists ridicule the morality the Bible teaches, and many, even Christian psychologists, no longer find anything wrong with lifestyles and actions that affront God. Some preachers ridicule Christians who try their best to be biblically grounded, and because of their visibility, these preachers lead many Christians farther from God and closer to secularism. There are any number of things, from so-called science to society's insistence on being politically correct, designed to confuse our thinking.

What lies hidden and unheralded is the fact that thousands of scientists, philosophers, psychologists, and other professionals are Bible-believing, dedicated Christians. Many highly educated scholars hold firmly to God, His Word, and His morality. We must not let ourselves be confused by the cacophony of voices trying to convince us that Christianity is moronically outdated.

In defending ourselves against the evil ones, we need to remember that the loudest and most obvious attacks aren't always the most effective. Sometimes their best attacks are, instead, quite subtle. These spirit beings confuse you by telling you that the Bible is true and that you should believe and obey it, but they suggest that the interpretation of a certain passage isn't what you've always thought. They convince you that, rather than condemning a pondered action, the passage under consideration actually allows it. This argument is especially easy to believe when you are strongly tempted to commit the act. I've seen Christians go through convoluted reasoning to justify things such as homosexuality, fornication, greed, and divorce.

The confusing of the intellect and the dulling of the reasoning come so close together that it's often hard to tell them apart.

THE APPLICATION FOR YOU

To see if Satan's forces are moving you toward destruction, ask yourself where you are on his master template. The following questions are designed to help you do that.

Remember, the template of Ephesians 4 has five stages:

1. Darkening of the understanding
2. Hardening of the heart
3. Loss of sensitivity
4. Immersion in sensuality
5. Spiritual destruction

A "yes" answer to any of the following questions may indicate that you are on the template and moving away from God and the light. Be honest with yourself. You don't have to hide anything from anyone; no one will know how you answer these questions but you...and God. Make sure you don't lie to yourself. Truth may be painful, but it's always freeing.

The Questions

1. Are you confused about what is true?
2. Have your beliefs about God, the Bible, or the meaning of Bible passages gone through major changes recently?
3. Do your new views justify doing things you once believed were wrong?
4. Are you reasoning quite differently than you did when you were at the most dedicated point of your spiritual walk with God?
5. Do things that once brought you pain or mourning now have little effect on you?
6. Is something in your life absorbing so much of your emotion that almost everyone and everything else are losing the levels of importance they once held for you?
7. Are you craving more of that something or someone which is becoming the focus of your life?

8. Is God losing His place in your life because the something or someone you are focused on is crowding Him out?
9. After you became involved with this person or thing, did your emotions about God increase for a period then gradually diminish so that you no longer feel a strong love for God?
10. Are you doing things you once thought were wrong, now wanting to do them more often, with greater intensity, and no longer think about whether they are right or wrong?

The Scoring

Questions one through three help you discover if your understanding is being darkened. If any are answered "yes," seek counsel to make sure you aren't being deceived.

Questions four through six help you see if your heart is becoming hardened and you are losing sensitivity. If you answered "yes" to any of these, seek counsel from someone who can help you discern whether you are buying a lie you very much want to believe. Your hesitancy to seek counsel may be a sign of how much you need it.

Questions seven through ten help you decide if you are becoming immersed in sensuality. I assume you aren't totally corrupted by your sin, or you wouldn't be reading this book. Before it's too late, seek spiritual counsel from someone you deeply respect as a person of God. Strong, mature, Christian intervention and prayer can still deliver you from Satan's grasp.

These aren't the only questions that can help you see whether you are being lured by Satan, but they are valuable indicators. They are keyed to the template of Ephesians 4 because I believe that particular template for temptation is one that Satan uses with many overlaying variations.

If you understand Satan's master template, then everything else in this book will make sense. Remember, first comes confusion of the intellect. Then comes the hardening of the heart.

Who does these things? We begin to answer that question in the next chapter. Then we delve deeply into the forces at work in this war.

Read on. You may find yourself.

CHAPTER THREE

What Are Angels?

Usually he came in with a grin, stretched to his full six feet four inches, handsome face tanned and glowing, strewing confidence around him like petals before a bride. But not that day. When he arrived that morning he sagged, looking bewildered, and stumbled straight into my office.

"You're not gonna believe this," he said.

Dennis Randall was my associate minister and a dear friend. He started his remarkable story by reminding me of the storm the afternoon before. Donna, his wife, had come by the church building with their children, so Dennis decided to leave work early to drive them home. To get home they had to travel down the aptly named Green River Road. Any good rain transformed it into a river with an asphalt bed and concrete beaches.

Driving slowly through the flood, Dennis spotted a man standing knee-deep in water next to a stalled car. His first thought was to drive past him because something about the guy made him uneasy, but his deep commitment to Jesus wouldn't let him. Warily, but dutifully, he stopped to ask the man if he needed assistance. The guy, an unkempt man who looked like some throwback to the 1960s hippie era, opened the door and got in.

"Where to?" Dennis asked.

"Wherever you're going," he replied in a low voice, slowly surveying Dennis, his family, and the contents of the car.

Dennis looked at the disheveled man again, thought about his reply, and decided he had just let the wrong man into their car. Why hadn't he trusted his instincts and kept going? There was obviously something different, something unusual about this guy. His apprehension shifting toward fear, Dennis found himself silently praying, "Oh, God, what have I done? Don't let him hurt my wife or my children."

Within minutes, they were through the water and onto an empty road surrounded by cornfields. Suddenly, in the middle of nowhere, the man quietly told Dennis to stop. Dennis intensified his prayer, "God, if he's going to attempt to harm us, he'll do it now where no one can see. Don't let him."

As the car stopped, the man got out and shut the door. Relieved, Dennis quickly pulled back onto the road and immediately searched out the hippie in his mirror to see what he was doing.

He was gone.

Dennis was puzzled, but he shrugged it off, thanked God for his protection, and drove home.

The next morning when he came out of his house, he found a small card under his windshield wiper with a passage of Scripture typed on it. He handed it to me. The card said, "Do not forget to entertain strangers, for by so doing some people have entertained angels without knowing it" (Hebrews 13:2).

Sitting in my office, visibly shaken, the card in his hand, Dennis looked at me and asked, "Do you think…?"

I don't know.

But I do believe it's possible. Dennis and Donna Randall, along with their three children, may have entertained an angel without realizing it.

If he was an angel, why was he here, so shabbily dressed and acting so mysteriously? Maybe it was just to show Dennis how true his faith was. Perhaps he was there as an object lesson in kindness for the children. Or maybe his riding in their car kept some terrible thing from happening. That's an interesting thing about God's angels: They are here to serve us, but most of the time we don't know who they are or what they do. They don't take on themselves the glory of explaining. That's why most people never know whether or not it was an angel who blessed their lives; just like Dennis can never know for sure if his hippie was an angel.

God didn't put angels here so they could get the praise; our praise and thankfulness should always go to Him. The angels have that straight. We should get it straight too.

There is another interesting aspect to Dennis's story.

I called him to see if I could use the incident for this book and also to make sure I was telling the story as it happened, that my memory hadn't embellished it over time. He said I had it right then added this postscript: "You know how I keep everything, Joe. Well, I've searched for the card that was on my windshield, wanting to examine it again, to read that Scripture once more to see if I could find a clue. Funny thing, it's disappeared…just one more mystery to add to the mystery."

Dennis is glad he stopped to help the stranger.

ANGELS ARE AMONG US

There was a time in my biblical studies when I argued that angels had left the earth a couple of thousand years ago and weren't around anymore. Now, in light of all the Scriptures that speak of angels' activities, it seems far-fetched to believe they are gone; but at that time I accepted without much question what I had been taught by others.

Today, I feel differently. After studying spiritual warfare for many years, I believe angels, both good and bad, are active and often present. Sometimes they even allow themselves to be seen, but most of the time, if not all the time, those who see angels don't know what they've seen.

If you want to conduct a deep study about angels, the best reference I have found is *A Study of Angels* by Edward Myers, Ph.D.[1] Myers presents a scholarly study that carries you into the Scriptures and that requires concentration—hardly a gentle bedside book. I strongly recommend it to every serious Bible student who wants to know more about angels. It's also a great study guide for a church class.

Because Myers does such a thorough job, I feel it redundant to tell you everything I have learned or know about angels. But there are a few things about angels that need to be pointed out in this book. I can't discuss the unseen world of spiritual beings (good angels, Satan, evil angels, and demons) without giving some basic biblical information about what angels are.

The following information applies to all angels, good and bad. In later chapters I write about the difference in good and bad angels and demons.

ANGELS AREN'T LIKE PEOPLE

In comparing Jesus to angels, the Hebrew writer tells us some interesting things about angels. His emphasis is that Jesus, as the Son of God, is superior to angels; but he also says that when Jesus became a human being, He accepted a position inferior to angels (Hebrews 2:7). That passage tells us that being a human is to be lower than the angels. Angels are a lower order than deity but a higher order than man.

Our popular image of Clarence, in *It's a Wonderful Life,* trying to get his wings simply isn't valid. Angels were created to be angels (Colossians 1:16; Psalm 148); we don't become angels when we die. Humans and angels are completely separate beings.

ANGELS AREN'T LIKE GOD

Angels are *not* God; they cannot do what God does. They are servant beings made by the Most High God, and none of them was made His equal. Therefore, angels have limitations, though they aren't nearly as limited as we are.

Unlike God, angels aren't omnipotent. God is omnipotent, and He can do anything. As He phrased it, "I am the LORD, the God of all mankind. Is anything too hard for me?" (Jeremiah 32:27). Angels can't make that claim because there are things that are too hard for them. For example, they were created and do not have the power to create. In speaking of Jesus, Paul, inspired by the Holy Spirit, wrote, "For by him all things were created: things in heaven and on earth, visible and invisible, whether thrones or powers or rulers or authorities; all things were created by him and for him" (Colossians 1:16).

Notice that Jesus, along with the Father and Spirit (Genesis 1:1–2), created *everything*. Neither angels, man, nor any other thing in all creation has that power. Only God is omnipotent; only He can create.

Unlike God, angels are not omnipresent. God is everywhere (Psalm 139). God isn't limited to a specific location or a specific point in the space-time continuum. Angels are limited: they have to travel from one place to another and can only be in one place at a time. For example, Gabriel *left* heaven to visit Zechariah; he wasn't in heaven and on earth simultaneously (Luke 1:19). Angels can even be intercepted, delaying their journey. The powerful angel who visited Daniel told the prophet he would have been there sooner, but he had been delayed for twenty-one days by the prince of Persia (Daniel 10). Though a powerful angel, he was obviously limited by both location and time. No angel is ever revealed in the Bible as having God's power to transcend space and time; angels aren't omnipresent.

Unlike God, angels aren't omniscient. God knows everything (1 John 3:20); angels don't. They didn't know what the prophecies meant that they delivered to the earth, though they "long to look into these things" (1 Peter 1:12). God knows when the end of the world will come, but angels don't (Matthew 24:36). While they apparently are privileged to know more than humans, they don't know everything. They aren't omniscient.

Why make all these points about angels? Simple. Since angels aren't equal to God, worshiping them as God is sinful.

That point is important to make because of the great interest that now exists in angels. Our idealized image of beautiful, winged angels is everywhere, from tiny gold angel pins on shoulders to credit cards picturing angels to be carried in your wallet. Angels abound on calendars and postcards. There are books about angels and songs about angels. The appeal of seeing or knowing angels has sparked a multitude of lectures and workshops, many of them teaching all sorts of crazy, unbiblical ideas. For instance, one workshop teaches people how to pray to their angels. That shouldn't happen.

The words of Paul are clear and apply to today's frenzied angel seekers. "The reality, however, is found in Christ. Do not let anyone who delights in false humility and the worship of angels disqualify you for the prize. Such a person goes into great detail about what he has seen, and his unspiritual mind puffs him up with idle notions. He has lost connection with the Head" (Colossians 2:17–19).

Beware of stories told by those who claim they have had contact with angels. Listen carefully to what they say. Those who replace God with angels, either in theology or practice, have gone beyond God's clear message. Angels are servants of God, not His replacement.

WHAT ANGELS LOOK LIKE

What do angels look like? It's hard to say, because angels can appear to humans in any form they wish. Consider a few examples:

- Satan appeared to Eve as a serpent (Genesis 3).
- Angels appeared as men to Abraham and Lot (Genesis 18–19).

- An angel appeared to Moses as flames in a burning bush (Acts 7:30).
- Angels can appear as wind or flames of fire (Hebrews 1:7).
- Angels can appear as horses and chariots of fire (2 Kings 2:11; 6:17).
- Angels can be invisible until they decide to reveal themselves to humans (Numbers 22:21–34).
- Angels can also be terrifying in appearance (Daniel 10:7–11).

There are more references, but these make the point. Angels can appear in any form they wish, perfectly disguised so that humans don't know who they are. When the angels in Genesis 19 came to the city of Sodom, the Sodomites thought them mere men. If an angel decides to appear as a man, a human being cannot know he's not a man unless the angel decides to reveal himself. In Hebrews 13:2, that point is made strongly: "Do not forget to entertain strangers, for by so doing some people have entertained angels without knowing it." Dennis won't forget.

What do angels look like? Anything they want to look like. They could be right next to you and you wouldn't know. They could be a flame on a candle, the wind through the window, a snake in the tree outside, or the stranger who knocks on the door. They could even stand next to you, invisible, weapon drawn, waiting to kill you just as the angel of God invisibly waited to kill Balaam.

Would you still like to see an angel?

I have mixed feelings.

Several years ago, both *Time*[2] and *Newsweek*[3] published articles about angels. Both made a similar point: If angels are appearing to men today, why are all the experiences good ones? Shouldn't some bad encounters be reported? After all, aren't some Bible references to angelic appearances stories of frightened people who didn't like what they saw?

Both of the secular magazines saw something that many Christians seem to overlook: angels, even good ones, can be terrifying.

Daniel learned that the hard way.

Daniel certainly wasn't a coward. He knew that the penalty for praying to God was being thrown into a pit of starving predators. But Daniel didn't think twice: It was God he served, and it was God he prayed to. Any consequence would be faced with courage.

Kings hadn't scared him, spending a night in close quarters with hungry lions hadn't made him flinch; but one look at an angel, and he fainted dead away. He describes it this way, "I had no strength left, my face turned deathly pale and I was helpless" (Daniel 10:8).

He fainted.

The angel aroused him, "A hand touched me and set me trembling on my hands and knees" (v. 10). The angel didn't want to talk to Daniel while he was on all fours, so the angel told him to stand up. "When he said this to me, I stood up trembling" (v. 11). Daniel still couldn't get control of himself and later in the conversation couldn't make his mouth work. The angel touched his lips so he could speak, then Daniel said, "How can I, your servant, talk with you, my lord? My strength is gone and I can hardly breathe" (v. 17). The angel had to give Daniel strength to stand up, then he tried to soothe Daniel's fear, "'Do not be afraid, O man highly esteemed,' he said. 'Peace! Be strong now; be strong'" (v. 19).

Somehow I get a kick out of that. Daniel the lion tamer was told not once but twice, "Be strong now; be strong."

For those who long to see angels, the story in Daniel 10, as well as other biblical stories of angelic visits, should be enlightening. Think of all the stories in the Bible about humans who came into direct contact with angels who weren't disguised. How many of them were excited and happy from the first moment? Not one. It would seem that meeting an undisguised angel is a scary occurrence.

And those are the good angels!

Think about it. If an angel disguises himself, until you check it out in the next life, you'll never know for sure whether you've encountered one. If an angel doesn't disguise himself, he'll scare you so badly that, like Daniel, you'll faint.

Are you finding that angels aren't exactly as you thought? And there is much more to learn about angels that isn't in this book. A fascinating study awaits those whose curiosity has been tickled. This book is about the role of angels in spiritual warfare, both on the good and bad sides. Angels are part of that war, but not the essence of it.

To this point, I have avoided the minefields of controversy. However, to give you a sense of how angels operate and what they are, we must move into areas pockmarked with diverse theories and wild guesses, requiring some speculation and providing excellent breeding ground for debate. It is not for controversy I write these next sections, but to reveal more about angelic power. The first is the way angels communicate with us; the second is their ability to procreate.

THE TONGUES OF ANGELS

Even if you never see an angel, it doesn't mean that one hasn't communicated with you.

What?

Angels don't have to communicate through your five senses; they can communicate directly into your mind. Don't believe me? Then explain the following verses.

> The angel of God said to me in the dream, "Jacob." I answered, "Here I am." (Genesis 31:11)

> But after he had considered this, an angel of the Lord appeared to him in a dream and said, "Joseph son of David, do not be afraid to take Mary home as your wife, because what is conceived in her is from the Holy Spirit." (Matthew 1:20)

> When they had gone, an angel of the Lord appeared to Joseph in a dream. "Get up," he said, "take the child and his mother and escape to Egypt. Stay there until I tell you, for Herod is going to search for the child to kill him." (Matthew 2:13)

> After Herod died, an angel of the Lord appeared in a dream to Joseph in Egypt. (Matthew 2:19)

Though they lived centuries apart, both Jacob and Mary's husband, Joseph, received messages from God through angels who visited their dreams. If an angel communicates directly into a dream, which of the five senses does he use: hearing, sight, taste, smell, or touch? The answer is: none of the above. Dreams are thoughts, which means the angel communicated directly into the thoughts of both Jacob and Joseph.

Realizing angels can communicate into dreams or thoughts opens new vistas of possibilities, doesn't it? Will it change your outlook? It changed mine.

I once had a person ask me if he should pray only silently. He said his preacher had told him that Satan and his angels couldn't know what happened in his mind and could only know what he prayed for if he prayed vocally. To avoid Satan's intervention, the preacher said, he should never pray out loud.

No one likes eavesdroppers, especially if there is any chance the intruder could be an evil angel, but it apparently makes no difference if the prayers are vocal or silent. Remember, angels communicated into the mind of Joseph. If minds can be communicated into, they can be communicated from. With the kind of power necessary to communicate *into* someone's mind, it would be a snap to detect thoughts communicated *from* someone's mind. I think it logical to believe that angels can "hear" our thoughts, just as God "hears" them when we pray silently. Spiritual beings don't use tongues or eardrums, they connect in a purer, less physical way. Angels and other spirit beings do not have human limitations. They aren't limited by barriers of ears, eyes, and noses, unless they choose to take on human form for various time periods. Placing our fleshly constraints on them isn't logical.

If you have agreed with any of my reasoning, you may be asking yourself a disturbing question: "If angels can project their thoughts into my thoughts, how can I know when an angel is communicating with me?" Or, "How can I know which thoughts to follow and which ones to reject? After all, my thoughts may be from me, from God, or from Satan. How can I tell the difference?"

Until chapter eighteen, when I address that question more specifically, let me share one guideline with you: If any thought comes to you that is contrary to the Bible, it isn't from God. It's unimportant whether it comes from Satan, one of his angels, or your own evil desire; because if you follow that thought, you are personally responsible for your sin. What is important is that you follow only the thoughts that are holy and in harmony with God's revealed will, His Bible. Your actions come from your decisions; they are your responsibility. Angels can't take control of your mind, because any thought they place there can be accepted or rejected—by you. "But even if we or an angel from heaven should preach a gospel other than the one we preached to you, let him be eternally condemned!" (Galatians 1:8).

If the angel who preaches this other gospel is condemned, what must be the punishment of the one who believes and follows?

Reject any ungodly or evil thought.

ANGELS CAN'T PROCREATE

When God made man, He gave him the ability to make more humans. "God blessed them and said to them, 'Be fruitful and increase in number; fill the earth and subdue it'" (Genesis 1:28). We humans can procreate; we can continue the creation process by bringing more humans into God's creation. When two people have a child, they bring a new spiritual being into existence who dwells in the body of the newborn child.

Angels apparently don't have the ability to have baby angels. They were created when God, Jesus, and the Spirit made them (John 1:3; Colossians 1:16), but they apparently cannot join in union with other angels to produce more angels. When the Sadducees questioned Jesus about the next life, he said, "When the dead rise, they will neither marry nor be given in marriage; they will be like the angels in heaven" (Mark 12:25; cf. Matthew 22:30).

Was Jesus teaching that angels don't have to marry each other but can enjoy each other sexually without a marriage bond? No, that isn't likely. Throughout the Bible, God says over and over again that all people who have sex with each other are to be married to each other. Jesus is saying that angels, who are in spiritual form, do not have the *capability* of having sex and, therefore, don't get married.

That leads to an interesting thought. If having sex is a peak experience of physical love here on earth, and if angels, who are on a higher plane, do not need or are not capable of physical union, perhaps physical love-making is nothing but a vague comparison to the ecstasy of heavenly life and the nonfleshly pleasures there.

Sex is a physical thing for those in physical bodies. That is why the Bible refers to those who join themselves in sexual union as having "one flesh" or "one body." The Bible speaks of those who marry as becoming one flesh. Paul also makes it clear that sexual union makes two bodies into one whether they are married or not: "Do you not know that he who unites himself with a prostitute is one with her in body? For it is said, 'The two will become one flesh'" (1 Corinthians 6:16; cf. Genesis 2:24; Malachi 2:14–15; Matthew 19:5).

Angels don't have sexual union. Sexual union is for those in the flesh. Sexual union produces one body, one flesh—an impossibility for angels, because they don't have bodies of flesh and bone.

Often when I make the point that angels can't have sexual union with each other, someone brings up the difficult passage in Genesis 6, in which there is an apparent reference to angels having sexual union with human women. While the meaning of the passage is hotly disputed, there is an explanation of how angels could have had sexual union with women from earth and still not have the ability to have sexual union with other angels.

Read this disputed passage.

> The sons of God saw that the daughters of men were beautiful, and they married any of them they chose....
>
> The Nephilim were on the earth in those days—and also afterward—

> when the sons of God went to the daughters of men and had children by them. They were the heroes of old, men of renown.
>
> The LORD saw how great man's wickedness on the earth had become, and that every inclination of the thoughts of his heart was only evil all the time. The LORD was grieved that he had made man on the earth, and his heart was filled with pain. (Genesis 6:2, 4–6)

For many years I have argued that the "sons of God" in this passage refers to the descendants of Seth, while the "daughters of men" refers to the descendants of Cain. The intermarrying of the two lineages corrupted the world, as the good people were terribly influenced by the evil people. While I acknowledge that the phrase "sons of God" generally refers to angels, I have long believed that in this passage, it more likely refers to the righteous men who descended from Seth.

I admit that my explanation doesn't answer all the questions, especially the implication that the intermarriage caused the Nephilim, the giants on the earth. Therefore, I will consider with you the possibility that "sons of God" refers to angels.

One thing is clear, if angels were involved in the process, they could not have been involved as spiritual beings; they had to have had some way of being physically intimate with those women. Angels cannot make a human woman conceive without a union of some sort.

The Holy Spirit worked a miracle on Mary, and she conceived a child without the normal human process. No male of any kind was involved; she was a virgin in every sense of the word. The virgin birth of Jesus through Mary is the only one recorded. She was unique; no virgin births involving the power of angels or any other spiritual being preceded or followed Mary's.

The children born in Genesis 6 weren't born to virgins upon whom angels had worked miracles. Sexual union took place; that's why the word *married* is used. Angels, as spiritual beings, can't have sex. That would, of necessity, mean that if angels are being described in Genesis 6, they took upon themselves human form complete with human capability.

Can angels do that?

Yes. Remember the angels who visited Abraham and Lot in Genesis 18 and 19? They not only looked like men but could do the same things men do. They could eat (Genesis 18:8; 19:3) and prepare themselves to sleep in bed. If spiritual beings in human form can sleep and eat and digest food, then it is also possible for them to have sex with human women while in human form.

Such a strange union would explain how their offspring were giants. It would also put special emphasis on the words of Jesus in Matthew and Mark when He said the resurrected dead wouldn't marry but would be like *the angels in heaven.* The angels who live with God in heaven have never married or had sex with any human. If any angels have had sex with women, if that is what Genesis 6 teaches, they were *evil* angels. And the result was a world so corrupt that God brought it to an end. He washed it clean with His flood.

Are bad angels still having sex with human women? I'll answer that question with another question: Seen any giants around?

It seems that the union of angels and women will never again be tolerated—if it ever occurred at all. With all Satan's power and dominion over the world, God is still more powerful, and there are certain things over which He continues to exercise magnificent control. In later chapters we will explore the power of Satan and the power of God. For now, don't lose sleep worrying about an evil angel forcing himself on you, because God takes care of His own. I'm quite convinced God will never again (if He ever did) allow an angel to have sex with any woman—Christian or not.

Remember,

> In all these things we are more than conquerors through him who loved us. For I am convinced that neither death nor life, neither angels nor demons, neither the present nor the future, nor any powers, neither height nor depth, nor anything else in all creation, will be able to separate us from the love of God that is in Christ Jesus our Lord. (Romans 8:37–39)

EVERYONE WILL SEE AN ANGEL SOMEDAY

If after all that's been written in this chapter, you still find yourself longing to see an angel, you will. In Luke 16, Jesus told of a poor man named Lazarus who died. At his death, angels met him and escorted him to his wonderful place in paradise.

At death, the righteous dead are met by good angels. At death, the wicked are also met by good angels.

Good angels? For the wicked dead?

Yes. Satan's angels afflict us while we live, but they don't want to go where the angels of God take those who don't serve Him. They'll be there soon enough. It is the responsibility of good angels to take the wicked to hell.

> The Son of Man will send out his angels, and they will weed out of his kingdom everything that causes sin and all who do evil. They will throw them into the fiery furnace, where there will be weeping and gnashing of teeth. (Matthew 13:41–42)

> To you that are afflicted rest with us, at the revelation of the Lord Jesus from heaven with the angels of his power in flaming fire, rendering vengeance to them that know not God, and to them that obey not the gospel of our Lord Jesus. (2 Thessalonians 1:7–8 ASV)

So, either good or bad, believing or unbelieving, you will meet the angels of God face to face one day. Either on the day the world ends or the day you die—whichever comes first. Whether you rejoice in your meeting or scream in terror will be decided by how you live now.

Understanding angels' existence and power does not lead you to victory in this personal, spiritual war. Only being armed with faith in Jesus can provide the spiritual power leading to the glorious march welcoming us home.

Knowing all the aspects of spiritual warfare can be of great benefit to you as you fight the good fight. Fighting effectively requires seeing the unseen.

Are you ready to learn how? Read on.

SECTION

2

FORCES AT WORK AGAINST US

CHAPTER FOUR

Is There Really a Devil?

Each day Randy waited furiously for the radio program to end so he could challenge me to a philosophical duel about my on-air commentary. He was a brilliant young man who worked for the radio station where I did a daily five-minute, religious broadcast. As an avowed and vocal atheist, Randy's previous exposures to Christians led him to believe we were all "nonthinking, judgmental, uneducated morons." Believe me, I'm using his milder and less offensive words to describe what he thought of Christians.

Randy didn't know quite what to do with me. Though a Bible-believing Christian, I thought, read, and questioned just as much as he. Convinced I was an able opponent, he would debate me concerning the existence of spiritual things and the beliefs of Christians. He especially disliked what I considered sin and openly mocked anyone believing there was a wicked being somewhere who influenced the evil in this world.

Our arguments were intellectual and philosophical, but I felt a deep emotion as I listened. Randy was convinced that he and others like him would someday bring about the world he longed for through enlightenment of the human race, not through reliance on God or by battling Satan. He pitied my faith and deeply resented my joy. I pitied his unfounded hope and knew with certainty that eons of history have proven his argument false. I think that deep within himself Randy knew he was wrong, because the hope he dreamed of never once evidenced itself in his demeanor. He was the saddest and loneliest person I had met.

A REAL DEVIL

You, too, may believe there is no such thing as a real devil. Forty-seven percent of those who consider themselves evangelical Christians, 69 percent of Catholics, and 65 percent of mainline Protestants don't. They think Satan is just a symbol of the evil that exists.[1] Believing there is a devil who is served by angels and demons is not popular in the religious world of modern America. But denying the devil's existence gives him unacceptable leverage in his efforts on earth today.

It is true that our faith must be in God and our reliance on Him. But blindly facing the attacks of a real and vicious enemy unarmed is foolhardy, unnecessary, and extremely painful. God Himself tells us in the Bible that Satan exists, warning against his deceit. Paul counseled that awareness of Satan's schemes keeps him from outwitting us (2 Corinthians 2:11) and that putting on the full armor of God enables us to stand against the devil's schemes (Ephesians 6:11).

I can't think of a word for those who believe in God but do not believe there is a devil. They aren't atheists. Although I don't know what to call them, I know how to describe them. I can accurately say they are spiritually naive. It would also be accurate to call them *vulnerable.*

Before you write off the idea of a real devil as some antiquated fundamentalist concept, think through a few implications of that denial. By denying Satan's reality, you also, of necessity, deny his power. But because you cannot deny the reality of evil, you must assign the power of evil to another source.

WHOSE FAULT IS IT?

We are living in a scientific age. And science says that if something can't be tested and empirically proven, it doesn't exist. Many think that since we can't scientifically prove the existence of the devil, he simply isn't there. For them, the problem of evil isn't a spiritual malady; it is a human malady. Correcting the problem, or at least improving the situation, calls for a human solution carried out by human beings. The solution to evil would then be something like: "If we could just get people to treat each other with equality and respect, then all evil would disappear." That's a wonderful dream and one of the basic arguments my young atheist friend made over and again. But the dream will never be fulfilled; history has proven the impossibility of the task. Many noble people have given their lives trying to convince humankind to love each other enough to eradicate evil. If we could ask them, "Did you succeed in removing evil from the earth?" what do you think they would tell us? Without doubt, they died for noble causes. But were there any lasting results? Evil, even the evil of human beings mistreating each other, continues unabated despite the efforts of all the dreamers who gave themselves to end it.

Something beyond our own human weakness is working to bring out the worst in us. Humans didn't invent evil, and humans will never eradicate it. It exists separate from us and only seems to originate from us because it has so thoroughly permeated us.

To believe there is no devil is to believe that the struggle for good and evil is totally within ourselves and that we have no one to blame but ourselves for any of the evil that we do.

Well...let's not go *that* far. Surely we can blame something for the evil that we do—even if we don't believe there are wicked spiritual influences.

It's Not My Fault

Instinctively, we want to believe we aren't evil and that no evil emanates from us. We want to believe that while we sometimes do evil acts, there is something outside ourselves prompting it, seducing us—something beyond our ability to control—"making us do it."

Lacking a devil to hate, modern man has found substitutes to blame for his problems. For example, if you believe evil is from humans, you must blame humanity for the evil in your own life. Perhaps you can blame your parents or significant others in your life, who were either poor role models or cruel abusers or too self-absorbed to give you what you needed. Maybe you believe your poor choices were forced on you by economic factors beyond your control. At the very least, it must be that you have done wrong not of yourself but because there was no one to stop you.

Denying there is a devil doesn't mean people don't think the factors of evil aren't influencing them; it just means they look for evil in other places.

Everything's My Fault

Those people who can't find someone or something else to blame turn inward and place inordinate blame on themselves. Because they sometimes act in ways that are wrong, they are compelled to find the root of that wrong. Finding no other justifiable target for their remorseful anger, their imagination convinces them *they* are evil, viewing every selfish desire as proof of their evilness.

Feelings of low self-esteem, wretchedness, and utter lack of worth or value are not uncommon in the world or in the church. If we see ourselves as unworthy, any difficulty in our lives or the lives of those we love brings with it the conviction that we brought the trouble on ourselves because of our moral deficiency. We mournfully accept our troubles as deserved punishment for our sinfulness. For example, if we are poor or struggling, we see our low station as a direct result of our own lack of goodness. If we have success or riches, we find ways to self-sabotage and lose everything because we just can't view ourselves as good enough to deserve the good things. We see good in others, yet in ourselves we see only a weak propensity for sin.

THE BALANCE OF BLAME

Have you seen the point yet? There is a real problem of evil, and it *cannot* be blamed on us. But at the same time, it *must* be blamed on us. There is a balance of responsibility. If you believe you are never at fault for your actions, you suffer from what the psychologists call a character disorder. If you feel that everything is your fault, you'll likely be labeled a paranoid or another kind of neurotic or psychotic.

Those of us who believe in the forces of evil are balanced. We believe that we are responsible for our own actions. "By his own evil desire, he is dragged away and enticed" is the way James wrote it in James 1:14. While accepting personal culpability, we also know that the temptations aren't coming from *within* us but are put *before* us.

And that distinction gives us the dignity to go on.

I am not happy when I sin, but I don't let myself buy into the lie that I am evil. God made me in His image, and He has forgiven me by His grace. There is a powerful evil force that knows my weaknesses, trying its best to get me to yield to them. My occasional yielding gives the evil forces only brief victory, though they hope for a longer, even eternal, one.

The knowledge that I am not my own worst enemy frees me from unbearable, unproductive, and overwhelming guilt. Knowing that other human beings are not the enemy frees me from the destructive forces of hatred and bitterness. Knowing there is a devil who is deceiving people into sin arms me for a successful fight against the real enemy. I know that a person who sins against me is responsible for his sin, but I also know that he is only acting at the prompting of another. I will deal directly with sin but will not dissipate myself spiritually by hating the sinner. My emotional weapons are reserved for the battle against one much larger than any human who wrongs me. My battle is against Satan himself and with his angelic and demonic hordes. I don't fight philosophically, living without hope, as did my young atheist friend; I fight spiritually, living in goodness, hope, joy, and peace.

SATAN IS REAL

Yes, understanding that Satan is real has contributed to my peace. As one person who listened to my tape series on spiritual warfare said, "It puts everything in place. Now it makes sense. So many questions are answered. Now I can rest from the battle I have been having within—a vicious battle with myself. I can also rest from the battle I have been having with people who have brought pain into my life. Now I understand who the real enemy is."

Beyond the philosophical reasons for believing Satan exists, the Scriptures are clear about who he is, where he came from, and what he does. In the next chapter, we'll examine his origin, and in the chapter after that, his power. You may not want to know about him, but awareness is in your best interest.

Diligently pray—and read on.

CHAPTER FIVE

Where Did Satan Come from, and Where Is He Now?

I wish I could have seen him back then—before the fall—although I'm quite convinced I don't want to see him now. Satan was God's glorious creation, full of wisdom and beauty. God trusted him enough to place him as the guardian cherub in the garden with Adam and Eve. It was in that garden he caused his own fall from heaven and the fall of all those angels foolish enough to follow as he lured God's new children from Him.

This understanding of Satan is a recent one for me. For many years I firmly believed that the devil has always existed. My arguments centered on the fact that if Satan didn't always exist, then, in essence, God created evil by creating Satan. But in my efforts to solve one philosophical problem, I created a host of others. Even so, I still thought it the better answer.

EZEKIEL'S PICTURE

It was while reading Dr. Edward Myers's book *A Study of Angels* that I found the truth about Satan I had been missing. I had always dismissed the prophecy in Ezekiel 28 as having nothing to do with Satan and everything to do with the king of Tyre. Myers unlocked the mystery, showing me that as Ezekiel gave the lament about the king, he also gave information about events in the Garden of Eden that aren't recorded anyplace else. Though the primary message is about the king of Tyre, this passage gives us an unusual glimpse into Satan's role in severing man from his direct and unlimited communion with God.

> You were the model of perfection, full of wisdom and perfect in beauty. You were in Eden, the garden of God; every precious stone adorned you: ruby, topaz and emerald, chrysolite, onyx and jasper, sapphire, turquoise and beryl. Your settings and mountings were made of gold; on the day you were created they were prepared. You were anointed as a guardian cherub, for so I ordained you. You were on the holy mount of God; you walked among the fiery stones. You were blameless in your ways from the day you were created till wickedness was found in you. Through your widespread trade you were filled with violence, and you sinned. So I drove you in disgrace from the mount of God, and I expelled you, O guardian cherub, from among the fiery stones. Your heart became proud on account of your beauty, and you corrupted your wisdom because of your splendor. So I threw you to the earth; I made a spectacle of you before kings. (Ezekiel 28:12–17)

The king of Tyre wasn't in Eden nor was he created. He was procreated just as we were. God didn't speak him into existence; other human beings brought him into existence through the process of human birth. Neither can the king of Tyre be described as a guardian cherub ordained by God. And since his existence began on earth, there is little likelihood he could have been expelled from the mount of God *to* earth.

Yes, it could be symbolic language, but the symbolism would be valid only if something happened in the Garden that this language symbolizes. And what would that have been?

God appointed a spectacular being to be the guardian cherub in the Garden of Eden, an astonishing being who was the absolute model of perfection from the day he was created until he sinned. His sin sprang from his pride.

While Ezekiel compares the king of Tyre to the devil in the Garden of Eden, he gives us a glimpse into what happened in the Garden and how Satan's pride led to his fall.

We know it was Satan's pride that led to his fall. In 1 Timothy 3:6, centuries after Ezekiel 28 was written, Paul instructs Timothy on choosing overseers of the church: "He must not be a recent convert, or he may become conceited and fall under the same judgment as the devil." Satan's conceit led to his fall, and Ezekiel tells us what he was conceited about.

SATAN'S MONSTROUS SIN

If Satan was a guardian in the Garden—and I am convinced he was—the fall of Satan occurred simultaneously with the fall of man. Satan was cast from heaven as humankind fell from grace. Ezekiel makes it clear that the events in the Garden led to his fall. Apparently, it was at this same time that rebellious angels followed Satan, forcing God to cast them to earth with him (2 Peter 2:4; Jude 6).

Satan's responsibility as the guardian in the Garden makes his sin even more hideous.

Occasionally I read or hear news about day-care operators being arrested and charged with child abuse. Such stories strike the very heart of a parent's great concern: "Can I trust the protection of my children to others?" When those we trust with our children's well-being become the predators, our primal urge is to punish quickly and severely. All loving parents want justice served.

Our human reaction toward those who hurt our children gives us insight into the gravity of the sin committed by Satan and the immediate and harsh punishment meted out by God. Satan abused God's children in the most awful way: He took them from the Father who loved them, and he brought pain, confusion, humiliation, and life-wrenching consequences into their lives.

In that singular act of abuse, which introduced sin into the world, Satan abused all children who would ever be born. In a similar way to the phenomenon that abused children often become abusive parents, the sinfulness of Adam and Eve was passed down to their children. Each generation polluted the next, with a cumulative effect that has become the very nature of man (Ephesians 2:3). It all started with the cherub God trusted as the guardian of His children. No evil existing in the world today *could* exist had sin never entered the world through Satan's proud, selfish exploitation of Eve in the beginning.

SATAN RULES THE WORLD

This being, who was once God's crowning angelic creation, still exists. Where does he live, since he can no longer live in heaven? The answer is clear: He lives on earth. That is where God cast him, and that is where he remains.

And he controls it.

We don't like to think in those terms. We want to think only about the power of God and His great love for us. We sing, "He's got the whole world in His hands." And there is definitely a sense in which that is true. "The earth is the LORD's, and everything in it, the world, and all who live in it" (Psalm 24:1). Perhaps our knowledge of verses teaching this happy thought is why we largely ignore John's frightening statement, "We know that we are children of God, and that the whole world is under the control of the evil one" (1 John 5:19). Satan doesn't *own* the world, but he does *control* it.

Read it again and weep. Satan rules the world.

Jesus knew that and called him "the prince of this world" in John 14:30. Paul would say it in these terms: "Take your stand against the devil's schemes. For our struggle is not against flesh and blood, but against the rulers, against the authorities, against the powers of this dark world and against the spiritual forces of evil in the heavenly realms" (Ephesians 6:11–12).

Did you notice that language? He says plainly that the devil's forces are the rulers, authorities, and powers of this dark world. Look around you with increased awareness. Satan's control of the world explains the evil abounding on it.

After I gave a presentation on spiritual warfare at a men's retreat, one of the brothers approached me—obviously agitated. "If the world is under the control of Satan," he said, "we might as well give up. Quit." My words had shaken him as I shared what the Bible taught about Satan and his angels. You may be having a similar reaction. You may be thinking, "How can Satan be in control? How can anyone believe such a foolish idea?"

Read the preceding passages again and ask yourself honestly what they mean. You will reach no other conclusion. Satan is in control of the world.

The word *world* is used with different meanings in Scripture. Sometimes it means the planet hurtling through space on which we ride. Sometimes it refers to the people who live here. "For God so loved the world that he gave his one and only Son, that whoever believes in him shall not perish but have eternal life" (John 3:16). As used in 1 John 5:19,

John 14:30, and Ephesians 6:11–12, the word *world* refers to the system or order ruled by Satan.

We use the word in similar ways in our English language. We talk about things like the world of baseball, meaning the system or order of baseball and all its peripherals. Satan has just such a world—a system and order that he controls. Here. On earth.

SATAN RULES THE AIR

Satan not only rules on earth, he also controls the heavens. No, not the third heaven where God lives, but the first heaven and possibly the second.

Three heavens?

Yes. Paul referred in 2 Corinthians 12:2 to a man who "was caught up to the third heaven." In the New Testament, the word *heaven* refers to at least three areas. The people of Paul's day used it to refer to any of those areas.

The first heaven is where the birds fly. It is the heaven referred to in James 5:18: "The heavens gave rain, and the earth produced its crops."

The second heaven contains the stars. It is the heaven referred to in 2 Peter 3:10: "But the day of the Lord will come like a thief. The heavens will disappear with a roar; the elements will be destroyed by fire, and the earth and everything in it will be laid bare."

The third heaven is where God dwells. It is the heaven referred to in 1 Peter 3:21–22: "Jesus Christ, who has gone into heaven and is at God's right hand."

Today we call these areas, or heavens, the *atmosphere, space,* and *heaven* (God's home). Inserting these more modern terms as you read about heaven or heavenly realms in the New Testament may be helpful. The context makes clear the meaning. Be aware that sometimes the word *air* is used instead of heaven, as in 1 Thessalonians 4:17: "We who are still alive and are left will be caught up together with them in the clouds to meet the Lord in the air." As in this verse, *air* usually refers to the place where the clouds are—the first heaven, or atmosphere.

Got all that? Now, how does it apply to our study of spiritual warfare?

In Ephesians 6:12, Paul called Satan's army "the spiritual forces of evil in heavenly realms," and in Ephesians 2:2, he called Satan "the ruler of the kingdom of the air." The use of the word *air* in this verse shows that

Satan rules the atmosphere. Thus, the first heaven (also called the world) is part of Satan's domain.

The control of the second heaven isn't as clearly explained. Is what we know as space also within the area of the "world" ruled by Satan, or is it completely out of his control? Any answer is conjecture, but at this point in my study, I believe that "space" is included in Satan's sphere of control. The many passages referring to the destruction of both the earth and the stars at the last day lead me to believe that space has been corrupted by Satan just as the earth has.

We know for sure that Satan's forces operate in the "heavenly realms." Clearly, Satan rules the first heaven, the atmosphere. My opinion is that he also rules the second heaven, space.

You might be thinking, "How interesting. But what possible good can this knowledge do me?"

Knowing that Satan controls the world, including the air, explains why this earth has become so corrupt. From reading headlines of world events, you know that evil operates freely in this world. If you find yourself asking why God allowed the world to become so corrupt, remember that it isn't controlled by God. Satan controls it, and Satan corrupts it.

This understanding gives deeper meaning to God's command: "Do not love the world or anything in the world. If anyone loves the world, the love of the Father is not in him. For everything in the world—the cravings of sinful man, the lust of his eyes and the boasting of what he has and does—comes not from the Father but from the world" (1 John 2:15–16).

If getting ahead in the world means sacrificing health, relationships, or your soul, remember whose world you're sacrificing for. When the pressures of the world get you down, remember who made it what it has become. If you find yourself wanting to become the richest or most famous person in the world, remember to whom you must pay homage to achieve that position.

This world is not our home. Our home is where God reigns.

JESUS WILL RULE

Does Jesus have sovereignty over the world controlled by Satan? Not yet. In Matthew 28:18, Jesus says, "All authority in heaven and on earth has been given to me." Later, the Hebrew writer and the apostle Paul clarify that for us. In Hebrews 2:8, the writer makes the strong point that

God has put everything under Jesus' feet. He quotes from Psalm 8:4–6 then writes, "In putting everything under him, God left nothing that is not subject to him. *Yet at present* we do not see everything subject to him."

Did you note those emphasized words? "Yet at present" not everything is subjected to Jesus, even though He does have all authority.

When will everything be subject to Him? In 1 Corinthians 15:24–27, as he was led by the Holy Spirit to write about the final resurrection, Paul says, "Then the end will come, when he hands over the kingdom to God the Father after he has destroyed all dominion, authority and power. For he must reign until he has put all his enemies under his feet. The last enemy to be destroyed is death. For he 'has put everything under his feet.'"

Jesus is reigning now, having been declared the Son of God with power at His own resurrection (Romans 1:4), but according to what the Holy Spirit tells us through 1 Corinthians 15 and Hebrews 2, there are still dominions, authorities, and powers that are not yet under Jesus' feet. Ultimately, they will be conquered and totally subjected to Him when He hands everything over to the Father.

Until then, the dominions, authorities, and powers ruling this world belong to Satan. No wonder the Bible calls this the dark world.

SATAN IS POWERFUL

The devil controls the world, has power in the world, and is using that power effectively. He and his angels use weapons of deception and delusion to manipulate. And they don't exist only in theory or theological treatise; they exist in fact. Even if you have accepted the fact that Satan really exists, you are unequipped for spiritual combat if you think him practically powerless.

Just how much power does he have? Are any limitations placed on him? These and other questions about Satan's power are examined in the next chapter.

Get your notebook and your Bible, then read on.

CHAPTER SIX

What Power Does Satan Have?

The lead paragraph of the news article immediately caught my attention.

> Lonnie Weeks Jr. yesterday told the jury that convicted him of capital murder that an "evil spirit" forced him to pump six bullets into state trooper Jose M. Cavazos on a dark Interstate 95 exit ramp.
>
> "I'm sorry for what I have done," he told a hushed courtroom in a barely audible voice. "I took an innocent man's life. What I did was wrong."[1]

We've become accustomed to seeing similar stories on television and reading them in the newspaper. A criminal declares, "A voice inside me kept screaming for me to do it," and it's up to the jury to decide whether he's crazy or cunning. They determine his guilt based on their decision. It happens often enough that hardly anyone stops to ask whether an evil spirit really could have spurred the offender.

After all, we're too sophisticated to believe the "devil-made-me-do-it" plea. Our law doesn't recognize such a plea as valid, and anyone claiming such nonsense is either insane or trying to appear to be. Demon-driven people exist only in the movies, right?

Can the devil have that much power over a human being—enough power to make him shoot another person six times? Before I ponder that question, let's examine several passages.

WHAT SATAN DOES

Consider the following scriptures, paying particularly close attention to the emphasized words:

> Satan rose up against Israel and *incited* David to take a census. (1 Chronicles 21:1)
>
> ...this woman...whom Satan has *kept bound* for eighteen long years. (Luke 13:16)
>
> Simon, Satan has asked to *sift you as wheat.* (Luke 22:31)
>
> The devil had already *prompted* Judas Iscariot, son of Simon, to betray Jesus. (John 13:2)
>
> As soon as Judas took the bread, Satan *entered into him.* (John 13:27)
>
> Ananias, how is it that Satan has *so filled your heart?* (Acts 5:3)
>
> The god of this age has *blinded the minds* of unbelievers. (2 Corinthians 4:4)
>
> ...the ruler of the kingdom of the air, the spirit who is now *at work in* those who are disobedient. (Ephesians 2:2)
>
> ...the devil, who has *taken them captive* to do his will. (2 Timothy 2:26)

When these familiar verses are put together, they make a frightening list. These and other verses make it clear that Satan can do things to humans—such as, incite, bind, sift, prompt, enter, fill, blind, work in, and take captive. Don't underestimate Satan. He is a powerful being who can lead people to do wrong.

But did you notice the words carefully? Read in context, these passages show Satan manipulating rather than controlling. The only people he can *make* do things are those who are possessed by his demons. He must *seduce* everyone else.

The topic of demon possession is considered in chapter nine. For now, grasp the point at hand: If a person isn't possessed by an evil spirit, he has control over his actions. Satan can't make him do anything. But don't underestimate Satan's power: He has tremendous influence on any person he is manipulating.

Lonnie Weeks Jr., the man whose story began this chapter, apparently isn't demon possessed. He sat in a courtroom, calm, in control of himself, and softly spoke of his penitence. Demon-possessed people in the Bible seldom had that kind of control. This leads me to doubt that a spiritual being *forced* him to shoot Trooper Cavazos. But that doesn't mean an evil spirit wasn't involved.

Evil beings prey on the weakness of human beings, even when those humans are not possessed by demons. The evil ones find success through manipulation, making it unnecessary to force our cooperation. The words *forced* or *made* are too strong for what they do through their manipulation. *Incited* or *prompted* come directly from the Scriptures and accurately describe their activities. No one is forced to yield to inciting or prompting, but they often choose to yield. Why? Because the evil ones know our weaknesses and exploit them to the fullest.

Think about it. What makes you angry? What makes you lust? What makes you despair? The evil ones know, and each time their innuendoes and promptings work, they smirk in triumph. They know how to use circumstances and situations to bring all that is weak or bad within us to full expression. Even when they can't make us do it, they are a part of our doing it.

Don't scoff. They've done it to you before…and they will again.

DON'T DOUBT SATAN'S POWER

Christians aren't immune to Satan's power and influence. If you think you are, you should remember the words of Paul: "If you think you are standing firm, be careful that you don't fall!" (1 Corinthians 10:12).

One of my old friends was in the audience when I lectured on spiritual warfare at a church in a large Midwestern city. I had always known Fred to be a student, willing to tackle any subject open-mindedly, with Bible in hand. That night my presentation touched a nerve deep within him, causing a strong, negative reaction. After the lecture, with not so much as a parting word of friendship, he carefully avoided me and slipped out.

Two weeks later, the minister of that church called to tell me why. Fred had interpreted my words as saying that people have no responsibility for their actions, that everything is the devil's fault. For days afterward, he brought up the subject with any church member he met and orated at great length about how no Christian can blame his sin on anyone but himself.

Listening to Fred's continual campaign, the minister realized that, in his great zeal to denounce my lecture, Fred was essentially arguing that Satan has no power to operate in the world today. While Fred would say that he believes the devil is real, he actually sees him as an ineffective, powerless figure who watches from the sidelines, posing no real threat.

Maybe you view the devil in the same way. In your conscientious effort to ensure that people don't discard personal responsibility, have you argued yourself into the theological corner of an impotent devil?

Let's think about it. If Satan is powerless, and if every wrong we do comes only from within ourselves, how did Satan "prompt" Judas to betray Jesus (John 13:2) or "incite" David to number Israel (1 Chronicles 21:1) or "sift" Simon Peter by leading him to deny Jesus? (Luke 22:31). In each case, the person stood responsible before God for his own actions; but in each case, the Scripture is luminously clear as to the instigator. To shift sole responsibility to either the devil or the sinner is to misunderstand the battle, and therefore, to be inadequately armed for the spiritual battle and without the proper strategy for victory.

Slowly read the following scriptures again:

> The god of this age has *blinded the minds* of unbelievers, so that they cannot see the light of the gospel of the glory of Christ. (2 Corinthians 4:4)
>
> ...the spirit who is now *at work in* those who are disobedient. (Ephesians 2:2)
>
> ...come to their senses, and escape from the trap of the devil, who has *taken them captive* to do his will. (2 Timothy 2:26)

Has Satan "blinded the minds" of the believers so they cannot see his workings in the world today? If he was powerful enough to "take captive" the Christians that Timothy was teaching, he is powerful enough to take many captives in the churches today. Like Paul, we should tell each other to "come to our senses" and quit denying Satan and his power. We should bring out the big guns, urging each other to mobilize the forces available to the church today to combat Satan and his hordes.

Satan is big, he's bad, and he's mad.

That's the bad news. The good news is that Satan probably doesn't know who you are.

SATAN ISN'T GOD

That's right, Satan couldn't possibly know every human alive—or, for that matter, every Christian on earth. Satan doesn't have the same characteristics as God. He, too, is an angel. And like the angels we discussed in chapter three, he is not God's equal.

God is omnipotent: He is all-powerful. Satan isn't; his power is limited. He couldn't attack either Job or Peter without asking permission (Job 1; Luke 22:31). When God cast him out of heaven, Satan couldn't force his way back in. When he attacked Jesus at his birth, Michael the archangel defeated him in battle (Revelation 12). Satan is limited enough in power that God makes this promise: "God is faithful; he will not let you be tempted beyond what you can bear. But when you are tempted, he will also provide a way out so that you can stand up under it" (1 Corinthians 10:13).

God is omnipresent: He is everywhere. Satan isn't. Just like every other angel, he can only be one place at a time; he can't be everywhere at once. Because of that limitation, the devil may never have been in your presence. Do you doubt that? Think of every story you remember from the Bible about angels. They always had to travel from one place to the other. In Daniel 10, the angel was delayed more than three weeks between the time he left heaven and the time he reached Daniel. Angels aren't like God the Father or the Holy Spirit; they can't be everywhere at once. Satan can only be in one place at a time, and he has to travel from one location to another.

God is omniscient: He knows everything. Satan is limited in knowledge. When Jesus took human form, He abandoned some of His power of godhood and no longer had all knowledge. Jesus pointed out that angels don't have all knowledge either. In speaking of the end of the world, He said, "No one knows about that day or hour, not even the angels in heaven, nor the Son, but only the Father" (Matthew 24:36). Peter also tells us that angels don't know everything, and he wrote that the angels who delivered prophecies longed to know what the prophecies meant (1 Peter 1:10–12). Satan, like every other angel, doesn't know everything—and that must be terribly frustrating for him!

DON'T DARE SLANDER HIM

Even with these limitations, Satan is mighty enough that God Himself gave us strong warning about him. Through Peter, He wrote about people ignorant of the power of spiritual beings:

> Bold and arrogant, these men are not afraid to slander celestial beings; yet even angels, although they are stronger and more powerful, do not bring slanderous accusations against such beings in the presence of the Lord. But these men blaspheme in matters they do not understand. They are like brute beasts, creatures of instinct, born only to be caught and destroyed, and like beasts they too will perish. (2 Peter 2:10–12)

You might read that passage and think that God is only telling us not to blaspheme good angels. But a passage in Jude reveals that He is referring to every celestial being, including Satan. Look at the similarity in the language to 2 Peter.

> Dreamers pollute their own bodies, reject authority and slander celestial beings. But even the archangel Michael, when he was disputing with the devil about the body of Moses, did not dare to bring a slanderous accusation against him, but said, "The Lord rebuke you!" Yet these men speak abusively against whatever they do not understand; and what things they do understand by instinct, like unreasoning animals—these are the very things that destroy them. (Jude 8–10)

If the archangel Michael, the strongest good angel we know anything about, is careful not to bring a slanderous accusation against Satan, what should that tell us? I cringe when I hear preachers talk about Satan as if he were some cur dog to be beaten and scorned. He's evil, but he's also powerful, and that power deserves a healthy respect from all those who may have it unleashed on them. Peter warned that men who slander Satan are obviously false teachers; they surely don't know the teachings of God.

The next time you think it's funny when someone dresses as a buffoon devil with horns and a pitchfork, remember God's warning about slandering celestial beings more powerful than you. Also remember it the next time you tell some zany joke about God or Jesus or the Holy Spirit. None of these celestial beings desires to be mocked. And all of them, even the angels, have more power on this earth than you.

Respect all spiritual beings—even evil ones. Satan is powerful; and we're not to doubt him, dismiss him, or disparage him.

DON'T LOOK NOW

We have learned that Satan is limited—he is not God's equal—but he's still staggeringly powerful. He's not all-knowing, but he's absolutely brilliant by any human standard. He's not everywhere, but he lives somewhere in the world to which he has been cast down.[2]

Before you breathe a sigh of relief that Satan's home may be far from you, remember that Satan doesn't have to be everywhere at once. He has legions of angels, demons, and people who work for him. While Satan may not have personal knowledge of you, there is no doubt that one of his evil servants knows you intimately.

There is a host of evil beings serving Satan. Paul said it this way:

> Put on the full armor of God so that you can take your stand against the devil's schemes. For our struggle is not against flesh and blood, but against the rulers, against the authorities, against the powers of this dark world and against the spiritual forces of evil in the heavenly realms. Therefore put on the full armor of God, so that when the day of evil comes, you may be able to stand your ground, and after you have done everything, to stand. (Ephesians 6:11–13)

The devil has divided the world into powers, dominions, and authorities. In the next chapter, we will explore what that means.

Never lose awareness that the hordes faithful to Satan are spread throughout the world; and that means that you get personal attention—whether you want it or not.

Keep your eyes open and read on.

CHAPTER SEVEN

What Do Satan's Angels Do?

Indignation dripped from every word Anne spat at me, "Well, they may be able to kill *you,* but they certainly can't kill *me!*"

It was one of those weekend church seminars to which I had been invited to speak on spiritual warfare. I flew in, got situated in my hotel room, and then made my way to the meeting room for the first session. Arriving early, I had a chance to meet most of the people present before the opening prayer. Anne was there as a guest of one of the members and had seemed pleasant enough when we first chatted.

That changed quickly when I began to discuss angels. The longer I spoke, the stronger her reaction. At first she turned to her host, casting a baleful eye when she disagreed. Gaining little support with that tactic, she started whispering rebuttals to my comments, gathering volume as she became more agitated. Finally, she could contain it no longer. "Are you for real?" she demanded.

"Is there something you disagree with?" I sighed, waiting for the attack to come. Nothing gets people so riled as treading on their long-held beliefs, even if you happen to be right. And I was.

Anne contended that evil angels are powerless to do any harm to Christians. She especially reacted to my statement that evil angels have the power to kill and that sometimes that power is used against Christians.

You, too, may believe that Christians are protected from Satan's flaming arrows. If so, you might want to think that position through a little more carefully. Several biblical examples show the power of evil angels to harm God's people.

SATAN'S ANGELS KILLED IN THE OLD TESTAMENT

Can Satan attack a righteous person to bring harm into his life? Ask Job.

The story told in the Book of Job makes it plain that Satan killed Job's children. Do you remember how he did it? "Suddenly a mighty wind swept in from the desert and struck the four corners of the house. It collapsed on them and they are dead" (Job 1:19). The storm system that killed Job's children also took its toll on his servants and sheep. "The fire of God fell from the sky and burned up the sheep and the servants" (v. 16). We would call fire from the sky lightning. (See Numbers 11:1; 1 Kings 18:38; 2 Kings 1:12.)

Satan controlled nature to kill the children, servants, and flocks of a "blameless and upright [man], a man who fears God and shuns evil" (v. 8). He even struck Job, the blameless man, with a terrible disease (2:7). Think about what that means. If Job's children could be killed and Job himself terribly afflicted with disease, then why would any person think her righteousness so strong that no physical attack from Satan could come to her? Job, the blameless, upright, God-fearing, evil-shunning man of God, took the brunt of Satan's attacks. If God didn't completely protect Job from evil, why would He completely protect you?

SATAN'S ANGELS KILLED IN THE NEW TESTAMENT

If you think that because those in the Old Testament had a relationship with God different from ours that He protects us differently than He did them, think again. The New Testament, too, teaches that Christians will suffer.

Jesus said, "Remember the words I spoke to you: 'No servant is greater than his master.' If they persecuted me, they will persecute you also" (John 15:20).

Paul emphasized it to Timothy: "In fact, everyone who wants to live a godly life in Christ Jesus will be persecuted" (2 Timothy 3:12).

The Hebrew writer gave strong warning and encouragement to Christians to remain faithful during persecution. He compared the suffering of Christians with the suffering of God's people in the Old Testament, reminding them of those who went before: "They were stoned; they were sawed in two; they were put to death by the sword" (11:37). He used the Old Testament stories to encourage Christians of his day to endure the persecution they were facing. Inspired by the Holy Spirit, he went on to tell them, "In your struggle against sin, you have not yet resisted to the point of shedding your blood" (12:4). Did you notice the use of "not yet"? The implication is chilling. The recipients of the Hebrew letter had "not yet" resisted to the point of shedding their blood, but that time was coming. History tells us that it did. Then he wrote, "Endure hardship as discipline; God is treating you as sons. For what son is not disciplined by his father?" (12:7).

God allows persecution of those He loves, using the persecution for His own purposes.

You may be thinking, "Sure, those passages mention persecution, but does persecution include death?"

For some, yes. Consider two high-profile examples. John the Baptist, the cousin of Jesus, was killed by Herod (Matthew 14:10). The apostle James, the brother of John and close friend of Jesus, was put to death with the sword (Acts 12:2). If Jesus let His cousin and one of His best friends on earth be killed, He will let Satan attack you also.

His warning to those facing the destruction of Jerusalem was no empty threat: "Then you will be handed over to be persecuted and put to death, and you will be hated by all nations because of me" (Matthew 24:9).

Pain, affliction, and even death are the fate of some Christians just because they chose to follow Jesus. Why? In chapter fourteen I show you passages that shed light on that age-old question. For now, *believe* that evil angels can bring you harm.

SATAN'S ANGELS CAN HARM YOU

To think that you will be spared persecution or that evil angels can't arrange your death is to think yourself better protected than the prophets, the apostles, and even Jesus.

Yes, you understood me correctly. Although the Bible doesn't specifically mention that Satan or his angels caused the deaths of John, James, Jesus, and the others, these evil beings were behind the acts. You know that Satan killed Jesus, though he did it through the mob who demanded His death and the Romans who executed Him. In the same way, the evil done to John and James (and you and me) is prompted by the evil one and his hordes. There are reasons for the harm that comes to us; it is not accidental. In chapter fourteen, I show you why I believe that and how God uses it for our good.

The Tools They Use

Satan works through nature, through circumstances, and through people.

When he destroyed Job's servants and camels, he did it through wicked people. "The Chaldeans formed three raiding parties and swept down on your camels and carried them off. They put the servants to the sword" (Job 1:17). In the direct context of that chapter, everything that was happening to Job, his children, his servants, and his possessions was done by the overt action of Satan.

He doesn't use only wicked people; he uses good people too. Satan used Job's wife and Job's friends—Bildad, Eliphaz, Zophar, and Elihu—to discourage him and weaken his faith.

Satan even used physical disease. "Satan went out from the presence of the LORD and afflicted Job with painful sores from the soles of his feet to the top of his head" (2:7).

To summarize, Satan and his angels have the power to:

- use evil people to harm you
- use good people to discourage you
- make you sick
- use nature (or disguise themselves as an act of nature)
- destroy property and possessions
- kill you or those you love

They Can Do It without Miracles

Notice that Satan and his angels accomplished their goals in the lives of Job and others without the use of miracles. That's right—by the classic definition of a *miracle,* no miracle took place. A miracle is a violation of a law of nature, such as the dead coming back to life or an amputated limb growing back. None of the things that occurred in the life of Job violated nature; rather, they occurred *through* nature. (In today's debate about miracles, this observation is important.) Angels can work without human detection, never needing a miracle to accomplish their task.

For example, an angel struck Herod with worms. "And he was eaten by worms and died" (Acts 12:23). Dying from a terrible infestation of worms isn't a miracle; it is consistent with nature as we understand it. When Satan's angels worked in Job's life, they worked in harmony with nature.

Occasionally, angels have been involved in acts unexplainable by nature—a burning bush that didn't burn up (Exodus 3) or a locked gate that swung open of its own accord (Acts 12:10)—acts that were obviously miraculous. But generally, angels accomplish their objectives through nonmiraculous means. From man's viewpoint, most angels' actions are works of nature. Only spiritual beings can see that these works of nature are actually caused by spiritual beings.

If you want a chilling thought to ponder, consider that what sometimes appears to be nature may instead be the handiwork of angels. Remember that Hebrews 1 says angels can be wind or fire. In the Old Testament the angels of God sometimes appeared as fire. The wind that killed Job's children and the fire from heaven that destroyed his servants might well have been wicked angels. I don't mean an angel *using* wind or lightning; I mean an angel *being* wind or lightning. An angel working as nature has not performed a miracle, though he controls the havoc that "act of nature" produces.

An angel appearing to be a natural phenomenon, such as wind or lightning, might explain some of the extraordinary stories you hear about nature. You've heard the incredible stories of tornadoes lifting people to safety without harming them, or hurricanes skipping over some things and targeting others, or other amazing stories about "natural" catastrophes. Was it really nature or angels appearing as nature?

Manipulation and Seduction

Do you know any person well enough to manipulate him or her? Do you know how to arrange circumstances or situations that will ensure a probable course of behavior? Of course you do.

My daughters are experts at it. They know how to get me to do practically anything they want. Of course, they can't *make* me do anything. Sometimes their manipulations don't work because I'm too sly or because they misjudge the situation, but overall, they're quite effective.

If another human can know you well enough to occasionally manipulate you, how effective could an angel be?

If you're thinking they can't manipulate you because they don't appear to you, think again.

When I was a young minister, I was taught that any spiritual communication must come through my five senses. I completely accepted the idea that if I couldn't taste it, smell it, touch it, see it, or hear it, it couldn't get into my consciousness. Faithfully, I passed on this belief by teaching others. The only difficulty with that idea is that it ignores some clear Bible examples.

As mentioned earlier, when God's angel spoke to Joseph, the husband of Mary, he did it through dreams (Matthew 1:20; 2:13, 19). Joseph didn't hear him with his ears, see him with his eyes, touch him with his skin, taste him with his mouth, or smell him with his nose. Yet the angel communicated with Joseph just the same. How? Through his thoughts. Dreams occur in the brain; they are thoughts. Here is an indisputable, Bible example of an angel communicating directly into the thoughts of a human.

Scary, isn't it? Does it make you wonder about all those people who firmly believe an evil spirit told them to do some awful thing?

If angels can communicate to us in our thoughts, it is logical to assume they can receive communication from us through our thoughts.

Realizing that angels can know my thoughts, why should I be surprised that they are so good at knowing my weaknesses? I have them, just as you do. I used to be amazed at the "coincidence" of my weaknesses being hit with just the right temptations at just the right times. But my study of spiritual warfare has shown me it wasn't coincidence at all. Evil spiritual beings gleefully manipulate me by presenting me with sinful opportunities just when I am least prepared to cope with them.

God doesn't tempt us (James 1:13); Satan does. Jesus told us to pray, "Lead us not into *temptation*, but deliver us from the *evil one*" (Matthew 6:13). Notice how each ties to the other? God keeps me from being led into temptation by delivering me from the evil one.

If you've been reading this book carefully, you know I believe that every person is personally responsible for his own sin. Being seduced is no justification for yielding to the seduction. But understanding who is seducing us and how well they know us helps us understand why these seductions are often masterpieces of temptation. It also makes us aware of how difficult it is to be sinless.

In chapters eleven through fourteen, we'll examine these seductions more carefully, raising our awareness of how to resist them.

WHY BAD ANGELS DO BAD THINGS

As you have seen, wicked angels can and will do harmful, evil things to people. They particularly like afflicting the people of God.

You might wonder why they want to bring pain and misery to us. There are at least three reasons.

One: We have opportunity to go where evil angels can never return. When Christians die, they will go to be with God in heaven, the third heaven, God's dwelling place. "The angels who did not keep their positions of authority but abandoned their own home" (Jude 6) can never live there again.

Two: If they can turn us from God and cause us to be lost, we will live under Satan's rule after we die. Consider that statement. The Prince of Darkness, who is of a higher spiritual order and is stronger than we are, will have complete control over us mere mortals because we will be in hell with his evil angels, dominated by them.

Occasionally I am questioned about that statement. How can Satan rule people if they're all in hell together? Think of it this way: If you were placed into a dungeon with other prisoners stronger and more powerful than you, could they rule you? You know they could, and if you have any knowledge of prisons, you know they would. The stronger dominate the weaker in prisons all over the world. Why would it be any different in hell? Yes, Satan and his angels will be in pain, too, but that isn't any consolation—it will only make them meaner.

Three: Satan and his malicious horde hate God and want to bring Him as much pain as they can. They delight in hurting God's children precisely because it hurts God.

Revelation 12 paints the picture clearly. Satan was cast out of heaven; he hasn't the power to attack God and take heaven from Him. When Jesus came to earth, Satan tried to destroy Him near the time of His birth, but Michael brought his army to protect Jesus and defeated Satan in a battle in the heavens. They probably battled in the second heaven—

space—though it may have been the first heaven—the atmosphere. Either way, it wasn't directly on the earth and certainly not in the third heaven, the dwelling place of God.

John refers to the birth: "She gave birth to a son, a male child, who will rule all the nations with an iron scepter" (Revelation 12:5). He says in symbolic language that God protected the newborn Savior: "And her child was snatched up to God and to his throne." Then he tells of the war that came as Satan tried to destroy the child:

> And there was war in heaven. Michael and his angels fought against the dragon, and the dragon and his angels fought back. But he was not strong enough, and they lost their place in heaven. The great dragon was hurled down—that ancient serpent called the devil or Satan, who leads the whole world astray. He was hurled to the earth, and his angels with him. (Revelation 12:7–9)

This isn't a reference to the fall of the angels that took place in the beginning, but it is pictured as just as great a loss to Satan. It refers to the battle to destroy the baby Jesus and to Satan's failure to accomplish his mission. Interestingly, as war was taking place in the heavens between the armies of Satan and Michael, Herod was killing all the male children under two years of age on earth.

I believe that any time there is a grand-scale, hideous act on earth, angels are fighting in the heavens above it. Some angels are fighting to continue the atrocity; some to end it.

Nevertheless, the point of Revelation 12 is that when Satan and his angels realized they could not successfully fight God or Jesus, they turned on us. John wrote it this way: "Then the dragon [Satan (v. 9)] was enraged at the woman and went off to make war against the rest of her offspring—those who obey God's commandments and hold to the testimony of Jesus" (Revelation 12:17).

It's simple. There is no way Satan can successfully fight heaven. He failed in his efforts to destroy Jesus while He was on earth, so he takes his anger and vengeance out on those who follow the God of heaven and obey the Lord Jesus. He can't hurt Them directly, so he hurts Them indirectly by hurting us.

Not only does he persecute us, he seduces us to hurt God. Did you know you can hurt God? When Satan or his angels entice us to sin, we hurt God. And God is hurt by our sin even more than he is hurt by observing our pain.

You might be thinking, "Do Satan's efforts to entice us follow any kind of order or plan, or are they simply haphazard?"

There isn't any haphazardness to it. Like any efficient army, Satan's forces are well organized and very effective. His organization of the world enables him to accomplish his objective: to persecute and tempt the people of God. Because, as an angel, he can't be everywhere, Satan divided the world among those angels who followed him.

POWERS, DOMINIONS, AUTHORITIES

Paul said our battle is "against the rulers, against the authorities, against the powers of this dark world and against the spiritual forces of evil in the heavenly realms" (Ephesians 6:12).

Satan has apparently divided the world into geographical areas and has given charge of those areas to various powerful angels. These angels are called princes or kings. Daniel's visiting angel gives us insight into the Ephesians 6 passage.

> Since the first day that you set your mind to gain understanding and to humble yourself before your God, your words were heard, and I have come in response to them. But the prince of the Persian kingdom resisted me twenty-one days. Then Michael, one of the chief princes, came to help me, because I was detained there with the king of Persia. (Daniel 10:12–13)

Later he continued,

> Soon I will return to fight against the prince of Persia, and when I go, the prince of Greece will come.... (No one supports me against them except Michael, your prince.) (vv. 10:20–21)

The words of this angel provide us with much information.

First, Michael is called a prince, but so are the two wicked angels, the prince of Persia and the prince of Greece. That suggests they are equal in power to Michael. It is appropriate that Satan would place in prominent positions on earth the princes or archangels who followed him in the rebellion. What better angels to lead the other angels of evil?

Second, referring to these angels in the singular doesn't mean they are alone. When the angel says that only Michael supported him, I don't believe he means the angel Michael came by himself. Michael is a warrior angel that leads his own army (Revelation 12). Saying that Michael came alone probably means that only Michael's army came, and not the other armies led by the other princes or archangels of heaven. We use that kind of language today. If I said that in the Gulf War of the early 1990s General Schwartzkopf fought against Saddam Hussein, no one would picture these two men in personal, hand-to-hand combat in the desert. Everyone would know I meant the armies led by these two men. I think the same type of language is used to refer to these angels. The prince of Persia and the prince of Greece are powerful angels leading powerful angelic armies. Michael does the same.

Third, if there were angelic armies led by princes over Persia and Greece, it would be logical that other princes rule other parts of the world. That would mean that today angels rule nations, or, at the least, continents. I think it entirely proper to believe there is a powerful angel ruling America, and that he is served by an army of evil angels. Less powerful angels report to more powerful angels; they report to the prince of America, and he reports to Satan himself. These angels are dispersed throughout our nation, working to serve Satan and hurt God by harming and undermining His people.

I made the point earlier in the book that Satan may not know you personally. But I believe that at least one of his angels knows you, targets you, and actively works to persecute you.

I readily admit that my conclusions are speculative, but they do provide a logical explanation for the work of Satan and the effect he has on the world.

Fourth, wicked angels sometimes interfere with the answer to our prayers. The angel told Daniel that he had been struggling for twenty-one days to get through to answer Daniel's prayer. Only when Michael came to his aid was he able to penetrate the barrier presented by the prince of Persia.

Sermons or classes on prayer often list the same three points: Sometimes God says yes, sometimes God says no, and sometimes God says wait. Let me add a fourth point, based on the story in Daniel 10, that merits consideration. Sometimes God's answer is on the way, but the forces of evil consider it so disruptive to their goals that they have waged a battle to stop it.

Daniel's prayer was answered eventually, but did you notice that he didn't stop praying during the interim? I believe that to be significant. While I can't prove it from any specific statement in the text, it seems that his continued prayers affected the efforts of the angel to get through. Perhaps some of our prayers aren't answered because when the evil ones delay the answer, we simply quit praying. Yes, I know that God can answer a short prayer offered only once, but I also know that Jesus taught us we should always pray and never give up. He even told parables about it (Luke 11:5–8; 18:1–8).

Fifth, the understanding that Satan divided the world into regions makes his offer to Jesus more understandable. Recall that in the temptation of Jesus in the wilderness, the devil took him to a very high mountain and showed him all the kingdoms of the world and their splendor. "All this I will give you…if you will bow down and worship me" (Matthew 4:9). The world is under Satan's control (1 John 5:19), and he felt very comfortable offering it to Jesus. What was he offering? He was offering Jesus the position of second-in-command. All Jesus had to do was worship Satan, and He would be placed just under him in his authority chain.

I don't think the passage is referring only to physical kingdoms of the world, but also to the spiritual kingdoms that Satan established to rule the world. Jesus would have been over all the wicked angels, even the princes, if He yielded to Satan.

Because the earth belongs to God, every kingdom on it is His by right. "O LORD, God of Israel, enthroned between the cherubim, you alone are God over all the kingdoms of the earth. You have made heaven and earth" (2 Kings 19:15; cf. Isaiah 37:16). But that doesn't prevent Satan from assisting and manipulating earthly kings who do evil. The angel who visited Daniel said that the angel, the prince of Persia, would soon be replaced by the prince of Greece (Daniel 10:20). Evil angels of great power, followed by angelic armies, assisted both the Persian and Greek kingdoms of earth. In that sense, Satan also offered Jesus the physical kingdoms of the earth. Either way, ruling the kingdoms meant ruling angels. Clearly, the intended lure of the temptation was control of the spiritual, angelic kingdoms.

This section—on powers, dominions, authorities—is placed at the end of the chapter on Satan's angels because it is the most speculative. Don't allow argument over any speculation to detract from the clear message of the power of Satan's angels: They hate us, they persecute us, and they tempt us.

Can they possess us? Sit down, buckle up, and read on.

CHAPTER EIGHT

What Are Demons?

The question hung in the air, unanswered, as Jamie tried again to distract me with a rush of words that said nothing. I didn't enjoy making him feel uncomfortable, but I wanted to hear the truth.

I understood his fear. We had just met, and he couldn't decide if he should trust me. But the longer he talked, the greater my frustration grew, and the more I wanted to hear the true answer.

"You're a missionary to a Third World country," I interrupted. "If they're gonna reveal themselves openly anywhere on earth, it'd be there. Now, have you or have you not dealt with a case you believed to be genuine demon possession?"

You may wonder why Jamie found the question so disconcerting. After all, missionaries talk about that kind of thing everywhere, even on national television. Jamie, however, was different. Most of the leaders in his religious fellowship do not believe demons are here on earth today. Without much questioning, they generally accept a doctrine that locks all spiritual activity into the first century. If Jamie admitted he had seen what he truly believed to be demon possession, he could easily find himself in trouble with his supporting church.

When I first asked this particular question, his hesitation was so obvious that it caught my attention, especially when he didn't answer negatively. I knew I had to dig deeper. Jamie had something in mind, and he didn't want to talk about it.

"Look, Jamie," I encouraged, "I'm not out to make any trouble for you or anyone else. I just want to know because of my own study. I don't know you, and your answer isn't going to sway me heavily either way. I'm a student in search of information, nothing more."

Hesitantly, Jamie began. Gradually the story leaked out. Yes, he'd seen what he believed to be demon possession. He detailed the place, time, and circumstances, explaining why he believed it really was a demon and not some other phenomenon. Then, in a quiet voice, he said, "When faced with it, I didn't know what to do. They were all there, the family, looking to me for deliverance…an exorcism, or something. Instead, I said a quick prayer and hustled out of there."

Bringing it up again didn't just cause him concern about his church; it made him feel guilty about abandoning the supposed demoniac and his family. I felt his pain.

Did Jamie face a demon? Are they here on the earth? Just what are they anyway?

The answer to that last question may be the most startling.

THE SOULS OF THE DEAD

Demons in the Bible are the souls of the dead who have come back to earth. The souls of the *wicked* dead not only roam the earth but can inhabit and control the bodies of the living. (See chapter twenty-one to learn about the souls of the *righteous* dead.)

That's a rather bold statement, isn't it? And, as I discovered, somewhat controversial.

Within months of the original publication of *Seeing the Unseen,* it was used around the world to study spiritual warfare. Missionaries from the western part of Africa invited me to spend a week with them discussing it. Missionaries in the Ukraine translated sections to use as pamphlets and tracts for evangelism. Churches across the United States and Canada built Bible classes around it. (Quite often these classes were for teens. Apparently teenagers are intrigued by this subject and really apply themselves to its study.) The responses from all these and more were positive, but every person who contacted me had the same question first on his or her list: "How in the world can you believe that demons are the souls of the dead?" Then they would immediately go into detailed explanations of why I should know that demons are fallen angels.

None of them convinced me; though for convenience sake, it would be easier for me if they had! I decided a long time ago that when I'm the only one who is right, it's time to reexamine my position. That's what I did, and the result is what you'll read in this and the following two chapters.

One of my chief sources of study for both the previous version and this one is a lecture given on March 10, 1841 by Alexander Campbell to the Popular Lecture Club of Nashville, Tennessee. His quickly jotted manuscript on demonology is still available in the October 1841 issue of the Millennial Harbinger.[1] I readily admit my reliance on Campbell's approach to explaining this subject and make liberal use of what he presented on that day.

THE MEANING OF WORDS

If we intend to understand what demons are, we must begin with an awareness of what the people in Jesus' day believed them to be. That is the *only* way to understand them correctly. A basic law of interpretation is that we must assign the *same* meaning to a word that was assigned by the people in whose time and place it was used. We can't go assigning *our* meanings to *their* words; we must accept *their* meaning if we are to understand *their* writings.

Dictionaries, grammar books, and translations are based on this fundamental law of interpretation. If they weren't, they would be of no value to us. How could we trust any translation from an ancient language that ignored this crucial principle?

This point is so very important that I ask your indulgence as I explain it further.

Have you heard a teacher or preacher speaking on the subject of the *talents* in Matthew 25:14–30 carefully explain that to people in the first century a *talent* was a measure of money? Why would a well-prepared teacher go to that trouble? Because the teacher didn't want us assigning our twenty-first-century meaning to the word *talent* (such as ability or aptitude) because it would change the meaning of the story. One man wasn't given five times more ability or aptitude than another; he was given five times more *money* to be responsible for. The parable is about having the courage to live up to the level of responsibility assigned, not a story about one person having more ability than another.

But the only way you could know that is to know what the word *talent* meant to Matthew's original audience. To understand what it means to us, we *must* first understand what it meant to them. That's just being a good Bible student.

You may be thinking, "But what if the populace of the first century misunderstood the meaning of the word *demon?* Can we not define it properly now if we believe the people back then didn't know what it really meant?"

Allow me to show you the fallacy of that kind of reasoning. If people in that time didn't know what a word really meant, then God couldn't teach them via that word unless He first explained *His* meaning. Otherwise, He would have meant one thing, and they would have understood something completely different. How then could He call them to the accountability of obedience?

Whenever Jesus or any inspired Bible writer used a word, expression, or passage in a way that the people of that day didn't normally use it, *they explained that they were using it differently!* Otherwise, their communication would have been useless. Jesus gives us a perfect example of this principle in the Sermon on the Mount. In the midst of explaining things that people misunderstood, Jesus said in Matthew 5:27–28: "You have heard that it was said, 'Do not commit adultery.' But I tell you that anyone who looks at a woman lustfully has already committed adultery with her in his heart."

We infer from what Jesus said in this passage that the men of that day thought that as long as they didn't actually have sex with women other than their wives, they didn't commit adultery.[2] That's why Jesus clarified what *He* meant by the word *adultery.*

Verbal or written communication is always based on specific meanings within specific contexts. When people employ the same meaning, they communicate. If each understands the word differently, they don't communicate. Therefore, to make His point clear, Jesus *had* to tell His audience that He was using the word *adultery* differently from how they understood it.

The same principle applies to our understanding of demons. We *must* accept that a demon is whatever the people in Jesus' day understood a demon to be unless Jesus or some inspired person changed the definition for them. Reinterpreting the word centuries later just doesn't work.

WHAT PEOPLE IN BIBLICAL TIMES UNDERSTOOD DEMONS TO BE

To best understand this, let's start with a short evolution of the word *demon*. According to some etymologists, the word *demon* descended from a very ancient verb that means "to discriminate, to know."[3] Early in its usage, it referred to a person of intelligence, a knowing one. For example, Aristotle was called "demon" as a special title of honor. With time, the word evolved to refer to a human spirit that had vacated its body at death and, therefore, been initiated into the secrets of another world not shared with living humans.

Alexander Campbell wrote, "Thus a separated spirit became a genius, a demigod, a mediator, a divinity of the ancient superstition according to its acquirements in this state of probation." The International Standard Bible Encyclopaedia says it this way: "[Demon] had two closely related meanings; a deity, and a spirit, superhuman but not supernatural."[4] Did you note that? Superhuman, but not supernatural. No longer in the flesh, they were freed from its limitations.

Many people of that era believed that the departed spirit became a sort of deity, but not a supernatural deity like God. They believed they were deity in the sense that they were now more intelligent and powerful than humans; therefore, superhuman. They were gods, but not God. "For the LORD is the great God, the great King above all gods" (Psalm 95:3).

In order to better understand what people of Jesus' day understood demons to be, let's look at some of the writings of biblical times.

Pagan Writers

Pagan writings of that era used the word *demon* to refer to spirits of dead people. Hesiod quoted Plutarch as saying, "The spirits of mortals become demons when separated from their earthly bodies." Hesiod also wrote of his own convictions: "The demons of the Greeks were the ghosts and [genius] of departed men...and although not actors themselves, they encourage others to act in harmony with their views and characters." Aristotle himself quotes Zenocrates, who referred to the souls of living men as demons who had not yet vacated their original bodies. Campbell also noted the definition of these pagan writers: "In this character Zoroaster, Thales, Pythagoras, Plato, Plutarch,

Celsus, Apuleius, and many others contemplated the demons of their times."

Old Testament Writers

The inspired writers of the Old Testament understood that the people of their day (and those for thousands of years before) believed that the souls of the dead could be contacted for superhuman knowledge. For example, note the reference to the spirits of the dead in this passage:

> When you enter the land the LORD your God is giving you, do not learn to imitate the detestable ways of the nations there. Let no one be found among you who sacrifices his son or daughter in the fire, who practices divination or sorcery, interprets omens, engages in witchcraft, or casts spells, or who is a medium or spiritist or who consults the dead. Anyone who does these things is detestable to the LORD, and because of these detestable practices the LORD your God will drive out those nations before you. You must be blameless before the LORD your God. (Deuteronomy 18:9–13)

Why is that passage important? Campbell writes,

> Hence we affirm that the doctrine of a separate state—of disembodied ghosts, or demons—of necromancy and divination, is a thousand years older than Homer or Hesiod, than any Pagan historian, philosopher, or poet whatsoever. And so deeply rooted in the land of Canaan, so early and so long cherished and taught by the seven nations was this doctrine, that, notwithstanding the severe statutes against it, traces of it are found among the Jews for almost a thousand years after Moses....
>
> Necromancy was the principal parent of all the arts of divination ever practiced in the world, and was directly and avowedly founded on the fact, not only of demoniacal influence, but that demons are the spirits of dead men, with whom living men could, and did form intimacies. This the very word *necromancy* intimates. The necromancer...was a prophet inspired by the dead. His art lay in making or finding a familiar spirit, in evoking a demon from whom he obtained superhuman knowledge. So the Greek term imports and all antiquity confirms....
>
> Ghosts who have visited the unseen world, and whose horizon is so much enlarged, are supposed to be peculiarly intelligent, and on this account originally called *demons,* or *knowing ones....*

> It is perfectly indifferent whether it was a pretence or a reality: for, mark it well, had there not been a senior and more venerated belief in the existence of a spiritual system...that disembodied spirits were demons or knowing ones...who ever could have thought of consulting them, of evoking them by any art, or of pretending in the face of the world to any familiarity with them! I gain strength by the denial or the admission of the thing, so long as its high antiquity must be conceded. I do indeed contend...that a belief in demons, in a separate existence of the spirits of the dead, is more ancient than necromancy, and that it is a belief and a tradition older than the Pagan, the Jewish, or the Christian systems—older than Moses and his law—older than any earthly record whatever.

A cursory examination of the Old Testament makes Campbell's point obvious: "When men tell you to consult mediums and spiritists, who whisper and mutter, should not a people inquire of their God? Why consult the dead on behalf of the living?" (Isaiah 8:19).

Campbell was right. The Old Testament refers to the belief that the dead have extraordinary knowledge and implies that those knowledgeable dead were the demons that people sacrificed to. Note the following verse: "They joined themselves also to Baal of Peor, and ate sacrifices made to the dead" (Psalm 106:28 NKJV).[5] And just verses later the psalmist continues: "They sacrificed their sons and their daughters to demons" (v. 37).

Sacrifices were made to the dead (verse 37 implies that "the dead" meant "demons"), and some of the people were so corrupted by the heathen practice that they even ate the sacrifices. Even if you doubt my belief that demons are equivalent to the dead in the above passages, at least you must agree that the corrupted Jews of the Old Testament made sacrifices to the dead and made sacrifices to demons. They also believed that through certain people, such as spiritists or mediums, they could make contact with the dead.

It is on that basis I call them to testify. These passages and others like them show that well before the famous pagan writers, people believed that at least some of the dead still roamed the earth in spirit form and that they could be worshiped as having greater power or knowledge than the living. That belief was prevalent in the day of Jesus, and neither He nor His apostles ever corrected it. When they spoke of demons, the people to whom they spoke understood those demons to be the souls of the dead.

Jewish Historians

Josephus, well-known historian of Jesus' time on earth, wrote, "Demons are the spirits of wicked men, who enter into living men and destroy them, unless they are so happy as to meet with speedy relief."

Philo wrote, "The souls of dead men are called demons."

The "Church Fathers"

Renowned church leaders during the first two centuries or so of the church's existence are sometimes called the "church fathers" or "early fathers." Among them were Justin Martyr, Ireneus, Origen, and others. Justin made this statement: "Those who are seized and tormented by the souls of the dead, whom all call demons, and madmen." Notice his words? In speaking of the early church, he said that "all" called the souls of the dead demons. That's clear evidence of what those in the early church believed demons to be.

Campbell writes, "Lardner, after examining with the most laborious care the works of these, and all the Fathers of the first two centuries, says, 'The notion of demons, or the souls of dead men, having power over living men was *universally* prevalent among the heathen of these times, and believed by many Christians.'"

Before examining New Testament passages that corroborate the above point, I need to recognize that not all who study the ancient koine Greek language reach the same conclusion as Campbell.

Did any writers of those times use *demon* to refer to anything other than the souls of the dead? Yes. There are references to demons being *gods.* Walter Bauer's well-known work on the uses of Greek words in the New Testament and other early Christian literature tells of some such references. In discussing the various koine Greek words for *demon,* Bauer points out that sometimes demons were considered to be "a deity, divinity."[6] He goes on to describe them as "independent beings who occupy a position somewhere between the human and divine." But another interesting phrase he uses for them is "ghost-like."

Notice that none of these uses of the word *demon* indicate that anyone of the era believed demons to be angels—fallen or otherwise. That belief came later. People believed them to be the souls of the dead or gods. There is no conflict in the two views. Souls of the dead gained a level of power and knowledge above that of living humans—making them gods in comparison to incarnate man. But demons weren't angels, and nothing in the belief that they were gods shows that people of that day thought them to be angels. Campbell concluded correctly that the people of the first century believed demons to be the souls of the dead.

SUPPORT FROM SCRIPTURE

Lessons from a Demoniac

The same story is found in Matthew 8, Mark 5, and Luke 8 and is told slightly differently by each writer. I'll paraphrase it here.

Jesus traveled across the Sea of Galilee, stepped off the boat, and was immediately confronted by a demoniac, a man inhabited by evil spirits. The man lived in the tombs, crying out day and night. The demons who possessed him abused him physically by making him cut himself with stones. They also gave him supernatural strength, thwarting the efforts of anyone who tried to subdue him. Whenever someone tried to chain him, he would tear the chains apart and break the irons shackling his feet.

When the man rushed up to Jesus, the demons immediately recognized the power in front of them and shouted,

> "What do you want with me, Jesus, Son of the Most High God? I beg you, don't torture me!"…
>
> Jesus asked him, "What is your name?"
>
> "Legion," he replied, because many demons had gone into him. And they begged him repeatedly not to order them to go into the Abyss. (Luke 8:28, 30–31)

The demons begged Jesus to let them enter the bodies of about two thousand pigs that were feeding nearby. Jesus granted the request. The demons entered the pigs, and the pigs rushed into the lake and were drowned.

What is so important about this Bible story, and what do we learn from it? Consider the following seven points:

First, demons can inhabit bodies, both human and animal. Not only do they have the ability, they have the desire. They didn't ask Jesus just to let them run free; they asked for permission to enter the nearby pigs. I assume they didn't ask for permission to enter another human because they knew Jesus wouldn't allow it. It would be unreasonable to cast them from one human into another.

The pigs' running into the sea and drowning brings up several possibilities. Perhaps the demons caused the pigs to drown so they could flee the area. Perhaps Jesus drowned the pigs to imprison the demons. Or maybe the demons were unable to control the pigs: They could force a human to do their bidding but had no medium with which to control the unreasoning, soulless swine.

I don't know which of the above explanations is correct, or even if something else altogether took place. I do know it's clear that the demons had a fondness for a body.

Second, they asked Jesus not to torture them. Luke couples their request with the statement, "For Jesus had commanded the evil spirit to come out of the man" (v. 29). Interestingly, they viewed leaving their host body as torture. Perhaps they saw the lack of a body as torture, or maybe they feared that Jesus would send them to torture as He cast them out. One thing is clear: They saw remaining in a body as the way to avoid torture.

Third, they repeatedly begged Jesus not to send them into the Abyss. That word isn't applicable to the nearby lake because it denotes something without a bottom, a pit so deep the end is never reached. Sometimes this Greek word for "abyss," *abussos,* refers directly to the residence of the dead (Romans 10:7). The demons feared that Jesus would send them into the bottomless pit—likely the world of the dead.

Fourth, the demons were numbered in the thousands. They said their name was "Legion," a Roman term for a unit of three to six thousand men. At least two thousand of them were in the man because that is the number of pigs that ran into the lake after the demons took them over.

Fifth, the demons hated their host's body and wanted to harm it. They caused this man to cut himself repeatedly. Other demon-possession stories in the New Testament tell of demons throwing their host bodies into the fire to burn them or into the water to drown them (Matthew 17:15–18). They wanted to be in the body but hated the body they were in.

Sixth, the demons kept the man in the region of the tombs. That area seemed to hold a special appeal for them.

Seventh, the demons possessed supernatural knowledge. They knew Jesus the moment they saw Him. An example in Acts 16 shows that demons could also predict the future accurately. The demon-possessed girl in that story made money for her master by soothsaying. Demons have knowledge that surpasses that of living humans.

These seven points combined present a strong argument for demons being the souls of the dead.

Think it through. Demons wanted a body and had the ability to enter and control it. They so craved being enclosed in flesh that more than two thousand of them were crammed into one person. They feared leaving the body they inhabited and had an even greater fear of the bottomless pit. They wanted to be in cemeteries, perhaps because some of their original bodies were there or because it was a city of the dead. They craved a human body but resented its still being alive. They punished their host.

Demons Are Not Fallen Angels

There is a common misconception that demons are wicked angels. The noncanonical Jewish writing known as the Book of Enoch indicates that demons are fallen angels,[7] and it appears that a veritable plethora of biblical commentators accept that view. In my opinion, they accept it not because of its validity but because of preexisting prejudices about the state of the dead. Every slice of history contains writers who express views contrary to the majority. In our study, we look to the majority for the common understanding of the time.

The logic from those who have interacted with me runs something like this: "Demons must be fallen angels because they *cannot* be the souls of the dead." So far in these informal debates, no one has offered any proof of his or her belief that demons are fallen angels. They give me no passages that indicate such, nor do they show me that the general populace of the people of Jesus' day understood demons to be such. Their primary argument, beginning to end, is that they *must* be fallen angels because they surely cannot be the souls of the dead.

It would seem that those who make such arguments would notice that in Acts 23:9 a teacher of the law clearly indicates that spirits and angels are *different* beings. And no one in the Sanhedrin questions his understanding! Paul was before the Sanhedrin when: "There was a great uproar, and some of the teachers of the law who were Pharisees stood up and argued vigorously. 'We find nothing wrong with this man,' they said. 'What if a spirit or an angel has spoken to him?' "

Did you notice his language? A spirit *or* an angel. He recognized that there were spirits on earth who are not angels.[8] And just what might those nonangelic spirits be? As we have shown from abundant sources, the people of that day believed that spirits were the souls of the dead.

If you can show me a passage (other than in the non-inspired book Enoch) that corroborates the belief that the spirits you read of in the New Testament, specifically demons, are angels I'll be very happy to see it.

Allow me to explain why it doesn't make sense to believe that demons are fallen angels. Notice that angels aren't predisposed to any of the things that demons are.

First, angels don't enter people; demons do. The only reference to any angel ever entering a human is John 13:27: "As soon as Judas took the bread, Satan entered into him." The context makes a figurative interpretation acceptable. If Satan actually entered Judas, this is the first and only explicit statement about an angel getting inside a human body. Every other reference to angels and humans tells of angels taking upon themselves the *form* of a human, never taking over a human.

Further, angels do not crave being in a human body because they can take any form they want, anytime they want; demons crave living in a human body. Why would two thousand angels want to be *one* human body when angels are superior to humans? Are that many of them that excited about demoting themselves? (Hebrews 2:9). What could possibly motivate them or their master Satan to decrease their active, available worldwide angelic forces by two thousand warriors just to torment one man? Angels apparently didn't fear that Jesus would cast them into the Abyss while He was on earth (though they will be cast there someday); demons feared that Jesus would send them there when He forced them from the demoniac. Angels have no predilection for cemeteries and tombs; demons seem to be attracted by them.

Are you convinced yet? There are still two more questions to consider.

CAN THE DEAD COME BACK TO EARTH?

Some argue that the reason demons cannot be the souls of dead is because the dead are locked up in the world of the dead and cannot return here. They usually refer to Luke 16:19–31, which tells the story about the rich man and Lazarus. After they were both in the realm of the dead, an interesting conversation took place.

> In hell, where he was in torment, he [the rich man] looked up and saw Abraham far away, with Lazarus by his side. So he called to him, "Father Abraham, have pity on me and send Lazarus to dip the tip of his finger in water and cool my tongue, because I am in agony in this fire."
>
> [As part of his reply, Abraham said,] "Between us and you a great chasm has been fixed, so that those who want to go from here to you cannot, nor can anyone cross over from there to us."
>
> He [the rich man] answered, "Then I beg you, father, send Lazarus

> to my father's house, for I have five brothers. Let him warn them, so that they will not also come to this place of torment."
>
> Abraham replied, "They have Moses and the Prophets; let them listen to them.... If they do not listen to Moses and the Prophets, they will not be convinced even if someone rises from the dead."

From these verses some make the following emphatic point: "Abraham said that the dead *cannot* leave the realm of the dead."

Of course, my reply is always, "Really? Show me the passage that says that."

Their first response is usually to look at me as if I were missing a few key brain cells. Then they read slowly and carefully the portion that says, "between us and you a great chasm has been fixed, so that those who want to go from here to you cannot, nor can anyone cross over from there to us." Finally, in triumph they raise one eyebrow as if to say, "Gotcha!"

I love to ask them to read it one more time and show me the part where it says that the dead cannot return to earth. The passage says clearly that the dead cannot go from one portion of the hadean world to the other. The righteous dead cannot go to the place of torment that exists on the other side of the chasm. Nor can the wicked dead cross that chasm to reach the realm of the righteous. There is a great chasm between those two places. But there is no reference to a chasm or any other barrier preventing them from coming to earth. Nothing—absolutely nothing—in that passage makes any reference to the dead being able or unable to return to earth. That matter was never contemplated in that parable.

"Wait!" someone cries. "It says that Lazarus couldn't go back to warn the rich man's brothers." But when that section is read more carefully, one finds that it doesn't say that either. It doesn't say that Lazarus *cannot* come back: It says that it wouldn't make any difference to the brothers if he did! Those are two very different matters.

You may be thinking, "Joe, you missed this one. It doesn't have to say that they cannot leave the world of the dead to come back to earth. If they can't go across the chasm from one part of the hadean world to the other, they cannot leave the place at all."

The flaw with that logic is that it is altogether suppositional. One who makes this argument does so by making the assumption that by being prevented from crossing to the other side of the hadean world, those in that world are imprisoned on *all* sides by some type of barrier. Proving that supposition wrong takes only a scripture or two.

Here's one:

> Then the woman asked, "Whom shall I bring up for you?"
> "Bring up Samuel," he said.
> When the woman saw Samuel, she cried out at the top of her voice and said to Saul, "Why have you deceived me? You are Saul!"
> The king said to her, "Don't be afraid. What do you see?"
> The woman said, "I see a spirit coming up out of the ground."
> "What does he look like?" he asked.
> "An old man wearing a robe is coming up," she said.
> Then Saul knew it was Samuel, and he bowed down and prostrated himself with his face to the ground.
> Samuel said to Saul, "Why have you disturbed me by bringing me up?" (1 Samuel 28:11–15)

If the dead *cannot* leave the hadean world, then Samuel could *not* have come to see Saul. And he's not the only dead person the Bible says came back to earth. In Matthew 17:1–8, we find that Moses and Elijah came back from the dead to visit with Jesus. And according to Matthew 27:52–53, when Jesus died, "The tombs broke open and the bodies of many holy people who had died were raised to life. They came out of the tombs, and after Jesus' resurrection they went into the holy city and appeared to many people." Interestingly, that word "many" in this passage means a crowd! Lots of folks came back from the dead that day.

So if you argue that Luke 16 teaches that the dead *cannot* leave the world of the dead, you have direct contradictions both in the Old Testament and New Testament. From these clear instances in biblical history, we can easily determine that the parable of the rich man and Lazarus wasn't intended to tell us that the dead cannot leave the world of the dead. As you've just seen, the Bible tells of dead people who *did* come back. Jesus told the story in Luke 16 to show the differences in the next world for those who are the good and those who are the wicked. He never reassured us that once they're gone, they can never return here.

DO THE DEAD HAVE KNOWLEDGE OF THINGS THAT LIVING PEOPLE DON'T?

A very scholarly friend of mine once pointed me to Ecclesiastes 9:5, 6, and 10 to convince me that my view of demons could not be correct. Those verses say:

> For the living know that they will die, but the dead know nothing; they have no further reward, and even the memory of them is forgotten. Their love, their hate and their jealousy have long since vanished; never again will they have a part in anything that happens under the sun.... For in the grave, where you are going, there is neither working nor planning nor knowledge nor wisdom.

He wanted me to understand that since the dead "know nothing" and have neither "knowledge nor wisdom," it would certainly be impossible for them to predict the future as demons are want to do. He also stated that the premise from which Solomon writes—the dead "never again have a part in anything that happens under the sun"—proves conclusively that none of them is on the earth.

Without arguing the language of Solomon (who in his distress makes highly exaggerated statements like "Meaningless! Meaningless! Utterly meaningless! Everything is meaningless" [Ecclesiastes 1:2]), I can prove that Solomon was lamenting his coming death and describing his own sense of doom and hopelessness rather than teaching us about the world of the dead.

How? By showing from Scripture that the dead are aware of what is happening on earth and that they occasionally have business here. Sometimes their awareness goes beyond that of living humans.

When Samuel came from the dead to visit Saul, he told Saul his future (1 Samuel 28:15–19).

> "I am in great distress," Saul said [to Samuel]. "The Philistines are fighting against me, and God has turned away from me. He no longer answers me, either by prophets or by dreams. So I have called on you to tell me what to do."
>
> [As part of his reply, Samuel said,] "The LORD will hand over both Israel and you to the Philistines, and tomorrow you and your sons will be with me. The LORD will also hand over the army of Israel to the Philistines."

Samuel could and did tell Saul exactly what would occur the next day. Though dead, he had awareness, wisdom, and knowledge. Quite a contradiction to Solomon's view of death, isn't it?

A similar thing occurred when Moses and Elijah visited with Jesus on what we today call the Mount of Transfiguration (Luke 9:29–31). "As he [Jesus] was praying, the appearance of his face changed, and his clothes became as bright as a flash of lightning. Two men, Moses and Elijah, appeared in glorious splendor, talking with Jesus. They spoke about his departure, which he was about to bring to fulfillment at Jerusalem."

These two back from the dead knew that Jesus was about to depart this world and that He was about to "bring to fulfillment" the mission He had come to complete. They even knew where it was going to take place. They were sent to visit with Jesus about it, indicating that they likely were involved in helping Him in some way. They had business on earth, even though dead for hundreds of years.

DEMONS, GODS, AND IDOLS

Earlier in the chapter, I explained that many people in Bible times believed that demons were a sort of deity, a god. Don't misunderstand; I'm not saying that demons are God. There is a difference between the God and a god. The gods in the Bible are entities inferior to the God of heaven but superior to mankind.

Consider this passage: "They made him jealous with their foreign gods and angered him with their detestable idols. They sacrificed to demons, which are not God—gods they had not known, gods that recently appeared, gods your fathers did not fear" (Deuteronomy 32:16–17).

In fact, there is a direct connection between idols and demons. An idol is nothing but a piece of wood or metal that has been designed into some image; offering to an idol was offering to nothing. But the creatures who stood behind those idols did exist, and they gladly accepted the sacrifices made to them, even though the people making the sacrifices may not have known of their existence.

Far-fetched? Keep reading. "They worshiped their idols, which became a snare to them. They sacrificed their sons and their daughters to demons. They shed innocent blood, the blood of their sons and daughters, whom they sacrificed to the idols of Canaan, and the land was desecrated by their blood" (Psalm 106:36–38).

Look closely. Sacrificing sons and daughters to the idol and sacrificing to the *demon* were the same thing.

New Testament passages make the same point.

> We know that an idol is nothing at all in the world and that there is no God but one. For even if there are so-called gods, whether in heaven or on earth (as indeed there are many "gods" and many "lords"), yet for us there is but one God, the Father, from whom all things came and for whom we live; and there is but one Lord, Jesus Christ, through whom all things came and through whom we live. (1 Corinthians 8:4–6)

Gods? Or, better stated, gods? Yes, there are many gods but only one God. The idol itself is nothing, not even a god, but there are gods who are worshiped through the idols, and these gods are demons. If God calls them gods, He must be telling us they have some power. At the very least, He is telling us to avoid them.

> Is not the cup of thanksgiving for which we give thanks a participation in the blood of Christ? And is not the bread that we break a participation in the body of Christ? Because there is one loaf, we, who are many, are one body, for we all partake of the one loaf.
>
> Consider the people of Israel: Do not those who eat the sacrifices participate in the altar? Do I mean then that a sacrifice offered to an idol is anything, or that an idol is anything? No, but the sacrifices of pagans are offered to demons, not to God, and I do not want you to be participants with demons. You cannot drink the cup of the Lord and the cup of demons too; you cannot have a part in both the Lord's table and the table of demons. Are we trying to arouse the Lord's jealousy? Are we stronger than he? (1 Corinthians 10:16–22)

Paul told the Corinthians they should not make such sacrifices because by so doing they were becoming participants with demons. You cannot be part of worship that makes you a participant with demons and also be part of worship that makes you a participant with God. God will reject you if you try.

So far, the points are:

- Demons are gods, but not God; He is vastly superior.
- Idols are nothing but wood or metal.
- Demons accept offers made to idols.
- Offers made to pagan idols are in reality made to demons.

Demonic Gods Today?

The preceding verses in 1 Corinthians were obviously written to Christians who lived in a society that worshiped pagan idols. I think there are applications in today's world.

If I misinterpret how these passages should be applied in my life, I prefer being too cautious to not being cautious enough. I become wary when I read these verses in light of Old Testament passages that condemn witchcraft, sorcery, divination, astrology, and the like. I choose to avoid certain things (although those things in and of themselves are nothing) because unseen beings are probably lurking behind them.

Remember, an idol was nothing, but those who sacrificed to it sacrificed to a demon, a false god. It is my opinion that there are parallels today.

Though I see the astrology section of my newspaper as nothing, I know God condemned those in the Old Testament who participated in activities that attempted to predict the future.

At night, the commercials for "psychic hotlines" inundate the airwaves. I think their phone number would be more revealing if it were 1-900-4A-DEMON.

I see the grotesquely cute "kitchen witches" that some folks put in their houses as nothing, but I know that God views witchcraft as detestable, a work of the flesh, and a sin worthy of death (Exodus 22:18; Deuteronomy 18:10–12; Galatians 5:20). There is nothing cute about any witch. As a Christian, I want nothing to do with a witch doll because of the being it represents.

I see the costumes of ghosts, devils, and goblins as nothing, but I know they represent beings that are demonic and devilish. Just like idols, such costumes are nothing; it's what they represent that chills me. My children aren't forbidden to participate in American cultural fall festivities, but they are forbidden to dress themselves as ghosts, devils, Draculas, or anything evil.

"Dracula?" you cry, "Don't you know vampires are just mythical characters? They can't really fly or turn themselves into werewolves! C'mon, Joe, aren't you getting a little far out here?"

Let's examine the symbolism. The mythical movie character Dracula hates light, fears crosses, and offers eternal life to those who follow him. Who do you think he reflects? If he doesn't represent the devil, what does?

I am not willing to say that everything I've listed above is sinful, but I can say that everyone I know who is a serious student of spiritual warfare has come to the same conclusions about them as I have. We so strongly crave light and symbols of holiness that we are repulsed by the very representations of evil and darkness. We have nothing to do with symbols of satanic beings.

The properties of wood, metal, paper, cloth, and plastic are nothing. Our concern is which are being glorified, sacrificed to, or worshiped through these lifeless symbols.

Avoiding the Power of Evil Spirits

Actually, it matters little to me whether or not you believe that demons roam the earth. If you know they are powerful enough for the Scripture to call them gods, and you know they are represented by idols, then you know that you need to avoid them—however they interact with mankind. It's time to discuss how these evil spirits can be avoided.

First, we must avoid their lies: "The Spirit clearly says that in later times some will abandon the faith and follow *deceiving spirits* and *things taught by demons.* Such teachings come through hypocritical liars, whose consciences have been seared as with a hot iron" (1 Timothy 4:1–2).

Demons aren't here just to possess and harm. They have a mission to find hypocrites with seared consciences whom they can use to spread lies. These hypocritical, calloused teachers lead Christians away from the faith. The doctrines these teachers espouse do not come from their own imaginations; they are given to them by deceiving spirits, demons. Not every lie has the right crafting to deceive. But for the unsuspecting, a master lie spun by master liars can be as believable as the truth itself.

Demons want to harm, but their ultimate mission is to destroy faith. They crave hurting the hosts they inhabit, but they *rejoice* in deceiving believers into abandoning the faith.

Don't let your heart become seared. Demons use hypocritical liars with hard, unfeeling consciences to spread their destructive lies. Make sure you aren't letting your heart become hard and your conscience seared, or they may use you.

Second, just as God's people were instructed in the Old Testament, we should avoid astrology, séances, and witches. We Christians have no reason to seek out or associate with any being who claims the ability to tell the future. Spirit guides and other novel approaches offered by New Age seers in New Age seminars are the work of evil. Sure, these "seers" see the "spirit guides" as good, but how else would Satan's forces disguise themselves?

Avoid all symbols of evil. Since the symbols must be offensive to God, whether demons lurk behind them or not, simply avoid all contact with or display of symbols of evil, including any kind of fortune telling or divination.

Third, avoid inner turmoil. Inner peace appears to interfere with the ability of evil spirits: "Whenever the spirit from God came upon Saul, David would take his harp and play. Then relief would come to Saul; he would feel better, and the evil spirit would leave him" (1 Samuel 16:23).

Whether it was because of the praise to God or the soothing music of an accomplished musician, the evil spirit chose to leave. Most likely it was because there was no dissension or discontent in Saul's heart. The wording of the last phrase, *"he would feel better, and the evil spirit would leave him,"* indicates it wasn't the music itself but the effect the music had on Saul that caused the evil spirit to leave. Peace is from God. Not only is peace a fruit of the Spirit, but our having peace also seems to affect the power spirit beings have over us. The more peace we have in our hearts, the less power evil beings have over us.

Is the right music a surefire method for removing the influence of evil beings? No. "The next day an evil spirit from God came forcefully upon Saul. He was prophesying in his house, while David was playing the harp, as he usually did" (1 Samuel 18:10). It wasn't the harp playing that drove away the evil spirit; it was the feelings Saul was having. When Saul was at peace, the evil spirit left him. When he was filled with jealousy or anger, it could come "forcefully upon" him, even if he were enjoying the music at the time. His jealousy (v. 9) made him vulnerable to the evil spirit, even while directly involved in the godly act of prophesying.

Could there be a message for us as we go through our hectic, emotionally charged days?

I believe there is. Allowing God's peace to overwhelm us and refusing to get caught up in the petty, jealous, angry emotions of our times gives us greater strength against spiritual attack. Praise and pray so you may find peace in God. David's songs of praise to God brought peace to King Saul. Keep a song of praise on your tongue and a thankful prayer on your lips, and if that brings you peace, the evil spirits won't want to bother with you too much. The peace within you that comes from praising God thwarts them. Just doing a spiritual act won't deter them. The spirit attacked Saul as he prophesied. Inner peace is the key.

Peace isn't only a result of the Spirit; it is a weapon of the Spirit.

CONCLUDING THOUGHTS

In the grand scheme of things, it may matter little as to what you believe demons are as long as you know that they serve Satan. But on another level, it does seem to me that it *is* important to know. With increased knowledge comes increased strength and power. With increased knowledge we can grow to broadened wisdom and improved effectiveness in our battle with the principalities and powers of Satan.

I've done my best to show you why I believe that demons are the souls of the dead.

- We've seen why it is crucial to effective Bible interpretation to assign the same meaning to words that the original recipients understood.
- We've examined what people of biblical times understood demons to be.
- We've examined Scripture and learned that: (1) the belief of the day was that demons were the souls of the dead and (2) demons are not fallen angels.
- We've seen that the dead can, in fact, return to earth.
- We've discovered that the dead do have knowledge of things that living people don't.

As with everything else in life, you should reach your own conclusion on the matter. If you decide to study further, don't be misled by the occasional mistranslation in the King James Version where you will see the word *devils* rather than *demon* or *evil spirit.* There is only one devil; there are many evil spirits. I simply ask one thing of you as you study: Be honest with yourself. Don't deny the reality of an argument just because your prejudice says that the conclusion of the argument cannot be right.

Now let's move on to more pressing matters about the activity of demons today. In the next chapter, we will examine whether demons still inhabit people.

CHAPTER NINE

Can Demons Still Possess People?

If she hadn't been so persistent, I'm sure I would have talked her out of the meeting. She and her husband had just completed an intensive counseling series at a Christian university, and part of their homework had been to read sections of the first version of *Seeing the Unseen.* They insisted I allow them to intersect my travels to gain my personal opinion about their situation. I responded that I rarely have free time during my journeys, and besides, if they knew me better, they probably wouldn't trouble themselves to travel across the street to get my opinion, much less halfway across the nation.

Not even a polite chuckle in response: She continued as if I had said nothing.

"We've been to every kind of specialist you can imagine. Gone through a battery of psychological tests. Interviewed with leading experts in their fields. Spent thousands of dollars and countless hours in evaluations, therapies, reevaluations, and 'Sorry we can't help you; we don't know what this is.' Our last counselor said that since every other possibility has been eliminated, it must be demonic and that we should find you to get rid of it."

"Me? Why me?"

"Well, you wrote the book on spiritual warfare that they use in their program. He said you'd understand and would help."

That put me in a dilemma. Yes, I had written that demons are still on earth, but I had also written that my belief had never found practical application. Chapter after chapter in the book contained stories of real events (disguised to protect identities, of course) in which my biblical knowledge had been dramatically deepened by personally engaging in spiritual warfare. But I didn't include stories of personally engaging in battle with demons because I had none. On that subject I wasn't writing about what I had learned from experience in the field, but from thoughtful study and reflection in the comfort of my upstairs study at home.

Therefore, while I was very happy to discuss via telephone my studies and findings with this couple; I was terrified to actually meet them. Thoughts kept running through my mind: "What if there really is a demon? Or maybe even a bunch of them! Maybe what they're thinking is demonic is only mental or emotional illness? How would I recognize whether it is or not? Could they just be wackos from the religious fringe who see a demon under every bush? Hey, why do they want to involve me in this? In *this* area of spiritual warfare I'm a theorist, not a practitioner!"

Finally, feeling guilty for my hesitancy, I agreed to meet them. After hanging up, I remembered a quote from Mack Christian, a mechanic friend who had already gone home to Jesus. Several years ago he was having a terrible time working on a part on my car because of where and how it was situated. He grinned at me and said, "Every person who designs a car should have to be a mechanic on it during its first year of production. The next year's version would be a *lot* more practical if they had to experience firsthand what it means to *do* what they *say* will work! Anybody can tell other folks how they *should* be able to fix something, but they don't understand how it works in the real world until they have to do it themselves."

I grinned myself as I played a mental picture of God smiling at Mack and saying, "Looks like Joe just realized that what you taught him that day applies to authors too."

Just before I answer the question framed in the title of this chapter in a practical, experiential way, please allow me to review some important truths about demons.

But first, I need to clarify our terminology. As we discussed in the previous chapter, in Bible times, *demon* meant any spirit of the dead—

whether wicked or righteous. However, contemporary usage of the word *demon* is confined to *evil* spirits. Therefore, for our remaining discussions about demons, we will use *demon* to mean evil spirit.

THEY ARE STILL HERE

For years I believed that toward the end of the first century, demons returned to the Abyss, where the wicked dead are kept, leaving the earth entirely. When I began to study spiritual warfare, I reexamined that belief.

Those who believe that demons no longer roam the earth often use Zechariah 13:1–2 as proof for that belief. It says, "'On that day a fountain will be opened to the house of David and the inhabitants of Jerusalem, to cleanse them from sin and impurity. On that day, I will banish the names of the idols from the land, and they will be remembered no more,' declares the LORD Almighty. 'I will remove both the prophets and the *spirit of impurity* from the land.'"

They argue that when God removed the prophets from the land, He also removed the unclean spirits. *Unclean spirits* is the way the King James Version translates the phrase under consideration; *spirit of impurity* is the translation found in the New International Version. People who believe that this verse teaches the removal of demons from earth believe that the prophets were removed from the land by the end of the first century. Therefore, they reason, the unclean spirits or demons were removed at the same time.

This is, at the very least, a very vague passage on which to base the belief that demons are no longer here. The only time one can know exactly what a prophet meant is when a New Testament writer explains his prophecy. When you read a phrase like "this is that which was spoken of by the prophet..." you can know, without doubt, the Lord's interpretation of the prophecy. Otherwise, human logic and reason become the avenue for determining the meaning of a prophecy. Those who have absolute faith in their logic have absolute faith in their interpretations. Personally, I have absolute faith only in God and view any human interpretation with caution. There is no New Testament reference indicating that this prophecy means the expulsion of demons from earth, and I fear the human interpretation that assumes such.

I think the rendering in the New International Version makes the meaning of the passage clear. A time was coming when God would remove the *spirit of impurity*—not *demons*—from the land of Israel. No reference—at least no clear reference—to the expulsion of demons is made in this verse.

If there is a passage that teaches the removal of demons from the planet, it would seem we could find it in the New Testament. The truth of the matter is that the New Testament simply doesn't mention or even imply the removal of demons from earth. Paul wrote Timothy: "The Spirit clearly says that in *later times* some will abandon the faith and follow deceiving spirits and things taught by demons" (1 Timothy 4:1). Paul wrote this to Timothy sometime after A.D. 65, warning that demons would still be doing their work in later times than that of the writing of the letter. That certainly shows that demons were active well into the end of the century. So where is the verse indicating their departure by the end of the century?

I searched and searched but could find no passage that clearly taught their departure. That missing verse was the *first* step in my new line of thinking. Its lack prodded me into rethinking the subject, but for a long time, I still didn't alter my theory. The reason was simple: I had never met a demon-possessed person. If they're here, why don't I run into them?

Time took care of that argument too. Although I had not witnessed demon possession personally, my thinking kept being challenged by people who had a different perspective.

Second, my eyes were opened by reading the book *People of the Lie,* the national bestseller by M. Scott Peck, M.D., who also authored the runaway hit *The Road Less Traveled.* Peck is a psychiatrist, well credentialed and widely read. One section of his book was titled "Of Possession and Exorcism."[1]

Peck's accounts didn't convince me, but they did open me to the possibility of demon possession. Already aware that there was no sound, biblical evidence that demons had left the earth since the time of the New Testament, I read his reasoning with openness. Dr. Peck, a trained scientist, argued that some cases of evil in human beings have no other explanation than possession by evil spirits. As I reflected on the evil in the world, I found myself becoming more willing to reconsider my stand.

With my awareness lifted, I began to listen to what I hadn't heard before.

Third, the experiences of those in other churches haunted me. There is a wealth of material available on current-day demon possession from both charismatic and Catholic churches. Even the secular media recognizes their expertise on the subject. While watching the television special "Angels Among Us," broadcast on NBC in May 1994, I heard a series of startling statements. Most of the special was so slanted toward the New Age movement that I paid little attention to it—until Reverend[2] John G. Horgan, a religious scholar, was interviewed. Immediately, he captivated me. He first told of a documented event in August 1914, where both the German and Allied armies reported the presence of visible angels over the battlefield, protecting the British army in a World War I battle. But what bolted me upright in my chair was his story of a demonic episode concerning a five-year-old boy who ranted in some unknown language. The child was audiotaped, and the tapes sent to linguists for study. In their analysis of the tapes, they discovered the child was using obscene profanities from ancient Hebrew, a language to which the child had no exposure. Horgan emphasized the documentation of the phenomenon, stating that they had the tapes as proof. His challenge was clear: If this wasn't a case of demon possession, give it some other believable explanation.

The special dug deeper into demon possession by interviewing Father James J. LeBar, Consultant on Cults for the Archdiocese of New York. He said that between the years of 1960 and 1989 there was little documentation of demon possession. In fact, in the year 1989 there wasn't a single case reported. That changed in 1990. In that one year, more than 250 cases were recorded. Because so many years had passed with little activity, the Catholic church was caught unprepared, having a shortage of priests trained to deal with the demonic problem.

For some time after the special, I sat thinking about the tremendous experience the Catholic church has had with demons and exorcisms. So have many charismatic and Pentecostal churches. Discounting their experiences because of my doctrinal differences with them didn't show great wisdom on my part. I don't have to believe Catholic doctrine to believe they have encountered satanic forces and faced them through the name of Jesus. I think it's time we look beyond the borders of our own religious heritages to see what our religious neighbors have learned that can be of value to us in this spiritual war.

Fourth, I found that there were many preachers—especially younger ones, who were unsure of their political clout and job security—who were searching for someone to listen to their accounts of the situations they had encountered. They felt they had fought demons, but they didn't know whom to talk to about their skirmishes.

Some readers will have difficulty understanding why these preachers couldn't talk openly. But any professional minister of any religious group knows why. The power structures and creeds of organized religion often keep their members from being honest with themselves or with the Word. It matters little whether the topic is demonology or worship, conversion or eschatology. Once the powers-that-be in any religious organization have spoken, it behooves members to accept without question. We don't want to admit it, but it's the truth. I've been there, and I know what it's like to struggle with interesting and challenging new thoughts, wanting to explore the Scriptures but fearing the reaction of fellow Christians. Sometimes their minds are so tightly closed that their belief becomes too holy to question, no matter what scripture you quote.

The preachers I talked with who believed they had encountered demons were from churches who believed that demons are no longer here. If they had dared speak openly of such things, they would have been viewed as "holy-rollers," or worse, theological liberals. But as my mind opened, they began to seek me out. Their stories were so similar that it was as if they had met together to concoct them. Yet the reports came from different men at different times in different parts of the nation. Quite often, they hadn't even heard of each other. But one after the other, they repeated strikingly similar accounts of what they had faced and what they had done.

The *fifth* prodding toward my reassessment came in the form of a statement by a missionary who had worked a long time in Third World countries.

> Why would Satan allow his forces to reveal themselves clearly in America? Americans think Satan a silly fool in a clownish red suit. Allowing demons to possess people and call attention to themselves in this country would be counterproductive. It is much wiser to let the people of America think of Satan as a farce than to drive them to God for deliverance from widespread demon possession. But in Third World countries, where the populace has no doubt that Satan exists, he has nothing to gain from a subdued approach. It is there that he unleashes demons to do their work.

I've been to several places in the world since the original publication of *Seeing the Unseen.* Among those travels I was privileged to visit the western portion of the continent of Africa and spend a little time in the countries of Togo and Benin. Not typical tourist spots to say the least. (My brother Greg travels with me as I go to Third World countries. In

Togo, he discovered firsthand that when in the darkness you unexpectedly encounter a drunken soldier pointing an AK47 at you and wanting money, it's one of those mission moments you cherish forever!)

The voodoo that worked its way into portions of the Americas originated in Togo and Benin. As human beings were captured and carried away to be sold as slaves, many from this region became inhabitants of the Caribbean. Rather than abandoning the demonic religion into which they had been inculcated, they evolved it to include some of the trappings of the Christianity to which they were exposed and expected by their owners to accept.

It's morbidly fascinating to experience their religion in its original setting, free from pseudo-Christian embellishments. Greg and I photographed a three-year-old girl with broad scars on her upper arms. The cruel slashes signified to everyone who saw her that her parents had given her in marriage to a demon. We saw idols with blood sacrifices scattered before them. As missionaries translated so that we could talk with villagers, we discovered that many things they do coincide perfectly with what I have learned in Scripture about demonology. For example, people sacrifice to their dead ancestors as part of their demon worship. (Notice the correspondence to the identity of demons as souls of the dead, which we studied in the last chapter.)

In one village of mud huts and thatched roofs, we were advised not to walk around a particular hut because a demon-worshiping group was gathered on the other side. The chief of the village grimly warned through a translator, "If you go around there and they see that camera around your neck, they will kill you on the spot."

I decided we had enough pictures for the day.

Greg agreed.

Why tell you about this openly demonic portion of the world? Because there *are* demons there—demons who possess people. And these demons are not confined to Africa. There are demons in other parts of the world as well—countries where Satan has nothing to hide because the populace knows he exists and fears his demons.

I won't tell you what many dedicated, loving missionaries from several Third World countries have told me they personally witnessed and done battle against. I've listened carefully to their whispers as they shared with Greg and me what they are afraid to tell their sponsoring churches in America for fear of being disbelieved. Or, more often, fear of being cut off from funding by sanctimonious Christians who would think they had gone native. I understood their hesitancy: If you haven't been to those countries to see, to feel the evil, to experience the undisguised power of the demonic, you might scoff at their experiences. There was a time in my life when I would have too.

Not now.

I've been in villages in the bush and met fetish priests (what Americans typically call witch doctors) and learned of their nearly unfettered power. I've also met a former fetish priest who gave up everything to come to Jesus and who knows things about the spiritual world that most Americans wouldn't want to know.

After listening, evaluating, praying, and sorting through and dismissing the abundant superstitions and apparent folktales of respective peoples, both Greg and I became convinced of the same thing many missionaries have come to know as real. A terrible force exists in this world and carries out malevolence against the populace in countries where they have no reason to disguise themselves. In America, a good portion of Europe, Canada, and similar nations where the populace demotes the devil to the goblin of children's dreams or the imaginary creature of movie directors, Satan would lose his advantage by clearly revealing his power. If you were fighting an enemy who didn't believe you existed, wouldn't that please you? Would you foolishly show yourself, or would you continue the guerilla warfare from hidden ambush?

Then don't think it unusual that the devil does the same.

There are people who live in the world who are possessed and demonstrate the characteristics of those demon-possessed in the New Testament era. I don't have to meet any of those folks to know that is true. The missionaries and those dedicated Christians living in villages, hamlets, or regions controlled by evil earned my respect. They have no reason to lie and every reason for living as righteous a life as possible. If you could meet them, you would quickly learn that they carry great credibility. They aren't deluded; they are clear-minded warriors in front-line battle.

I have no doubt their testimony is true.

Did you notice my line of reasoning? First, no scripture teaches that demons ever left the earth. Second, even a respected physician/psychiatrist like Scott Peck believes their existence is the only logical explanation for the evil in some people, and the exorcisms he has witnessed have brought about deliverance and healing for people whom psychiatry couldn't help. Third, many religious groups have well-documented cases of demon possession. Fourth, more and more preachers from churches who don't believe demons are on earth today are confronting what they believe to be demons. Fifth, many missionaries to Third World countries are convinced they have battled them.

None of these reasons is conclusive by itself, but when I consider them all together, I accept the current existence of demons. Surely, if they are no longer here, there would be one passage of Scripture that would clearly tell of their departure.

CAN DEMONS POSSESS CHRISTIANS?

If you're becoming convinced that demon possession *does* occur today, you may be wondering if it can happen to *you.*

Not if you're a Christian.

Acts 2:38 says that when we are baptized into Christ, we receive the gift of the Holy Spirit. Acts 5:32 also refers to the Holy Spirit whom God gives to Christians. Romans 5:5 says, "God has poured out his love into our hearts by the Holy Spirit, whom he has given us." Since a demon has to take control of a person to possess him, a demon certainly can't possess a Christian as long as the Holy Spirit lives in him or her.

The same protection is available to you. If you, as a penitent believer in Jesus Christ, were baptized into Him, you have received the Holy Spirit. You are a new creature who has passed from death to life. Paul said, "Don't you know that all of us who were baptized into Christ Jesus were baptized into his death? We were therefore buried with him through baptism into death in order that, just as Christ was raised from the dead through the glory of the Father, we too may live a new life" (Romans 6:3–4).

Paul explains further that our new life offers freedom from the control of Satan and sin: "We know that our old self was crucified with him so that the body of sin might be done away with, that we should no longer be slaves to sin—because anyone who has died has been freed from sin" (vv. 6–7).

The apostle Paul tells us that our relationship with God is secure: "I am convinced that neither death nor life, neither angels nor demons, neither the present nor the future, nor any powers, neither height nor depth, nor anything else in all creation, will be able to separate us from the love of God that is in Christ Jesus our Lord" (Romans 8:38–39).

There is no evil spirit strong enough to displace the Holy Spirit who lives in the Christian. Innocence doesn't repel these evil beings, but the power of the Spirit of God does. The Bible tells us of children who were possessed, but never of Christians who were possessed.

But there is another aspect of demonic operation that isn't the same as possession. The popular term for it in our time is *demonization,* and it *can* happen to a Christian.

DEMONIZATION

How could Christians possibly be demonized if the Holy Spirit is within them?

Because in demonization the Holy Spirit of God isn't displaced. The demon doesn't take control of the person as in possession but rather assumes a position of extreme influence and inordinate power over the person's decisions and actions. Demon-possessed people operate at the demon's whim and wish: They don't have the *ability* to resist. On the other hand, demonized people make their own decisions—they could resist if they knew how—but they *feel* as if they have no control over their actions because of the extreme influence demons exert.

The Devil's Foothold

We gain more insight into this concept in Ephesians 4:27, in which Paul admonishes Christians, "Do not give the devil a foothold." We need to know what Paul meant by "give the devil a foothold" to understand the Holy Spirit's admonition in that passage.

- The King James Version translates the phrase as "Neither give place to the devil."
- The New American Standard Bible has it, "do not give the devil an opportunity."
- Thayer defines this foothold as "a place, any portion or space marked off, as it were, from a surrounding space: metaphorically, opportunity, power, occasion for acting."[3]

With that insight, examine the verse in context:

> You were taught, with regard to your former way of life, to put off your old self, which is being corrupted by its deceitful desires; to be made new in the attitude of your minds; and to put on the new self, created to be like God in true righteousness and holiness.
>
> Therefore each of you must put off falsehood and speak truthfully to his neighbor, for we are all members of one body. "In your anger do

> not sin": Do not let the sun go down while you are still angry, and do not give the devil a foothold. (Ephesians 4:22–27)

In the context of telling Christians that we should be "like God," Paul solemnly informs us that if we cling to anger, we give the devil a foothold. From the translations and definition above, you can see that by sinfully clinging to anger, a Christian gives the forces of Satan a place, a power, an occasion for acting in that Christian's life.

Not satanic control, not possession. We still make our decisions. But by clinging to the anger, we have made ourselves more susceptible to satanic power. Tremendous power. We have presented opportunity for Satan's minions to lead us into more sin because of the vulnerability created by the sin we have not yet abandoned.

Be clear about this: Paul didn't say we've given our "flesh" a foothold. He isn't telling us that we've simply made ourselves weaker in our Christian walk and will, therefore, have more difficulty in dealing with everyday temptations. He says that we have given *the devil* a foothold. His hordes, minions, and spirits now have an access to us because we have allowed them an avenue to sneak inside our spiritual armor.

Because anger isn't the only sin mentioned in the surrounding verses (others mentioned are lying, stealing, unwholesome talk, bitterness, rage, brawling, slander, and "every form of malice"), it appears that any of these negative, sinful emotions creates a spiritual vulnerability within a Christian. As God admonishes us to become new and to seek to be like Him, He inserts a warning that we give the devil's forces[4] undue or inordinate influence over us if we cling to a sin that we should be ridding ourselves of.

Surely you've seen this in others if you haven't experienced it yourself.

- A sincere preacher who loves Jesus and wants to do right struggles with addiction to pornography, crying through the night because of the Web sites he visited earlier. He wants to quit, to never do it again, but when the desire hits him, he feels so much compulsion to go back to the porn that he feels he cannot resist.

- A woman who has given Jesus her heart and life occasionally finds herself screaming abusive words of scorn and hate at her children and doesn't seem to be able to stop. She hates herself for the abuse but doesn't have any idea how to prevent or stop the sinful behavior. It's as if at the times she does it she isn't herself and has absolutely no control.

- A sex addict enters one extramarital affair after another while abhorring himself and craving a loving relationship with his wife. He knows that what he is doing is wrong, but as soon as a new vulnerable woman enters the picture, he plots her seduction even as he prepares for his next Bible class at church.

Yes, these people are culpable. I am not in any way trying to suggest that they bear no responsibility for their decisions or actions. But what I finally came to realize is that many of these Christians (and quite a few non-Christians) face a force far more powerful than typical temptation. Unwittingly they left unsecured a portion of their personal and spiritual armor, allowing a Trojan horse to be placed within their gates. Operating from within the walls, unhampered by barriers and defenses, the devil's forces have their own room (foothold) inside the individual that gives the perfect vantage point for knowing just when and how to manipulate the individual into perennial sin.

Their manipulation is so powerful that the individual buys the lie that he or she cannot overcome the desire to sin. It's not uncommon for demonized people to report feeling as if another person is doing their thinking for them. They don't claim that "the devil made me do it." They simply feel powerless to control their own emotions and desires.

Inordinate Control

Demonization is control without complete command, inordinate influence that leads the person to feel irresistibly compelled and helpless even when he or she isn't.

Perhaps an illustration will make this clearer. A preacher friend once counseled a Christian lady who begged him to help her find a way to stop her affair with a married man. As he asked her why she didn't tell the man to leave her alone, she replied, "Oh, I have. Many times. And I think I'm over him. But eventually he comes for me again. When I open the door of my apartment and he's standing there, I lose all sense of reality. I no longer know what time it is, what day it is, or what I was going to do next. I am instantly his to do with as he wishes. It's like I have no will or control. No thought of consequences, of right or wrong. Whatever he wants, I will do without question."

If you think her description self-justifying, may I remind you of a passage? Talking about certain evil men, Paul wrote: "They are the kind who worm their way into homes and gain control over weak-willed women, who are loaded down with sins and are swayed by all kinds of evil desire" (2 Timothy 3:6).

Situations exist in which one human being can hold inordinate levels of influence over another. No, that doesn't justify the sin of the influenced person. The "victim" could take control of his or her decisions and actions. But as long as the evil influence prevails, the person believes that he or she is incapable of exerting discipline and self-control. If you were dealing with the situation my preacher friend faced, I'm quite sure you would tell the lady that she had to get completely away from that man, that she could have no contact with him whatsoever. As long as a person possesses seemingly irresistible influence over another, we know that the victim's freedom and subsequent spiritual health can never be achieved until the evil one is removed decisively from his or her life.

Some people carry nearly unbelievable ability to get other people to do as they wish. Paul says the devil has this ability too: "Those who oppose him [the man of God] he must gently instruct, in the hope that God will grant them repentance leading them to a knowledge of the truth, and that they will come to their senses and escape from the trap of the devil, who has taken them captive to do his will" (2 Timothy 2:25–26).

Come to their senses? Captive? Do his will? What is the Holy Spirit saying through Paul?

"Come to their senses" comes from the koine Greek word *ananepho* (an-an-ay'-fo), which means to become sober again. "Captive" is how the NIV translates *zogreo* (dzogue-reh'-o), which means to take alive or make a prisoner of war. And to do Satan's "will" comes from *thelema* (thel'-ay-mah), which has to do with purpose, decree, or volition.[5]

In this passage, the Holy Spirit refers to those who act as if they are drunk and no longer controlled by their own senses and intelligence. He says that they are that way because they have been taken prisoners of war. (Dare we call it spiritual war?) As benumbed prisoners, they weaken to the point that they yield their will to the will of their captor. Yes, they are responsible, but they don't feel that they can do anything to change because they have allowed themselves to become victims of satanic "brainwashing."[6]

These aren't good people falling short on occasion. These are people entangled in satanic snares to the point that they yield their wills. I've worked with people like that. They think they have no control, feel that they cannot stop. They are like those whom Peter said are mastered, entangled, or overcome. This isn't the everyday Christian struggle with flesh. It is much more than that. It is a person overcome in his struggle with evil to the point he becomes a slave of depravity.[7] "They...are slaves of depravity— for a man is a slave to whatever has mastered him. If they have escaped the corruption of the world by knowing our Lord and Savior Jesus Christ and are again entangled in it and overcome, they are worse off at the end than they were at the beginning" (2 Peter 2:19–20).

Any person can do evil. Some commit evil for so long that they willingly become evil. The two passages I referred to above could very accurately apply to those who are willingly evil, but they also apply to those who are demonized. The demonized are people who want to do right but cannot find within themselves the ability to allow the power of God to free them from their continual sin. They are in an up-close and personal battle against something that is real—something not of themselves, something stronger than they.

Rather than thinking in terms of temptation, think of these demonized people as being infected by imponderable influence. They are afflicted by demons who have taken advantage of an available foothold, and these demons have every advantage because by living within, they know the person's strengths and weaknesses.

How can people by their own power overcome an enemy who easily accesses their thoughts and emotions? How can they ignore a being who can whisper into their unconscious repetitive suggestions appealing to their weakest character? Like obsessed people, the demonized feel helpless, hopeless, and heartsick. They simply don't know how to overcome their sins. I guess you could say that in comparison with the rest of us, their temptation is to the tenth power!

Is There Help for the Demonized?

If you've been a Christian for a few years, you can make your own list of nearly incomprehensible actions you've either personally experienced or witnessed in people who you know love Jesus. No, not random acts that seldom, if ever, get repeated. Not that kind of temptation that every human faces. These sinful actions spring to life, subside into remission, and spring to life again. No one, including the sinner, seems to understand why he or she continues to struggle, why he or she cannot overcome the temptation or defeat the repetitious sin by the power of God.

I could attempt to give a list of symptoms or signs of demonization, but I am convinced that any such list would be used to hurt rather than help. Besides, lists can be wrong. I believe it much better to use spiritual discernment to discover that one is demonized rather than to use any so-called symptomatic list. That's why I write here in principle rather than in specific tests or analyzations. Some people who may appear to be demonized really are emotionally, psychologically, or physically ill. Why torment them with the rituals or ravings of well-intentioned but overzealous Christians who may actually exacerbate the problem? (Harm has been done and surely will be done again.[8])

Even with that warning, I emphasize that the *only* way those who are demonized will be made whole is when the power of God comes to deliver them from the evil beings who have a foothold within them. Until that happens they will suffer impulsiveness, intemperance, and self-created indignities.

You can preach to them, teach them, chastise them, pray for them, call them to accountability, and restrict their every movement without ever solving the problem. You can medicate them to reduce the boundaries of their sinful behavior or overmedicate them to the point of inertia, but their problem still isn't solved. Until we finally realize that demonized people are not mentally or emotionally ill, nor are they hopelessly evil, but instead that they need freedom from demonization, they have little hope of spiritual recovery.

If a person is truly demonized, nothing will ever free the person—whether Christian or not—from that recurring sin until the demonic has been soundly defeated by the power of Jesus.

If up to this point you haven't believed anything I've written in this book, your experiences with your own recurring struggles or with people you love prove the correctness of that preceding paragraph, don't they? You've known that something else had to be done, known that you and other helpers didn't know how to achieve victory. Frustrated, disappointed, drained, you've come to the brink of completely giving up. Now that you have a different perspective of what power drives the recurring sin and how that power has such control, you can finally see the spiritual solution.

Oh, the couple at the beginning of this chapter? They give the perfect example of what we'll study in the next chapter. You'll meet them again there and learn their fate.

CHAPTER TEN

How Do Christians Overcome the Demonic Today?

As we prayed for her, she slipped from her chair and puddled on the floor. Her husband quickly moved to the floor with her and lifted her head into his lap, cradling her as he would one who was dying.

In a sense she was.

She moaned, cried out in pain repeatedly, and dripped tears enough to have washed the feet of Jesus. A clear phlegm-like substance seeped from her nose and her mouth, slowly covering her clothes. Sometimes her sobbed words were understandable. Sometimes they were so garbled that no one could make sense of them.

Sometimes other sounds coursed through the room that none present wanted to think about.

All the while, we continued to pray aloud. We called on the power of God. We asked Him specific things on her behalf. We repeatedly relied on the name of Jesus. So that she would not feel that we were trying to control her freedom or actions, we occasionally asked her if she wished us to stop, if she wanted us to leave.

No.

Whenever she said that word, it was always clear. She was in great pain, but she would not have us stop.

She wanted to be free.

I refuse to give any more details in this book about what happened that day. All I can tell you at this point is that she was the wife in the couple I mentioned at the beginning of the last chapter. In just a few pages, I will tell you the result of our interaction, but first I want to give some very practical warnings about dealing with demons.

DEMONS ARE REAL, AND THEIR POWER IS TO BE RESPECTED

1. To Deny Demon Possession Is to Deny Scripture

As a Bible-believing Christian, I must believe that people deny the inspiration of the New Testament when they explain away its demonic stories as misconceptions about diseases and the superstition of a simple people. While demons sometimes caused diseases or physical maladies, the demons were quite different from the malady itself. When Jesus spoke with the multitude of demons who called themselves Legion, they had identity, knew who He was, and begged Him not to cast them into the Abyss. Unless the New Testament writers fabricated the story, demons were real beings. Therefore, only those modernists who deny the inspiration of Scripture would deny that demons actually existed as real beings. The Scripture presents them as such, and all those who accept Scripture as the Holy Writ of God must accept them that way as well.

My guess is that nearly every Bible-believing Christian who read the above paragraph mentally gave it an amen.

But many Bible-believing Christians do deny the existence of demons today, using the same logic as those modernists who deny that they really existed in the New Testament era. The modernists say that in the New Testament, people who thought they had demons or met demons were simply superstitious and uneducated. Today many Christians say the same about those who truly believe they have encountered demons. These skeptics often justify their beliefs by citing a case where some overzealous Christian tried to cast out a demon when obviously the problem wasn't spiritual but emotional, psychological, or physical. They cry, "See! It's just superstition. Not demons! You guys need to accept the great strides in science and quit living in the darkness of religious fanaticism. Demon possession ended in the first century."

If you think that way, keep reading.

2. Mistaken Diagnosis Doesn't Mean That Demons Don't Exist

It is undoubtedly true that many overzealous Christians—even ignorant and superstitious Christians—have claimed to have dealt with demons when no demons were present. What they encountered was nothing more than their own misunderstanding or misconception. Calling something a demon doesn't mean that it is. And it is undoubtedly true that some Christians have been badly hurt either emotionally, psychologically, or physically by those who assaulted them in an effort to remove the alleged demon.

But that doesn't mean that demons don't exist.

Citing misdiagnosis and severe treatment of a supposed demoniac no more proves that demons aren't here than a jury's mistaken conviction of a murderer and his subsequent execution prove that there are no murderers. The occasional failure of our legal system doesn't mean that a jury cannot examine evidence and come to a logical conclusion as to the guilt of a defendant. In like manner, an occasional failure on the part of overzealous or misinformed Christians doesn't mean that none of us could ever correctly deduce that an individual is possessed by a demon or demonized.[1]

Those who deny that spiritual warfare in our day includes the demonic typically relegate all human problems to the realm of the physician. Those who believe that spiritual warfare continues to involve the demonic all too often look for and find demons where none actually exists. Extremes on either side do not prove that either view should be discarded altogether.

When the true problem is physical or psychological, no one will cure the person by "casting out demons," because the problem isn't demonic. But at the same time, professionals who employ all that modern medical, pharmacological, and psychological science offers will continue to find that their methods will never heal some patients, because their problem isn't physical or psychological at its root. They aren't sick because of natural reasons, but because of supernatural reasons—specifically, demonic attack. People whose sickness is supernatural can be cured only by spiritual means.

3. Possession Is Rare and Must Be Proven!

It is common knowledge that the Catholic church has the most research and writings on the subject of demonology. While my own understanding of the Bible often puts me in conflict with Catholic views or doctrines, I find that some of their points hold great value to us who are non-Catholics. For example, though the Catholic church believes a person may be possessed by demons, they are likely the most skeptical group when it comes to believing that a specific individual is demon possessed. Because so many zealous people have attributed other human problems to the demonic, the Catholic tests to determine possession are quite extreme. In the General Rules Concerning Exorcism, they state:

> Especially, [the exorcist] should not believe too readily that a person is possessed by an evil spirit; but he ought to ascertain the signs by which a person possessed can be distinguished from one who is suffering from some illness, especially one of a psychological nature. Signs of possession may be the following: ability to speak with some facility in a strange tongue or to understand it when spoken by another; the faculty of divulging future and hidden events; display of powers which are beyond the subject's age and natural condition; and various other indications which, when taken together as a whole, build up the evidence.[2]

Maybe we should be as careful in our assessment of demon possession ourselves. When the Holy Spirit describes cases of demon possession in the New Testament, they are extreme and unusual. That's why I said earlier that I've never encountered true possession.

But I have encountered the lesser level that I mentioned in the previous chapter. It isn't possession but demonization.

4. Gradual Awareness of a Lesser Level of Demonic Activity

Catholics and Protestants alike are aware that while demonic possession is rare, there are other ways that demons operate. In the previous chapter, I explained the type of demonic activity that we called demonization. It isn't possession and doesn't require an exorcism, as exorcisms are normally considered. But it does take Christians fighting the power of Satan by the power of the Holy Spirit.

5. Overcoming Demons Requires Preparation and Spiritual Authority

Preparation

If that last paragraph makes you want to grab your Bible and go looking for a demon to deal with, slow down! Demons aren't weak, ineffective beings that any Christian can just saunter up to and order around. In dealing with demons, I recommend that we adopt the attitude expressed in Jude 9: "But even the archangel Michael, when he was disputing with the devil about the body of Moses, did not dare to bring a slanderous accusation against him, but said, 'The Lord rebuke you!'"

If the most powerful good angel we know anything about didn't confront Satan by his *own* power but instead said, "The Lord rebuke you!" we surely should maintain a respectful fear. Just because I know the name of Jesus and am a Christian doesn't mean that I am equipped to fight Satan's forces directly. In Ephesians 4, Paul makes it clear that becoming equipped requires training by those who are more mature. A couple of chapters later, in Ephesians 6, he tells us that facing evil requires armor and an offensive weapon. He goes on to let us know that when we are fighting spiritual war, we should involve intense prayer, even to the point of praying "in the Spirit" (6:18).

If you wish to fight the devil's forces (and I hope you grow to that point), you will have to operate under the authority of Jesus, or you yourself will be defeated as you attempt to free others.

Spiritual Authority

Does it take a priest or an ordained minister to confront the powers of Satan? No. The early church father Origen "expressly stated that even the simplest and rudest of the faithful sometimes cast out demons, by a mere prayer or adjuration, and urges the fact as proof of the power of Christ's grace, and the inability of demons to resist it."[3]

Not only did Christians confront the powers of Satan in the era just after the first century, I can show you biblically that people in the New Testament did it as well—people who were *not* apostles or ordained ministers, people who operated in the name of Jesus.

How do we do that? Read on.

OVERCOMING THE DEMONIC THROUGH THE AUTHORITY OF JESUS

When the disciples of Jesus in the New Testament cast out demons, they relied on authority and faith. Can we do the same today? Do we have the authority of Jesus to deal with demons?

Jesus Shared His Authority with Others

For years I argued that only the apostles and those on whom the apostles laid their hands had the authority to cast out demons. Of course, at that time, I believed that demons left the planet in the first century and hadn't been back since. To be completely honest, I must admit that my belief that they were gone grew directly from my belief that no one on earth had any authority to deal with them. My logic was simple: If we don't have the authority to cast them out, God must have made them leave so that we could maintain some type of spiritual balance.

Several of my compatriots still believe that, though their beliefs contain a contradiction they usually don't realize. They believe demons to be fallen angels. They believe fallen angels still operate on the earth. But they don't believe that demons can possess or affect people. (I'm not sure, but I think the name for that is compartmentalized thinking.)

While I believe we have the authority to deal with demons today, please don't think I believe that any person has authority like Jesus had when He lived in a human body. Any reasonable observer who experienced His personal ministry could see and recognize His unequaled authority and power. "All the people were amazed and said to each other, 'What is this teaching? With authority and power he gives orders to evil spirits and they come out!'" (Luke 4:36).

Jesus' Threefold Ministry Purpose

But Jesus didn't come to do all the work Himself. In the ninth chapter of Matthew, Jesus demonstrated that His ministry focused on three things:

- healing the sick
- casting out demons
- preaching the good news of the kingdom

As He sent out the apostles, He told them to focus on the same three areas. "He gave them power and authority to drive out all demons and to cure diseases, and he sent them out to preach the kingdom of God and to heal the sick" (Luke 9:1–2; cf. Matthew 10:1–8; Mark 6:7–12).

The apostles became His team, taking the gospel to the world. But those twelve would not be enough. Even in those ancient days, the world contained vast numbers of people who needed to see the power of God and hear His saving gospel. So Jesus sent more workers to gather the harvest: "After this the Lord appointed seventy-two others and sent them two by two ahead of him to every town and place where he was about to go" (Luke 10:1). He told them, "Heal the sick who are there and tell them, 'The kingdom of God is near you'" (v. 9).

Notice that He told this group of seventy-two to do two of the three things that He and His apostles focused on—healing the sick and preaching the good news of the kingdom. What about the third focus, driving out demons? "The seventy-two returned with joy and said, 'Lord, even the demons submit to us in your name'" (v. 17).

The seventy-two continued with the same three components of the strategy that guided Jesus' mission.

The Purpose of Jesus' Ministry Focus

Why these three areas? Why did Jesus, His apostles, and His larger evangelistic team concentrate on these three things?[4] Obviously I cannot speak for God, but I am happy to share my opinion! He apparently concentrated on these three areas to show His power:

- over nature (healing the sick)
- over Satan (casting out demons)
- to save souls (establishing His kingdom on earth)

By attacking on those three fronts, His new army of evangelists directly combated the evils that Satan had brought to the human race. Satan's tempting of Eve brought about physical maladies. His evil spirits inhabiting humankind gave him diabolical control over individuals. His introducing sin to the earth through Eve and Adam brought about the spiritual downfall of the human race. By attacking and defeating the devil's forces on these three battlefronts, Jesus gave clear indication to Satan that the war was on.

Jesus said to the seventy-two: "I saw Satan fall like lightning from heaven. I have given you authority to trample on snakes and scorpions and to overcome all the power of the enemy; nothing will harm you. However, do not rejoice that the spirits submit to you, but rejoice that your names are written in heaven" (Luke 10:18–20).

Of course, not only did He serve notice to Satan, He also served notice to the population of this world that His power was available to free them from the bondage of sin. They could now be saved, freed from demonic power, and given a life that would last forever (in a new body on a new earth to come). No wonder thousands responded to the good news and became Christians. They had the opportunity to gain back everything Satan had stolen from them.

Jesus' Ministry Focus Is Still Effective Today

In my opinion, that is why those three dimensions of ministry are still so effective in evangelism. It also seems to explain why a church ignoring any of the three prongs of Jesus' spiritual strategy proportionately loses the ability to attract people to Jesus. People still want to be well, to be delivered from Satan's minions, and to be in heaven forever. Ignoring their physical, spiritual, or eternal longings is to ignore the very ministries that made the church grow so rapidly in the New Testament.

That three-pronged attack on Satan's world is just as needed and just as powerful today as it was in the first century. And God's power and authority are available for the battle.

Authority Comes in the Name of Jesus

When Paul cast the demon out of the girl in Acts 16, he cried, "'In the name of Jesus Christ I command you to come out of her!' At that moment the spirit left her" (v. 18). There is power in His name.

Jesus had authority. He gave authority to the apostles. Then He gave it to the seventy-two. Did anyone else receive it, or were those all that He needed to continue the threefold mission?

The answer can be quickly ascertained from the New Testament. Yes, other Christians received Jesus' authority to combat disease, demons, and spiritual death.

Philip

When the apostles realized that they were too busy to take care of the physical needs (specifically feeding widows) of the Jerusalem church, they asked the church to appoint men to take that responsibility. One of them was the evangelist Philip (Acts 6:5–6). Shortly after his appointment, "Philip went down to a city in Samaria and proclaimed the Christ there. When the crowds heard Philip and saw the miraculous signs he did, they all paid close attention to what he said. With shrieks, evil spirits came out of many, and many paralytics and cripples were healed. So there was great joy in that city" (Acts 8:5–8).

The Man John Saw

An unnamed man cast out demons to the consternation of the apostles who didn't know him.

> "Teacher," said John, "we saw a man driving out demons in your name and we told him to stop, because he was not one of us."
>
> "Do not stop him," Jesus said. "No one who does a miracle in my name can in the next moment say anything bad about me, for whoever is not against us is for us. I tell you the truth, anyone who gives you a cup of water in my name because you belong to Christ will certainly not lose his reward." (Mark 9:38–41)

This unnamed believer was working miracles—specifically casting out demons—in the name of Jesus, and Jesus wanted him left alone. He employed the authority of Jesus' name to do these wonderful works.

The thing that upset the apostles was that he didn't fit their conception of how and when Jesus grants His authority. Nor does he fit the perceptions of most Christians of our time.

He wasn't meant to.

His story shows us that no matter who we are (even an apostle), we have no right to decide whom God will use or how He will use him or her.[5] Nor will He allow us to make rules about what He can do and what He can't. God refuses to live by our logic or deductions.

Sometimes our human system of interpretation can lead to some devastatingly wrong conclusions. Wouldn't it be terrible to erroneously establish a doctrine that kept us from accessing the power God wants to give us?[6]

Authority Comes through Relationship with Jesus

Now let's look at people who could work miracles in the name of Jesus although they had no relationship with Him:

> Not everyone who says to me, "Lord, Lord," will enter the kingdom of heaven, but only he who does the will of my Father who is in heaven. Many will say to me on that day, "Lord, Lord, did we not prophesy in

> your name, and in your name drive out demons and perform many miracles?" Then I will tell them plainly, "I never knew you. Away from me, you evildoers!"(Matthew 7:21–23)

Some conclude that these people claim to have done something they never did and that Jesus cast them away because of their lies. That view doesn't fit the context. Why would anyone tell an outright lie on Judgment Day? These people aren't lying; instead, they are deluded. Because they could do certain wondrous things in the name of Jesus, they assumed they had a relationship with Him. Jesus made it clear that it isn't what we do in His name that makes us His; it's whether we have a relationship with Him.

But the point is obvious. Here are people whom Jesus said would show up on Judgment Day proclaiming that they worked miracles in His name. He doesn't tell them they didn't; just that they missed the point: Him.

Interesting that we deduce who can and who can't, while Jesus says that some who can aren't even His!

Are we indicating that just calling out the name of Jesus gives a person the ability to cast out a demon?

No.

> Some Jews who went around driving out evil spirits tried to invoke the name of the Lord Jesus over those who were demon-possessed. They would say, "In the name of Jesus, whom Paul preaches, I command you to come out." Seven sons of Sceva, a Jewish chief priest, were doing this. One day the evil spirit answered them, "Jesus I know, and I know about Paul, but who are you?" Then the man who had the evil spirit jumped on them and overpowered them all. He gave them such a beating that they ran out of the house naked and bleeding. (Acts 19:13–16)

The wording indicates that some of the demons did actually leave when these characters commanded them to do so in the name of Jesus. But they eventually met a demon who was too savvy to yield so easily. Instead, he beat them bloody. The very name of Jesus carries authority, but some demons are so powerful that it takes more than employing His name. There must be spiritual authority in the individual as well.

Where does that come from?

Read on.

Authority Is Connected with Faith in Jesus

In three of the Gospels, we find various perspectives of an unusual event. Though Jesus had given the apostles power over demons, they couldn't cast a particular one out. This particularly violent demon had lived in a boy since his childhood, causing seizures and suffering. It robbed him of the faculties of speech and hearing. Occasionally, the demon would try to kill the boy by throwing him into water or fire. After the apostles' failure, the boy's father asked Jesus to cast out the demon, and He did. Of course, the apostles wanted to know why they couldn't do it themselves. Let's examine a few words from Matthew's and Mark's perspectives to see what we can learn. (I quote only where each writer recorded important words in different ways. To compare word for word in context, you will need to use your Bible.)

We begin with Matthew.

> "O unbelieving and perverse generation," Jesus replied, "how long shall I stay with you? How long shall I put up with you?"...
>
> Then the disciples came to Jesus in private and asked, "Why couldn't we drive it out?"
>
> He replied, "Because you have so little faith. I tell you the truth, if you have faith as small as a mustard seed, you can say to this mountain, 'Move from here to there' and it will move. Nothing will be impossible for you." (Matthew 17:17–21)

Now examine Mark's account.

> Jesus asked the boy's father, "How long has he been like this?"
>
> "From childhood," he answered. "It has often thrown him into fire or water to kill him. But if you can do anything, take pity on us and help us."
>
> "'If you can'?" said Jesus. "Everything is possible for him who believes."
>
> Immediately the boy's father exclaimed, "I do believe; help me overcome my unbelief!"...
>
> After Jesus had gone indoors, his disciples asked him privately, "Why couldn't we drive it out?"
>
> He replied, "This kind can come out only by prayer." (Mark 9:21–29)

(Luke's account adds little for our specific purpose [Luke 9:38–43].)

Notice the reason for the apostles' failure: lack of faith.

Jesus referred to unbelief three different times in these accounts.

- The unbelief of the people in general—"unbelieving generation."
- The unbelief of the apostles themselves—"You have so little faith."
- The unbelief of the boy's father—"'If you can'? Everything is possible for him who believes."

Jesus instructed the apostles about this failed exorcism as He would do so again later about a withered fig tree (Matthew 21:21). He used the opportunity to teach them that faith as small as a mustard seed can move mountains. To make sure they didn't think He was speaking metaphorically but was offering them a way to employ the very power of heaven, He said to the apostles, "Nothing will be impossible for you."

Nothing? Let's see: If nothing is impossible, then everything is possible. Right? Yes! In Mark's account, He used that very phrase: "Everything is possible for him who believes" (9:23). But this time He wasn't speaking to apostles but to the father of the demoniac boy!

Since the father wasn't one of Jesus' apostles or a minister of any kind, we can comfortably say that the promise wasn't just to those whom Jesus gave special gifts or authority. Furthermore, the promise wasn't just to the apostles or the boy's father. It is to all who believe! When Jesus said "for him who believes," He included every believer, not just a select few.

If in our minds we relegate that wonderful promise only to those of biblical times, our own disbelief in its availability shields us from accessing God's amazing power. He offers it to those who believe, not to those who disbelieve or doubt.

Don't go fighting demons without the kind of faith Jesus discusses here. Although they called on the power and authority of His name, the apostles' own lack of faith prevented their success in that spiritual battle.

Why did Jesus say, "This kind can come out only by prayer"? Comparing His statement about faith on this occasion to His similar statement at the cursing of the fig tree answers that question.

Jesus replied, "I tell you the truth, if you have faith and do not doubt, not only can you do what was done to the fig tree, but also you can say to this mountain, 'Go, throw yourself into the sea,' and it will be done. If you believe, you will receive whatever you ask for in prayer" (Matthew 21:21–22).

It's still a matter of faith. The purer our faith (the less doubt we have), the more of God's power we can call into spiritual battle. I didn't say that; Jesus did. Does that mean that His power is limited by our faith? No. He is all-powerful whether we believe or not. But He makes it clear that He chooses to direct His greatest power to those who go in His name, who know Him, and who believe without doubting that He will do the impossible.

If you want to be a spiritual warrior, continually deepen your faith in Him and your relationship with Him. That's where He gives His authority—not to titles but to faith working by love.

CONFRONTING DEMONIZATION

At the beginning of chapter nine, we will introduced a couple who came to me because they were convinced demonization existed in their home. Specifically, they believed the wife to be demonized. As you recall, all types of experts, evaluations, and the like had indicated that her problem was neither mental, emotional, nor physical. With all those possibilities exhausted, they discerned that demons were present and asked my aid in overcoming them.

Discovering Footholds

Since I believe that a demonized Christian must have opened the door through some type of foothold, I interviewed her at length about any sin that she refused to quit or release. Based on my understanding of Ephesians 4:25–32, I specifically asked many questions designed to discover the existence of things such as:

- Lying
- Anger
- Stealing
- Slothfulness
- Unwholesome talk
- Bitterness
- Rage
- Brawling
- Slander

- Every form of malice
- Refusing to forgive

Carefully, I pointed out that if she were clinging to one of those evils, she gave the devil's forces a foothold within her. No matter how much we believed or prayed, until she "closed the breech" in her spiritual armor, the demons could come right back in. We read the scripture in which Jesus talked about how much worse the reinfestation is than the initial demonic presence (Matthew 12:43–45).

During the course of our conversation, I discovered that she held an intense hatred toward her stepfather who had repeatedly sexually molested her. She had never forgiven him and felt that she never could. The longer we talked, the more obvious it became to everyone in the room that her hatred and unforgiving spirit created the foothold that allowed her to be spiritually violated. That's how demons continually lured her into the same sin repeatedly. She felt helpless, out of control. I explained that by believing that she could not forgive her stepfather, she was believing a lie. She wasn't possessed but demonized. She was responsible for her actions and must take a firm stand against the devil's schemes. At the same time, we needed to separate her from her tormentors (demons) so she could have peace and time to heal.

Praying with Intense Faith

After a couple of hours of talking and studying, my "gentle instruction" led her to repentance. She finally understood that her lingering rage toward her stepfather caused him no punishment at all but was leading to her own spiritual failure. She forgave him, and then we all sought God in an intense prayer full of faith. She took responsibility for her own actions and admitted to herself that while she often felt out of control, she really did have control. She had been allowing her anger, hurt, and emotional confusion to so fog her mind that she repeatedly made sinful decisions. Now that she was in the process of forgiving her father and clearing her mind of her hurt and pain, she was beginning to remove the foothold. Now we needed to separate the evil beings from her just as surely as we would separate her from a lover who exercised undue influence over her. With her agreement and participation, we went to war through prayer.

During an hour or so of prayer, we did what Paul did and, in the name of Jesus Christ, commanded the demon to leave her.

I never asked its name. Never used any holy or sacred objects. Used no rituals or recitations. Did no binding by my own power or strength. (Like the archangel Michael, I called on the Lord to do the rebuking.) I and the minister who was there to assist called faithfully and regularly on the name of Jesus and in faith expected God to do all that had to be done to set the woman free.

He did.

She has been free for more than two years at the time of this writing and suffered absolutely no reoccurrence of the problems that led her to ask for help.

As directed, she went home and told her minister what had occurred and asked him to guide her in spiritual growth so that the demon could not return.

What if It Wasn't a Demon?

You may be thinking the same thing I felt for months after that encounter. What if the experts were wrong? What if the problem was emotional or psychological? Maybe all we did was offer her a form of positive suggestion instead of real deliverance?

Finally, I reached what I believe to be a sound and safe conclusion to the matter.

First, we did no harm.

- Neither the minister nor I tried in any way to convince her that she was demonized, thus causing further mental or emotional confusion on her part.
- We carefully considered the professional opinions of the medical doctors and psychologists who had examined her. We checked and double-checked to make sure that we did nothing contrary to their advice or opinion. While I don't rely on doctors to give me spiritual counsel or to make the final decision on spiritual matters, I do give great respect to their training and expertise.
- We did nothing to restrain her, unduly agitate her, scare her, or embarrass her. She had complete control of her actions and freedom at all times.
- We did all we could to make her comfortable and safe.

Second, spiritual victory was won.

- Her problem had not been solved by the medical or psychological experts she had seen for years but was solved by confronting the demons she believed she had.
- Since we cannot see demons except on the radar of faith, we didn't look for an evil being to come snarling and tearing as proof that evil beings manipulated her. We believe that the *results* of the spiritual effort to remove demons proved its validity. Her problem was finally and completely solved.
- The woman and her husband have a wonderful marriage for the first time in twenty years.
- Her spiritual life is dramatically different now. She has a strong, faith-filled relationship with Jesus that is the guiding light to her life.

If you scoff because we saw no grotesque, drooling demon and cannot prove scientifically that he was ever there, I guess you'll scoff forever. I offer no other proof of our efficacy than the incontestable results in the woman's life. If I were to tell of things we saw, heard, smelled, and the like, I would only denigrate an act of spiritual war. Besides, since we have no examinable proof such as videos, you would have to take my word anyway.

And that, my friend, is an act of faith.

Why should you have faith in my veracity if you lack faith in the power of God to bring deliverance to one of His children?

The Thing to Remember

Demons aren't buffoons, goblins, or timid trolls. They are very real and very effective at their work. Sometimes demons have to be confronted directly; and by this very writing, I am encouraging Christians to have the faith to fight them. But not just anyone should attempt such a confrontation.

Only those who are spiritual, godly, and mature should attempt it.

They should never do it by thinking they have enough power on their own. It scares me terribly every time I hear some Christian say something like "I bind you" or "I cast you out." If the demon decides you aren't full of the power of God, you may just find yourself taking quite a beating.

The power of God is given to those who have faith that isn't riddled by doubt or personal sin. Everything is possible for the person who believes. But a person who thinks he or she has faith may discover something very different when face to face with one of Satan's minions.

Even with the greatest of faith, sometimes periods of prayer must still precede the demon's departure. If the apostles had to pray to get certain kinds out, be sure that you may have to do some very intense praying yourself.

When and if you decide to take on the demonic, make sure that the person with whom you are working does enough self-analysis to know where his or her foothold originates. Until that sin is confessed, repented of, and abandoned, you do little good to confront the demon. The opening left unclosed simply waits for the return of the evil.

As God delivers a person, setting him or her free, that person *must* pursue God in every way—learning, growing, praying, maturing. It will be the only path of life that will provide spiritual safety.

CHAPTER ELEVEN

Are Some Humans Empowered by Satan?

His loathing drifted about him like a fine mist, warning away any who might come near. As I watched him, I had the eerie sensation that he was crawling toward me, an evil predator stalking me on the stage where I stood speaking. Not only did he wear his hair and beard in likeness to the infamous Charles Manson, he had the same malignantly glazed eyes. I thought again how serious this warfare is and how strongly the enemy hates me for warning Christians about it.

I was speaking in a seminar for a church in Canada. They had rented the auditorium of a local college and had advertised to the community that I would be speaking on spiritual warfare. The three days had gone well, and the size of the audience had increased each service. Several people were studying, drilling me after each service with tough questions. God was glorified, and lives were changing.

It was during the last service that I noticed the man seated toward the middle of the room, glaring at me with unbridled, undisguised hatred. I didn't remember seeing him before and, at first, couldn't imagine what I'd done to upset him. As he became increasingly agitated by the things I said, I began to be aware that we were on different sides of this spiritual war. His evil intensified his presence, making his gaze horrific. Though I tried not to look at him, I felt myself hypnotically drawn to watch him, just as a mouse watches an approaching snake.

I even peeked during a prayer.

His steadfast stare hadn't broken; no bowing to pray for this guy. His malevolent eyes never left me, no matter where I moved in the auditorium, no matter what was happening.

My uneasiness grew as I thought of my wife and children. They had come on this trip with me, making a vacation of the speaking tour. The notion kept running through my mind that I had to protect them from this man. The custom of my then three-year-old daughter was to run into my arms after the closing prayer. If he decided to attack me, and she or my other children were nearby, they would likely be harmed.

Just before the end of the service, I moved to the very back of the auditorium, motioning my wife to join me. As the closing comments were being made, I told Alice to gather the children and stay away from me until everyone had left.

"Why?"

"There may be trouble, and I don't want you or the children hurt," I tried to say it nonchalantly.

Alice didn't believe in being nonchalant. Her voice was frightened—"What kind of trouble?"

"There's a man here who's very angry, and I think he may try to hurt me. Just get the children and stay away from me."

During the last prayer I didn't peek. I couldn't. I was praying too hard. I prayed for deliverance and protection for my family, myself, and all others present. When the prayer ended, I opened my eyes and searched him out.

He was gone.

"Who was he?" you ask.

I don't know.

"Who do you *think* he was?" you pursue.

I have no idea.

"Then," you may be thinking, "why did you tell the story?"

I'll answer that question, but it will take me awhile.

SATAN USES EVIL PEOPLE

When Satan attacked Job, he used nature, and he used people. His use of nature is chilling to think about. A great wind killed Job's children, lightning killed his servants and flocks, and an awful disease struck Job himself. His use of evil people is just as frightening. Raiding bands from the Sabeans and the Chaldeans killed Job's servants and stole his animals. The first two chapters of Job make it clear that each action was at Satan's bidding. Not only did Satan use wind and lightning, he actively and purposely used people.

How did Satan get the Sabeans and Chaldeans to do his bidding? He manipulated them through the same process we discussed in earlier chapters. Those raiding parties probably thought they were at just the right place at just the right time to catch Job's forces unsuspecting. Or perhaps they had planned the raids months in advance and believed everything that happened was the result of their own strategy. We know better. Satan used their circumstances and their nature to lead them into destructive raids, decimating Job's fortune.

That idea isn't such an unusual one, is it? Satan often uses people.

When Satan decided to kill Jesus, he used both the Jews and the Romans. He manipulated each group through their own selfish interests. He skillfully maneuvered them around their laws to put a respectable framework on their actions. It wasn't the Jews alone who killed Jesus, and it wasn't just the Romans. Satan was an integral piece of the whole puzzle. Those people bellowing for His crucifixion were not driven by civic duty or pharisaical fear; they were shrieking emissaries of the evil beings who joyfully used them. They didn't know they were pawns of Satan's forces. Remember Jesus' dying words: "Father, forgive them, for they do not know what they are doing" (Luke 23:34). Jesus knew.

Being Satan's pawn doesn't justify sinful actions. The people shouting for Jesus' crucifixion stood responsible for their actions; otherwise, Jesus wouldn't have needed to pray for God to forgive them. But they didn't realize what they were accomplishing for Satan; they didn't understand the full significance of what they were doing.

The people Satan uses are responsible, but they could never achieve the horrific things they do if he didn't empower them. That's right, empower.

SATAN EMPOWERS THOSE HE USES

Satan not only *uses* people; he *helps* them do what he wants.

Remember how he helped Judas? After guiding him through the beginning of the betrayal process, he finally took greater control. "Satan entered into him" (John 13:27). While it's not clear whether Satan actually entered Judas or whether this is a figure of speech, the point is clear. Satan was boldly using Judas to attack Jesus. Everything Judas did was prompted by Satan. Before there was any reference to a possible possession, Satan had already used Judas to make the arrangement with the priests to start the betrayal process. He doesn't have to be *in* a person to *use* that person.

In chapter six, "What Power Does Satan Have?" you read several relevant passages about how Satan uses us to get what he wants. I will remind you that Satan does things through people. He is the "spirit who is now at work in those who are disobedient" (Ephesians 2:2). When he works in or through a person, Satan uses his power to help them.

How does Satan empower a person? There are at least three ways.

Intensified Personal Traits

This first method may not seem so potent at first thought, but after consideration, you may conclude that it is the most powerful empowerment of all. It is definitely a common tactic of evil beings.

Using this tactic, Satan inflames people's passions to a point of dramatically increased strength. Using their own selfishness and their individual personality traits, he builds within them a strength and motivation that overpowers any opposition to their proposed sinful actions. David's life provides an example.

> Satan rose up against Israel and incited David to take a census of Israel. So David said to Joab and the commanders of the troops, "Go and count the Israelites from Beersheba to Dan. Then report back to me so that I may know how many there are."
>
> But Joab replied, "May the LORD multiply his troops a hundred times over. My lord the king, are they not all my lord's subjects? Why does my lord want to do this? Why should he bring guilt on Israel?"
>
> The king's word, however, overruled Joab. (1 Chronicles 21:1–4a)

Joab was right to tell David he shouldn't number the people. No military threat prompted this census. It apparently was done simply because of David's pride. He wanted to "know how many there are" (2 Samuel 24:2). The *New International Version Study Bible* gives this commentary on David's census:

> It is evident that his action was motivated either by pride in the size of the empire he had acquired or by reliance for his security on the

> size of the reserve of manpower he could muster in an emergency or, more likely, both. The mere taking of a census was hardly sinful (see Numbers 2:2–3; 26:2–4), but in this instance it represented an unwarranted glorying in and dependence on human power rather than the Lord.[1]

David knew it was the wrong thing to do. "David was conscience-stricken after he had counted the fighting men, and he said to the LORD, 'I have sinned greatly in what I have done. Now, O LORD, I beg you, take away the guilt of your servant. I have done a very foolish thing'" (2 Samuel 24:10; cf. 1 Chronicles 21:8).

God considered David's command to Joab to number the people "evil in the sight of God; so he punished Israel" (1 Chronicles 21:7). God became so furious at David's arrogant pride that He sent an angel to kill 70,000 men of Israel with a plague.

You read why David did it: Satan incited him. In Hebrew, *incite* means "to stimulate." It carries with it an implication of seduction. Satan stimulated David, seducing him. His will power became so strong that he ignored any counsel encouraging him to face his sinful action. Satan urged him on by fanning his passion and his pride. He used David's weaknesses against him by appealing directly to them. By increasing his inner motivation, he empowered David to sin.

Satan *uses* our selfish desires: "For everything in the world—the cravings of sinful man, the lust of his eyes and the boasting of what he has and does—comes not from the Father but from the world" (1 John 2:16). Feeding and intensifying our cravings gives us greater power and ability to sin.

This first empowerment by Satan intensifies the person's own traits—especially those that are selfish. If you think that isn't empowerment, answer this question: How many times have you seen a person accomplish some difficult task, against overwhelming opposition, just by his own intense motivation?

David's strong, prideful, inner motivation overruled all objections, bringing great misery to seventy thousand families in his nation.

Evil Angelic Escorts

But Satan's empowerment involves more than using a person's own inner drives. The second type of empowerment is equipping those who serve him with evil angelic escorts to help them in their duty. Read the following well-known story in a new light, this time paying particularly close attention to the words.

> When the servant of the man of God got up and went out early the next morning, an army with horses and chariots had surrounded the city. "Oh, my lord, what shall we do?" the servant asked.
>
> "Don't be afraid," the prophet answered. "Those who are with us are more than those who are with them."
>
> And Elisha prayed, "O LORD, open his eyes so he may see." Then the Lord opened the servant's eyes, and he looked and saw the hills full of horses and chariots of fire all around Elisha.
>
> As the enemy came down toward him, Elisha prayed to the LORD, "Strike these people with blindness." So he struck them with blindness, as Elisha had asked. (2 Kings 6:15–18)

I like this story, don't you? The good angels revealed themselves to the servant in warrior form—horses and chariots of fire—giving him reassurance of God's deliverance. What a great God! But the story also gives us a glimpse into how Satan empowers those who serve him.

When we tell this story to our children, we usually make it sound as if there were more good angels with Elisha than there were evil Aramean soldiers trying to capture him. But a careful reading shows that the army of God didn't outnumber the Arameans; that isn't what Elisha said at all. He said that "those who are with us are more than those who are with them." He didn't tell the servant there are more who are with us than there are *of* them. He said there were more with us than *with* them.

If those horses and chariots of fire on Elisha's side were angels—and no one doubts they were—his statement to the servant is clear. He told him there were more good angels with them than bad angels with the Arameans. This means that the raiding army apparently was escorted by evil angels but that Elisha was protected by a larger host of good angels. Elisha knew the good angels outnumbered the evil angels and asked God to make that clear to the servant.

You may be asking, "If evil angels were present, why didn't they reveal themselves?" God's purpose was to encourage the servant, not frighten him, and the sight of an evil army of angels wouldn't have comforted him at all.

"Did the bad angels flee when the good angels were revealed?" you ask. Not likely. Surely they knew of the presence of God's angels long before the servant saw them, yet they hadn't fled. Elisha's words indicate they were still there with the Arameans, because he referred to those "with" them.

The point is that the raiding band sent to get Elisha, the prophet of God, had a supporting group of evil angels with them. Satan's power was available to them through the agency of angelic presence. From our discussion in chapter seven, we know that angels can do tremendous things without the use of miracles. They use nature and people. Evil angels manipulate and intensify the desires of people. They coax people into evil actions. Then, Satan's angels offer protection to evil people as they commit those evil actions prompted by the evil angels.

Evil people surrounded by evil angels presents a disquieting thought.

Anything that gives the wicked more power is frightening, isn't it? Yet God warns us about power even greater than that. He warns of the most intense empowerment Satan can give.

Power to Deceive Even the Righteous

Without getting into a lengthy discussion of the identity of the "man of lawlessness" in 2 Thessalonians (that would simply distract us from our study), let me mention a third type of Satan's empowerment.

Whoever the "man of lawlessness" was or is to be, he has great power through Satan. "The coming of the lawless one will be in accordance with the work of Satan displayed in all kinds of counterfeit miracles, signs and wonders, and in every sort of evil that deceives those who are perishing. They perish because they refused to love the truth and so be saved" (2 Thessalonians 2:9–10).

Satan is so intense in his desire to destroy God's people that he will even empower this "man of lawlessness" to work apparent miracles. Satan's counterfeit miracles aren't the equal of God's miracles, and Satan isn't omnipotent like God is. But his miracles defy the logic and power of human beings. They can even deceive the righteous if the righteous aren't clinging tightly to the truth.

While this doesn't appear to be a continuing method of Satan, but one limited to a specific person and time, it does show his desire to empower and enable people to shatter God's followers.

So, how does Satan empower those who serve him? We've discussed at least three ways. First, he intensifies the traits of a person, giving him strong motivation to overcome all obstacles. Second, Satan encamps his angels around the wicked, escorting and assisting them in their wicked deeds. Third, when God allows, Satan uses all his power through a human being, even the power of apparent miracles, deceiving and destroying those who love God.

MANIFESTATIONS OF EMPOWERMENT

When I first realized that Satan camps his angels around those who serve him—in exquisite mimicry of a holy God surrounding His people with His angels—I found myself reaching some uncomfortable conclusions: There are people on earth who constantly have evil angels "inciting" them, just as Satan incited David. These evil angels cultivate and nourish selfish passions and desires, growing them into powerful inner motivations that have little control. They protect people in their efforts and escort them in their paths.

For some, these desires manifest themselves in deviant forms, leading them beyond normal human selfishness into an evil that transforms them. They become sociopaths and vicious criminals. Others, in stark contrast, manifest their evil desires by taking upon themselves the cloak of superior self-righteousness. Both groups fear neither God nor man, or if they do, they retreat into madness, huddling in a corner of their mind where neither God nor man is allowed.

Angels of Darkness

Let me tell you the story of one young man who couldn't have done what he did without evil beings manipulating and using him, destroying his life and the lives of others. I must tell his story carefully; I have no right to bring more pain to anyone involved.

Talented, poised, and outgoing, he was the last person anyone would suspect of doing anything wrong. When the heartbreaking details were finally made public, all those who knew him—and especially those who loved him—were shocked.

He would drive to other cities and buy neighborhood shopper magazines. He wasn't interested in buying anything, but he used the community paper to reach his ultimate goal—a teenage girl at home alone. He would call the number listed, asking about the advertised item. If a teenage girl answered, telling him he couldn't come over, he knew she was alone. With great charm and disarming wit, he would dissolve her fears, clearing the way for him to drop by.

He would then kidnap her, drive her back to his city, and keep her in bonds while he repeatedly assaulted her. He videotaped everything. After a few days, he would drive her back to her community and release her.

Until the next-to-last one.

He put her in the shower stall and shot her.

It wasn't until his next victim escaped that the world found out about his crimes. Arrested and taken before a judge, this handsome, outgoing young man with the charming wit now cowered in confusion and fear.

What went wrong? How did such a bright, young man from such a good and wonderful family wind up with such a sad, wasted life? I can't answer those questions, though I wish I could. But I do know that somewhere in his life, his own desires were so fed and twisted by unholy beings that they became aberrant. He was no longer the young man his mother had raised him to be; he broke her heart and the hearts of all who loved him. He became a criminal, seeking out victims and having little trouble finding them.

How can a serial criminal find victims so easily? What gives them that special charm that allows them to easily disarm even the wary? How do they know where to go and who are likely targets? In the case of this young man, how did he always know the right number to call, always find a girl alone, and always know the right words to get past her defenses?

By now you know my opinion on the matter. I believe that Satan's angels can lure some people into abnormally strong desires. I also believe they aid and abet those people, supporting the desires driving them to sin. When you believe spirit beings are helping and guiding people to the darker side of human desires, you are not amazed at their superior hunting skills and disarming ability to charm their prey. From reading the earlier chapters on angels, particularly the one about Satan's angels, you know they are acutely aware of weaknesses in those they stalk. Guiding a deluded person to take advantage of weaknesses in a fellow human would be simple.

We have all seen cases where someone was at the wrong place at the wrong time with the wrong person, resulting in a lack of resistance to sin with that person. Do you really think their being in that tempting situation was just a coincidence? I certainly don't—at least not always. Satan's angels lead people with similar weaknesses to each other precisely to increase the likelihood of sin. In the same way, when they control a person through his intensified evil passions, they lead him or her to people whose own weaknesses make them viable targets for his passions.

I'm not saying there is no such thing as coincidence. I am saying that "coincidence" doesn't happen nearly as often as we think. God's angels influence people toward good places and good situations; Satan's angels use their influence to just the opposite effect.

Perhaps you can now understand why the angry, hateful man in the Canadian audience caused me such concern. If he wasn't an evil angel, and I have no reason to believe he was, he was an evil human being, encouraged by evil angels to induce fear and terror in those around him.

While I surely wouldn't want to enter battle with an angel, I'm not terribly excited about fighting a human they are helping either. Having seen what evil people can do to good people, I don't live in the fantasy that they can't hurt me or my family. I know that bad beings do bad things to good people. I know God has promised it won't be beyond what we can stand, but He never promised complete deliverance from them. When I saw the hate in the man's eyes, I prepared for engagement.

You see, he and I work for different sides, each governed by a different commander. I prayed for deliverance, and God answered—blessed be the name of the Lord. But I know that no soldier is more important than the battle; some of us will suffer and some of us will die.

This isn't a game; it's war.

Some people on this earth work diligently for Satan, seemingly unaware that Satan will hurt them just as much as he wants to hurt us.

Angels of Light

Not only are obviously evil people used and empowered by Satan, but many who are veiled in cloaks of self-righteousness are tools of the devil for far-reaching pain and disaster.

Some of the best nourished and most protected by evil angels are leaders in churches and communities. Who hasn't known some "super-religious" person who has done more harm than any ten openly sinful people could do? These people are driven by inner feelings that force them to control and hurt, putting on the "cloak of righteousness" that gives them the justification they need for their actions. They often become ministers or church leaders, seeking positions of leadership in whatever they do. Although these folks do highly visible good works and are viewed as pillars in their communities, inwardly they are evil people who have bought Satan's lie so completely that they don't even know it is him they serve. Rather, they think of themselves as mighty servants of God.

If they chose to see, they could know that their master is Satan; their allegiance is obvious to those who are open to God. These desiccated hypocrites don't have love as the strongest emotion in their lives or their words. Rather, they feel hatred, anger, and a consuming need to control; evil beings use their power to magnify these negative, selfish emotions. These passions and the resulting actions vividly tell of their true spiritual condition, but they never get the message. They don't wake up in the morning thinking of the good they can do; they think about the people they must attack. To them attacking is a tool; their barrages bring the spiritually weak and naive under their control. Like Diotrephes, they have such control of their congregations that they will put out of the church any member who welcomes a brother they refuse to welcome (3 John 9–10). They exert just as much control over their own family members. Their legacy isn't a blessing; it is a tragedy of broken people.

These seared consciences don't live in God's real world populated with real people; they live in a world of their own making. They will do whatever it takes to make the people around them conform to that world, and they force everyone and everything to be what they demand.

Satan's angels help. Using their power to manipulate, they help the hypocrite control those who come under his influence. They give him sinful doctrines that further control God's people, keeping them from the blessings God offers them (1 Timothy 4:1–4).

It is likely that this kind of empowered evil person does much more harm than those who are in bold print on the tabloids at the grocery store or those whose pictures hang in the post office with rewards offered for their capture.

THEY HURT THE ONES THEY USE

Believing that Satan's angels use people isn't the same thing as believing that they bless them. They *use* them—in every sense of the word.

It would be logical to believe that some people have blessings that come from Satan. After all, if he rules the world (1 John 5:19), he can use its bounty for his own purposes. When he tried to lure Jesus into worshiping him, he offered earthly rewards for His submission.

But to think that Satan is actually pleased with those who serve his cause and that he wants to bless them out of some sense of kindness and appreciation is to misunderstand him altogether. He protects people who sin and gives them tools to help them sin more, but he takes all that away when it suits his purpose.

At Satan's whim, he not only removes angelic protection from those following him, he exposes them to pain and ridicule. This is especially true when the person being used still has a position of influence in the Christian community.

He's a very selfish master.

Proverbs 5 shows how Satan's offered pleasure turns to terrible pain. It paints a graphic picture as an adulterer bemoans his foolishness: "I have come to the brink of utter ruin in the midst of the whole assembly" (v. 14). Not only did his sin hurt him physically and spiritually, it hurt him emotionally before all the other people of God. And all of us who have been Christians for years know there is yet another dimension to that hurt: The assembly is also hurt by the sin.

Today, *assembly* refers to the church. We've seen the pain and confusion that come to the church when a member is publicly exposed in some grievous sin. When that member is a leader, nationally known, the impact is felt by all churches, even churches not remotely associated with that member. Satan must rejoice as he watches these well-known figures tumble into his lair—a chilling mental picture.

Exposing the sinner doesn't just hurt him, it hurts the people of God. The strong are saddened, the faith of the weak is undermined, and the hypocrites are encouraged in their hypocrisy because they feel superior to the exposed sinner.

It can cripple an entire church for a long time. I'll give you an example.

William and Frank

"How does it feel," I asked him, "to be used like that?"

For a long time he didn't answer; he just looked at the table between us. Then in a voice mixed with sadness and defiance he said, "I guess I was used. And I don't like it."

Frank was one of my best friends. "Kindred spirits" was the phrase I often used to describe us. I love him dearly and always will. As an elder in his church, he had been a guiding light to the congregation and its focus. That was no longer true. We sat in a restaurant, unhappily, while I did my best to bring him to his senses. He had left his wife and children for a woman and a lifestyle contrary to everything he had ever taught or been.

Of course, the church was hurt by what he did. They had quickly removed him from the eldership and had "disciplined" him by removing him publicly from their membership. He was openly living in sin, and though he didn't like what his church elders had to do, he knew they were following the biblical example in 1 Corinthians 5. He also knew I had made a special trip to that church urging his fellow elders to take those steps. I wanted him back; I wanted him to see the unseen forces at work.

The turmoil experienced by Frank had been the prelude to the real attack on that church a few weeks later. Their preacher, William, was arrested on a morals charge, and the newspapers had a heyday with the lurid details. The church reeled in shock. William had been in that church for years. Some of their deacons had been baptized by him when they were teenagers and had stood before him with their brides on their wedding days. No one could believe he had done it. The crushing truth descended when he admitted his guilt and resigned his position.

An industrious reporter looked deeper and found a past buried in the records. The probe revealed that William had been arrested on the same charges in nearby cities but had never gone to jail or been exposed in his hometown. He had been sinning for years, living another life with the gleeful support of the bad guys.

"Frank," I continued, "how long did it take the evil ones to set you up with this woman? You didn't abandon your family and your Lord after a one-night fling; this has been building for a long time. They watched you and learned your weaknesses. Then they put you in the right place with the right person to plant the seed that has grown into your disobedience.

"I'll tell you how long they worked on it," I continued. "Ten years. That's how long they've been protecting William in his sin, helping him, keeping him from being exposed. Doesn't it make sense to you why they expose him now? They waited until you, the charming elder everyone loved, rocked the church with a scandal and paved the way for the second wave. Then they turned on William, as they always planned to do. The two of you in quick succession. An evil one-two punch. You'll never know how many weak Christians will lose their faith over this. You'll never know how many people this church would have reached who now will never be reached for Jesus. You'll never know how many weak marriages will crumble because you and William won't be there to help save them. As a matter of fact, the influence of your sins will help weaken them.

"What you *will* know is the heartache and troubles this church will face for years. Even though you don't go there anymore, you'll hear about it. You were used. Your sin didn't hurt just you, your wife, your daughters, and the woman you're sinning with. It's impact is reaching out, hurting hundreds, if not thousands, of people."

I paused, then repeated my question: "How does it feel to be used?"

What about You?

I'll ask you the same question.

If you are continuing in a sin, Satan is using you. The fact that you haven't been caught or haven't experienced any negative consequence doesn't mean God has decided you may continue in this sinful thing. It means that you are protected by powerful spiritual beings who don't want you to stop. Using all their power of influence, manipulation, and control of nature and circumstances, they aid you. They want you to enjoy yourself. Whispering soothing rationalizations to calm your guilty conscience, they stroke your indignation and your desire. They bring every evil blessing they can.

God's angels are busy too. They are planning bad things for your life if there is any chance that such things will bring you to your spiritual senses. God chastens those He loves, and He's preparing a chastening for you in an effort to deliver you. Believe me, I know; I've been chastised severely in the past.

But while God's angels prepare for the battle to save you, evil angels continue assisting you in your sin. And when the time comes when they can get the most effect from it, these evil angels will expose you and bring you to ruin. They're just waiting for the time that will create the greatest impact and bring the most harm to the most people.

How long will they wait?

Years. Months. Days. Minutes. They are as patient or as swift as they need to be to accomplish their fiendish goals.

So, how does it feel to be used?

Good? It should. They make sure it is pleasurable in the short term; otherwise, they couldn't entice you. They want you to be addicted, reaching the point where my words or the words of any other godly person harmlessly roll off your conscience. They'll addict you, use you, and then destroy you.

It's not just you they will destroy. If they only wanted you, they'd destroy you now. No, they play the waiting game—continuing to abet your sin, wanting to hurt as many as possible. They're using you to hurt your parents...or your spouse...or your children...or your best friend. They may even use you to hurt people you hardly know. If you were a mighty servant of God at one time, they will use you to hurt people you could never know. Your influence for evil will be at least as far-reaching as your influence for good has been.

Feeling sad because of my words? They'll use that too. If they can, they'll make you despondent enough that you'll run away, maybe even kill yourself. Can't you see their game? Even that act of shame is used by them to cause great harm in the lives of many. Killing yourself doesn't stop their ability to use you for harm; it increases it.

The only way you can prevent them from using you any longer is to repent, seek God, and confess your sin before they can expose it—as they did in their hideous scheme with Frank and William.

STOP HIS USE OF PEOPLE

Satan and his angels do empower people in their wickedness. The only way we can slow that strategy is to bring as many people to God through Jesus as we possibly can. The truth of God is the ultimate weapon, effectively and efficiently defeating the lies of Satan.

Take the offensive by letting God defeat Satan in your life. Then share Him with others so He can be victorious there. He won't force His way on anyone—even you—but He stands ready to enter if you'll only open the door.

Frank finally opened the door of his heart to God. He called one afternoon to tell me, "I can't think of any other word, Joe, so I'll just call it a miracle. God is in my heart again. I'm living in harmony with Him again. It even appears my wife is going to take me back. Satan used me before to cause harm. God will use me now for whatever He wants."

Will you, too, open your heart to God as you close it to Satan? Quit believing Satan's lies. Quit being the pawn of evil beings. Beg God to show you the light, filling your heart and mind, taking your life.

Beg Him now—before it's too late.

SECTION

3

FORCES AT WORK WITHIN US

CHAPTER TWELVE

Why Do Christians Sin?

They tell me Charlie never did enter the ministry; he went to work for the railroad instead. I hope it wasn't because of the night he went to the fair with me. It would be a shame if that's what kept him from being a preacher; the man in the pew could have used someone who understood him.

We were both freshmen at a small church-related college in the deep south in the tumultuous year 1967. He was there to "make a preacher." I was there because the preacher at my home church had nagged me into enrolling; well, that and the fact that my girlfriend had dumped me. I figured I'd stay for a quarter or so until she came to her senses, then I'd go back home.

Just wanting to do my time and leave, I wasn't any too happy to discover that the campus was overrun with eighteen-year-old Christian storm troopers who eyed me as a potential target for evangelistic assault. On their own for the first time, overflowing with excitement about their new venture, they were eager to take into combat the righteous fervor that had driven them to pursue this educational route. Immediately, they began to search for heathens to convert—and my lack of fervor made me suspect. Before long I was a full-fledged mission project whose soul was sought with a vengeance.

I wasn't really that bad. I didn't smoke or chew, had given up drinking for school, and hardly ever cussed. But for lack of anyone more interesting, my fellow students looked on me as a campus reprobate. It seemed unimportant to them that I had committed myself to Jesus just months before. Because I didn't have their zeal and because I didn't fit their pattern, I wasn't one of them...at least not yet.

Their first attack was so subtle I didn't see it coming. Not ready to take on the tasks my mother had been doing for me, I used all my charm to talk some coeds into doing my laundry each week. Well, I thought it was my charm. Soon I discovered they did it because they had chosen me as their first mission project. They returned every shirt and pair of pants with neatly typed scriptures from the King James Version planted in each pocket. They never asked me if I read the verses or even if I knew they were there. It appeared they were trying to convert me by osmosis—get the truth next to me and somehow it would seep into me. I never did anything to discourage them. Why would I? I didn't mind being a walking Bible in return for my laundry and ironing. Gradually I found my niche in the school, learned to avoid the most intense students, and was doing okay.

The coming of the state fair in the late fall changed all that.

The day the fair opened, the leading members of the campus Preacher's Club walked unannounced into my dorm room. They called themselves Pi Sigma Delta; we knew them as a group of fiery young Bible majors who had appointed themselves as guardians of our souls. These neophyte scholars had decided I was too spiritually weak to be allowed to visit the fair unchaperoned. After all, it was very likely I would gamble for one of those stuffed zebras and lose my soul. They informed me that Charlie, a freshman Bible major from a rural section of Alabama, would go with me. Charlie didn't look enthused about the prospect, ducking his head and turning a little red around the edges, but as a good soldier he would do his duty—and so would I if I knew what was good for me.

That's how I found myself ambling along with Charlie that evening, miserable and grouchy. He wasn't having such a good time himself because he had to watch me instead of having fun on the rides. Every time we passed a mechanical monster tossing screaming, laughing victims about, he would growl under his breath and glare at me. I didn't care. He could have threatened to flog me, and still I would have refused to go on the rides with him. All I could think of was that stuffed zebra and my resentment for his standing between such a wonderful prize and me. Of course I hadn't even *thought* of a stuffed zebra until they said I couldn't have it; now I craved it.

Things livened remarkably for us when we came to a carnival barker doing his best to draw a crowd.

"Hurry, hurry, step right up, pay one dollar, and see the show." Behind him were several scantily clad young women—smiling, winking, and wiggling.

I felt a small stirring of interest.

"What are they gonna do in there?" Charlie mumbled through his labored breathing.

Casting a glance his way, I saw his glazed, wide-eyed stare glued to pieces of those swaying beauties. He seemed hypnotized by their sensuous undulations. Seeing a chance to gall this young preacher, I told him what they were going to do. Graphically.

"In front of all those people!?" was his strangled reply.

"That's why they charge a dollar, Charlie," I replied with a wicked grin.

He ripped his eyes from the nymphs, turning to look intently at me. "How do you know that? You ever been to one of these shows, Beam?"

My little plot died a quick, anguished death. Instead of embarrassing and angering Charlie, I had set myself up for purging at the hands of Pi Sigma Delta. Chagrined, I dropped my head as I admitted to Charlie I had been to a "girlie show" a year before. Then, recovering, I defiantly raised my chin and pointed out that I had since become a Christian and had been forgiven of all sin.

With as much piety as he could muster, he quivered, "Good church folks would never go in a place like that."

"You're right, Charlie. Man, you're right." I carefully crafted into my voice the devout tones I was learning at school so Charlie would know how sorry I was I had previously involved myself in such sordid practices.

I'm not sure he heard anything I said. He was again intently concentrating on the girls, and one of them, a blond with a saucy smile, was giving him the biggest come-on smile I'd seen in all my adolescent years of riotous living. "Oh, no," I inwardly pleaded, warning bells ringing in my head, "Don't look at him like that. Who knows what he'll do?" I felt a growing terror as I thought, "He's gonna start preaching. I just know it. He's gonna start preaching."

Incredibly, hesitantly, he slowly smiled back at the brazen blond; it was only a small one but definitely a smile. He hesitated, looked up the midway, looked down the midway, then whispered, "Let's go in there."

"Charlie! I'm surprised at you!"

"How can I preach against it if I don't know what it is?" It was nearly a shout. He was defiant: mouth set, eyes blazing and determined. It was obvious he wanted no argument, just agreement.

And that's exactly what he got. I was happy to follow him. This was *better* than a stuffed zebra! Besides, I had no guilt or responsibility in this. The preacher students themselves had said I was spiritually weak, and if my chaperon, my spiritual guide and protector, was going in there, well, who was I to question? I, the campus reprobate, was being shown the light.

Quickly reaching into my pocket, I pulled out a dollar and thrust it at the cashier. He glanced at it and grated, "A buck, buddy. It cost a buck." Too late, I realized the paper in my hand wasn't money at all; I'd unsheathed one of those scriptures the coeds had diligently planted for my deliverance. There, in front of the tent of temptations, I was waving a Bible passage!

Maybe the coeds knew exactly what they were doing all along.

The passage, James 1:13–15, sternly pointed its finger at me and thundered that lust leads to sin and sin leads to death. *Death*—my eyes couldn't let go of the word. I wasn't sure what the verse meant, but there was one thing I knew without doubt: If lust and death were tied together, I was teetering on the brink of disaster. Panic sliced through me; I was only eighteen—far too young to die.

"I can't go, Charlie."

"Why not?"

"I found this scripture in my pocket…"

"Well, for Pete's sake, don't show it to me!" he yelled.

I didn't show it to him. I just slid it back into my pocket and stood there rooted to the ground, speechless. Charlie handed over his dollar, resolutely walked up the stairs, and disappeared through the curtain into the world of the enticing blond.

When he emerged thirty minutes later, I stood waiting.

Neither of us said a word. We just looked at each other for a long moment and then started for the car. There was nothing to say. It had been a night of learning for both of us, and we each had serious thinking to do.

As we drove back to campus, I gently stroked my new, stuffed zebra.

I can't tell you what Charlie learned that night; you'll have to ask him about that. As for me, the scripture I found in my pocket became one of my greatest teachers in the years that have passed since that night. I wish I could say the verses so penetrated me that I never sinned again—but you would know better. You haven't met a Christian yet who has reached sinless perfection, and you, like the rest of us, struggle with temptation. We Christians love God, follow Jesus, and cry out for the power of the Spirit in our lives. We want to do right and dream of the time when we are so spiritually mature that the devil can find nothing to tempt us with. And still, we sin.

TEMPTATION—FROM SATAN OR FROM ME?

But where does sin originate? Should we blame ourselves or Satan?

A young man preparing for ministry once informed me that he had been taught that James 1:13–15 shows clearly there is no devil or any evil influence that tempts us. According to a teacher in his graduate school, the idea of a devil was fabricated by certain writers in the New Testament because they wanted to remove mankind's personal responsibility for their own evil actions. "Temptation and sin arise from within man," he argued, "and James proves it. The passage clearly says that each one is dragged away by his own evil desire. There is no devil and certainly not one strewing temptation in our way. We sin because we want to. We are the culprits."

I don't know who's teaching this young would-be preacher, but he is not equipping him properly to serve as an effective warrior in our spiritual battle. Satan and his forces are real. Later on in this chapter, I'll explain why his teacher was wrong by explaining the temptation process.

We have enough scoffers in the world whose rhetoric obscures Satan's meanness. We positively don't need any more people in the church helping him. Actually, the doctrine taught to this aspiring young minister will aid the enemy. When anyone uses any passage to teach there is no devil—that all the evil we do originates from within us—the devil smiles, appreciating the assistance.

How does teaching that doctrine help Satan? It helps by heaping more guilt and self-loathing on struggling people, causing them to view themselves as worthless and hopeless. Satan is the accuser, using guilt and shame to destroy those who sin (Zechariah 3:1–2). Telling people that all sin originates in them because they are intrinsically evil accomplishes the same evil goal. Convince us we are evil at heart, and you will simultaneously convince us we are worthless and hopeless.

How this supposed scholarship devastates Christians who are entangled in sin was evident in a phone conversation with Stephanie. It began like many others: "You don't know me, but a friend gave me your tapes on spiritual warfare. Would you have a few minutes to talk?"

Over the next hour I listened as Stephanie told me she was worthless and had no reason to continue living. When I counseled her to seek help from her local church, she told me *they* were the ones who had convinced her she was no good. She explained, "See, I still want to sin, even though I also want to do right. My preacher says my strong desire for this sin shows I have an evil heart. He says he's given up hope for me."

She had recently been living with a man who degraded her both mentally and spiritually, but now she lived alone. When she aborted his baby, he abandoned her. Throughout the affair she continued going to church, keeping up appearances so no one knew her living circumstances. No one knew about the pregnancy either. Finally her sin and guilt were too much to bear. Unable to cope any longer, she took her sick and hurting soul before the church, unloading all her sin and pain, confessing and begging for help.

Their reaction shocked her.

Mothers no longer allowed their children near her. Her best friend told her never to call again, severing their friendship. The preacher called her into a private meeting to tell her that all her sins were the result of her evil heart. "You can still come to church here; God knows you need it. But don't expect anyone to have anything to do with you. We now know you and what you're like. You won't fool us again."

Already overcome with guilt, she now felt hopeless. If God's people felt that way about her, how must God feel? "If I'm going to hell anyway, why not just go now? I have no reason to live."

Isn't it interesting that not one member of that church saw her as a woman who had been *seduced* into sin? No one stood up to fight Satan's army for her, to rescue her from the battle and the ensuing terror. They saw her as evil, even though she was begging for forgiveness and spiritual help. How could they do that? Easy. When you believe that all temptation comes from within a person, it is only logical to believe that a person's actions tell you what she is. "We now know you and what you're like. You won't fool us again." Since Christians should reject evil and refuse to associate with it, that church simply did what they thought right. They viewed her as evil and added another rejection to her young life: God's.

I'm quite sure the young would-be preacher who informed me that there is no devil would disagree with the behavior of that church. In reality, however, they were just following his own reasoning. If all sin comes from within me, then *I* am evil rather than being a person who *does* evil. If through either God's grace or my own self-control, I keep my sinful heart in control, the church should maintain fellowship with me. If I don't control the sinful urges and I demonstrate that lack of control repeatedly, the church has no option but to remove me, even if I beg for their help. My continued sinning would reveal a heart too evil to be allowed to affect the impressionable young or spiritually immature.

"Ridiculous," you say? No. I've seen the results of that kind of logic for too long, and so have you. We have created a chasm separating philosophy about theology from its practical effect on how people live, and it's time we changed that. God never gave a doctrine or teaching that destroys His children.

That's right, destroys.

What do you think the young man who was taught there is no devil could have said to Stephanie if he had heard her confession? If she had come before his church, hot tears of shame running down her blazing cheeks, could he have comforted her with words like, "You've sinned. I won't try to whitewash what you've done; we both know it was wrong, and now you are carrying the pain of it. But you are not an evil person. It's true that if a person does evil long enough, she'll become evil; but by the grace of God you have stopped before you reached that point. You've been tempted by evil beings who knew your weaknesses and planted evil in your heart. You've experienced the consequences of following those desires. But God is loving. He doesn't view you as an evil being but as a struggling sinner. He loves you and will forgive you. Now forgive yourself and accept His love"?

If he could have said those words, he also could have admonished the church to stand with her and surround her with the love of Christ. The sin would have been viewed separately from the sinner.

But as long as this young man believes that all sin originates from our own hearts with no outside seduction, he can't say those words. He deals with sin by putting all blame on the person. He would have left this hurting young woman, who was seeking solace, hopelessly and helplessly consumed with unquenchable guilt.

He might have had compassion, but if he had spoken to her honestly he would have said, "You've sinned. That sin came totally from your own evil desire. No one else, especially some nonexistent devil, had anything to do with it. Now pray that God will change your heart. Of course, you've greatly offended Him, but because He's so wonderful, He can love you in spite of the fact that you've personally outraged Him by who you are and what your nature leads you to. If you let Him remove those sinful desires, He will. But every time you feel them again, you'll know you've shut Him out and have let your own true evil nature take over again." He would then have told the church to warily watch her, avoiding her until she proves her sinful desires are in check. If her struggle too soon resurfaced, Satan would win. The church would abandon her, and in her despair, she would give up.

Believe me, it happens; ask Stephanie. She gave up. Her preacher convinced her she was evil at heart and that there was no hope for her. He used those exact words. That left it up to a stranger, hundreds of miles from where she lived, to talk her into putting down the gun she cradled in her lap. By the grace of God, I helped her see how Satan's forces had led her just where they wanted her and how they were about to have a victory celebration as soon as she despondently pulled the trigger.

Stephanie wasn't evil. She did sinful things that were evil, but those actions weren't because she is innately corrupt. Her guilt and pain showed her good heart, bruised by sin. A heart susceptible to evil isn't the same as a heart that is evil. Some theologians believe the Bible teaches that people are worthless and helpless, evil by nature. The Bible does teach we are sinners, but it doesn't teach we are worthless. It is important to remember that sin came *from* Satan and *through* Adam. It did not come *from* Adam (Romans 5:12–20). It doesn't come from you either.

If you've followed my point, you know I'm not saying that we should teach people they have no responsibility for their sins or that we should never hold people accountable for their sins. I am saying we should teach there is an outside force seducing them into sin. If that sin is yielded to long enough, a person can become evil. But he didn't start out that way, just as Adam didn't. Christians struggling with sin aren't evil, though they do evil things. The evil doesn't begin in their hearts but takes root there after being planted by beings who want them to sin.

The passage in James 1:13–15 doesn't take Satan's power away, nor does it say all temptation arises from us. A careful consideration of the passage and an understanding of the genealogy of sin doesn't discredit evil influences at all. Just the opposite is true: This verse makes it easier to understand how the evil forces do what they do.

THE TEMPTATION PROCESS

If the young man who believed that temptation arises from within ourselves was wrong, then where *does* temptation come from? The passage in James 1:13–15, which he used to support his view, actually shows that temptation comes from *Satan.* "When tempted, no one should say, 'God is tempting me.' For God cannot be tempted by evil, nor does he tempt anyone; but each one is tempted when, by his own evil desire, he is dragged away and enticed. Then, after desire has conceived, it gives birth to sin; and sin, when it is full-grown, gives birth to death."

Several years ago Warren Wiersbe divided the passage into four parts: desire, deceit, disobedience, and death. I challenge you to stop reading here, go back to the passage, and see if you can figure out how the passage naturally divides itself as Wiersbe suggested. Go on, try it. It will breathe life into the passage for you.

Back already? Did you see the process? Look at it like this:

Desire is easy. I know you saw it: "By his own evil desire" is the phrase where it's found.

Deceit may be a little tougher. You'll find it in "dragged away and enticed." I explain what those words mean later in this chapter.

Disobedience is another way of saying "gives birth to sin."

Death, naturally, is found in "when it is full-grown, gives birth to death," referring to the ultimate consequence of sin.

You see, temptation is part of the devil's strategy; it doesn't simply originate within us because of our own sinful nature. Temptation starts outside us before it gets inside us. Misunderstanding this means you'll find yourself battling you—thinking yourself your own enemy—rather than directing your anger and frustration where it should be aimed.

What a revelation! James's inspired words expose how Satan tempts us; not surprisingly, the temptation process of James 1 fits perfectly into the template of Ephesians 4 that we discussed in chapter two: Desire and deceit confuse the mind. Disobedience hardens the heart to the point that all sensitivity is lost. When sin becomes "full-grown," a person is so immersed in sensuality that he reaches spiritual death.

HOW SATAN USES DESIRE

Temptation uses desire to confuse the understanding. Before the heart can be hardened, the mind must be confused; and there are few things, if any at all, that can confuse as quickly and thoroughly as desire.

For example, have you ever *really wanted* to do something you knew was wrong? Everyone has. If you're anything like me or the hundreds of people I've talked with, you've gone through similar struggles.

As you face the temptation, hesitating, the spiritual in you whispers, either in thought or emotion, "Don't do this; it's wrong. Turn right now, and get out of here!" You know you should run away, and you want to flee; but you also want to stay.

Before you can take action to free yourself, the flesh counters, "Yeah, it's wrong. But if you walk away now, you may never get another chance at this as long as you live. You'll always wonder what it would have been like. Do it now or regret it forever."

In a logical debate with yourself, the spiritual would win; but you aren't debating—you're craving. The longer you think, the weaker you become. If you walk away now, you'll feel an emptiness and longing; but if you yield, you can *fill* that emptiness. The desire seems to take a life of its own, demanding control, compelling you to act before the opportunity is gone. Soon, your reasoning becomes confused, blurring the line between good and evil, right and wrong.

You may even find yourself thinking or feeling, "Surely God is a gracious God. He loves me. He'll forgive me even if I do this." You don't dare think about it too long, or your understanding will spotlight the error of your logic and stop you. To keep that from happening, you shut down your intellectual processes and switch to the emotional. Since it is desire that drives you, you give in and sin. You find yourself doing the sin but, at the same time, feeling detached from it. It's almost surreal. You experience the pleasure, but it has a dreamlike quality. Only later when the sin is past and when guilt creeps in where desire reigned only moments before, you reconnect with your real world.

Unless, of course, the guilt is overwhelming. Then the surreal, otherworldly feeling continues because you cannot face the reality and pain of what you have done.

Eventually the guilt subsides, and you remember just the pleasure of the sin, forgetting the pain and guilt that came with that first experience. The evil beings wait patiently for you to reach this state, and when you get there, they infiltrate your emotions, bringing the temptation to you again. Coming at just the right time in just the right way, they are consistently effective. Again, as the reasoning, logical, intellectual part of you starts to lose, you find yourself wanting the sin again. Only this time, you want more of it, oblivious to the fact that it will take more to reach the high you got last time.

The process of destruction has begun. You are on the way. Satan's forces provoke you at just the right time—when you are weak and when your emotions are running high, making you especially vulnerable. After a while they don't have to be as cunning, because you help them by rationalizing the sin, decreasing your guilt. Your heart will gradually harden. With time, you will be immersed in sensuality.

It starts so simply and so small. Just get the desire strong enough to confuse the thinking.

Not all temptations work just this way; there are other methods. You may be surprised at two I list at the end of this chapter. But they always follow a pattern, and it usually fits the template of Ephesians 4.

ANALYZING DESIRE

The pattern in James 1 is simple and effective. When a person's desire is aroused to a level overruling his logic and noble intent, his *want* is turned into *lust.* If a person can be lured into increased desire, his desires gain the power necessary to drag him away.

Lust—we all know that word; just the sound of it implies that something wrong is about to happen. *Lust* connotes evil; no one wants to be accused of lusting. Remember Jimmy Carter's statement while he was president, "I have lusted in my heart"? The press had a field day caricaturing the religious Carter as a secretly dirty old man. *Lust.* What a nasty sounding word. We all do it, but none of us wants to admit it.

Just what does it mean?

We Americans, especially Southerners, have a word in our vernacular that makes the idea quickly understandable—the word *craving.* A craving is a desire so strong that it consumes a person. Craving isn't just wanting something; it's longing for it.

This doesn't mean that all craving is evil. It isn't inherently bad to want something or someone with great longing. There are good and holy cravings just like there are evil cravings. As Paul wrote Timothy, "If anyone sets his heart on being an overseer, he desires a noble task"

(1 Timothy 3:1). That koine Greek word translated "desire" is similar to our English word *craving.* If Paul said those craving the position of overseer were craving a noble task, we know a person can crave something that is noble and holy.

If desire can be for something good or for something bad, we could be in a quandary. How can a person *know* if her craving for something or someone is good or evil? Is a strong desire from Satan or from God?

For those honest with themselves, it's not complicated at all to know the difference between good cravings and evil cravings. In any soul-searching self-analysis, there are three aspects of your desire you should consider: its focus, its strength, and its pending consequences.

Focus

How do you check the focus of a desire? When you find yourself badly wanting something, honestly answer these three questions:

- What actions will this desire lead me to?
- What will I do if I let this consume me?
- Are those actions right or wrong according to the Bible?

If you find yourself headed toward any action that is sinful, the desire driving it isn't from God—and you know it.

One of my friends told his secretary she could no longer work for him. As I asked him about it, he replied: "Joe, I found myself getting closer and closer to her. I started thinking about her when I wasn't at work and bringing her little presents when I traveled. I looked forward to talking with her. I never had a sinful thought about sex or leaving my wife or anything like that. But one day it dawned on me that I'd boarded a train, and I didn't want to go where it was headed. The only way not to go there eventually was to get off the train now while I've still got my wits about me."

It's a wise and self-honest man who sees where his desires are taking him. It's a spiritually mature man who will change the path.

Strength

Once you know the focus of your craving, check out its strength. You recall from chapter eleven that one way satanic beings empower humans is by magnifying their desires so they will be driven to overcome anything or anyone standing in their way. Honestly answer these questions:

- If God put something in my way to prevent me from getting this, would I find a way past the obstacle?
- Are wise and godly people counseling me against this action?
- Am I violating my own judgment or conscience?
- Am I sacrificing spiritually important segments of my life?
- Am I avoiding spiritual events or people?

If the answer to any of these question is "yes," admit that the desire has enough strength to lead you into great harm—and most likely will.

Good desires overcome obstacles, too, but the obstacles in their path are usually different. If you aren't sure whether the barriers in the way of a desire are from God or Satan, ask these questions:

- Who benefits if this doesn't happen, God or Satan?
- Who would be pleased if I don't do what this desire leads me to, God or Satan?
- Which people in my life are encouraging me, spiritual or worldly?

Pray for wisdom and seek the counsel of several people who are spiritually mature (Proverbs 15:22). If you are open, God will let you know if He is hindering you in the pursuit of your craving. Remember: *A sinful desire refuses to consider whether the barriers that prevent its completion are from God.* If you won't even consider that God could be trying to stop you, you are already playing with a loaded weapon. If you have a desire strong enough to overcome any barrier, even if the desire is from God, you're already sinning. Even if you haven't yet acted on your desire, if it's that strong, God has a name for it: sin (Matthew 5:27–28; 1 John 3:15).

A few years ago I angered a couple when I refused to perform their marriage ceremony. My refusal was based on the principle currently being discussed. The man had been married before; his marriage ended when his wife left him for a lover. In the course of premarital counseling sessions, I asked the young man, "If God spoke directly to you and told you not to marry Sarah but to go back to your previous wife, would you?" I wasn't telling him he had to go back to the first wife; I just wanted to gauge the strength of his desire for Sarah. Would he put her before

God? He thought only for a minute, then answered, "No. Even if God told me to, I wouldn't go back. I love Sarah, and I'm going to marry her." That might be a wonderful line in a television movie, but it chilled me. I wanted no part in a marriage where a man loved his wife more than he loved God. If God placed a barrier to that marriage, this young man would find a way around it. He said so. As far as I'm concerned, that marriage shouldn't have taken place until God was enthroned over it.

Any desire that won't consider God or His potential guidance—including barriers—is sinfully strong.

Pending Consequences

The last step of the three-part test is to examine the end results of the desire.

For example, Paul refused to eat meat or drink wine—things he had a right to—if by doing those things he would harm another believer (1 Corinthians 8:13; Romans 14:21). But he also confronted Peter in front of everyone when Peter acted the hypocrite (Galatians 2:11 ff.). He was sensitive to hurting any brother, but he was also quick to confront, even if the brother would be embarrassed in front of the church. He wasn't inconsistent. He had strong, spiritual reasons for doing each. The results were always godly.

If your desire is leading you to actions that will hurt others—parents, spouse, friends, church, or anyone else—then the pending results of the desire tell you the desire is wrong. Godly desires lead to godly actions that lead to godly results. Jesus hurt His mother when He wouldn't quit preaching and come home (Matthew 12:46–50). But his desire was holy; it had strong spiritual motive with a positive spiritual result. A man leaving his wife for another person isn't good; it's driven by an unholy selfishness that has no strong spiritual motive at all. The results devastate the man, his wife, and the person he is involved with.

Most desires have recognizable and predictable consequences when fulfilled. These anticipated consequences powerfully indicate whether the desire is good or bad.

Ask yourself,

- Who will be affected if I fulfill this craving?
- How will they be affected?

- What spiritual or biblical justification do I have for bringing this consequence into their lives?
- What will be the consequences in my own life—especially spiritually?

So, have you gotten the point? When all three components are honestly scrutinized, you will have a clear idea of whether your craving is good or evil. Use the test for yourself when you are craving something or someone. Use it for others when they seek spiritual counsel from you. It works.

If you crave something good for you or others and you won't violate any spiritual, moral, or legal principles to get it, that usually indicates a good craving or desire. If you crave something harmful to you or others and that craving is strong enough to push you to transgress spiritual, moral, or legal principles to get it, it's an evil lust or craving.

Evil desire thinks only of what it wants and how to get it; consequences will only be considered when they occur.

A LUSTFUL EXAMPLE

Let me illustrate. A few years ago, I was invited to eat with a group of Christians after Sunday morning services in their rural community. Three weeks prior, my doctor had given me strict orders to reduce cholesterol and weight for the sake of my health, my energy, and my family. "If you don't change now, one day you'll drop dead, and your baby girl will grow up without a daddy." Mention any of my daughters, and you have my complete attention. As each dish came around, I refused the ones flavored with or fried in fat and opted for the low-fat, low-calorie (and low-tasting) foods. The good sisters kept insisting I eat until I had to explain the reason for my choices. The brother to my left, his overfull plate in danger of capsizing its load, sighed and told me his doctor had told him to change his eating habits too.

"I know I shouldn't eat this stuff," he said, "but I can't help it. When I try to eat right, I start craving what I can't have. I can tell you right now, if I don't eat this, I'll be miserable all afternoon thinking about it and wishing I had. It may kill me—I've already had one heart attack, and they tell me my cholesterol level may mean I'm going to have another—but I've got to have it. It's just too good."

"What is your cholesterol level?" I asked.

"A little over 600." He got the words out just before shoveling a new load into his mouth.

I laughed, thinking he was exaggerating, until his wife somberly confirmed everything—even the unbelievable cholesterol level. That's a perfect example of lust, evil desire, or craving leading to the sin of gluttony.

If you desire something that is harmful to yourself or others, if you will override all obstacles to have what you want, and if you have no concern for the consequences, you have an evil craving.

Evil cravings are not just for food, of course. Lust wears many hats, and the focus of desire can cover the gamut from chocolate to power—anything or anyone. Some women crave the husband of their best friend. Some men crave women who aren't their wives. Others crave money or fame or prestige. It makes no difference what it is, when it is focused on the wrong thing, has enough strength to drive it past all barriers, and doesn't care about the consequences as long as it gets what it wants—it's sin.

SINFUL DESIRES PRETEND TO BE GOOD

Insidiously, evil desires often masquerade as noble emotions or causes. As one shattered wife told me, "When I confronted my husband and his lover, he was angry and she was indignant. 'I love your husband!'—I can still hear her saying it. To her it justified the eighteen months of cheating. She made it sound downright virtuous that he would leave me and the children for her. How can anyone think like that?"

They think like that because lust convinces them to buy the lie. They aren't about to test their wants by the light of Scripture or wisdom. In chapter two I wrote about the lies that destroy us if we believe them. How can Satan's forces get us to believe and embrace those destructive untruths? By hiding the lie in pretty wrapping, it becomes so alluring that we are consumed with craving to open it. The evil ones inflame our passions, overruling our logic and our faith.

How can they do that? They drag us away and entice us.

HOW SATAN USES DECEIT

According to those who know koine Greek better than I, the words in the phrase "dragged away and enticed" in James 1 have to do with baiting a hook or a trap. To understand what James means when he uses those words, think about why baited traps work. Why does a rabbit ignore the warning signs and enter a trap? Why does a fish allow itself to be lured to its destruction? Because the bait is so alluring, the animal proceeds in spite of its caution or its instinctive fears. Enticement overpowers and leads to being dragged away.

Dragged away, the phrase James uses, is a good description of deceit. When a person wants something badly enough, he will buy the lie that justifies his action. It isn't easy to deceive people who haven't had some emotional arousal. Just ask a con man. Cool, calm, and collected people driven by logic aren't easy marks for the deceptive tactics of confidence men. Manipulators ignore those people to look for more susceptible ones. When a person can be lured to a high level of desire, she will ignore all warning signs, letting her emotions drag her into a devilish trap. If greedy humans know how to arouse these desires to take advantage of people, what do you think powerful *spiritual* beings can do?

Deceit is Satan's most powerful tool. It makes everything else work. Without it, his seduction of Eve wouldn't have worked, bringing sin into the world; without it, he could never entice those who love Jesus to hurt Him by their sin.

Satan's lies allow us to justify our behavior *because they darken our understanding.* And those lies are always designed to lead us from God—away from His love and protection.

Satan can't take us from God's hand (John 10:28), so he must seduce us into leaving. His forces spend massive time and effort in those seductive processes. If we could always see his unseen forces, we would remain on guard, alert to their evil presence, but they are too smart to let themselves be seen. They operate quietly, behind the scenes, seducing us with their lies.

Be aware that seduction isn't always in the realm of pleasure, sometimes it's more effective if it hurts.

PAIN, RELIGION, AND OTHER TRAPS

In this chapter, we've broadly discussed how Satan uses desire to bring us under his control. In the next four chapters, we will delve more deeply into Satan's malevolent dance of deception and learn how desire and deceit work together, causing disobedience.

In chapter thirteen, we will discuss how Satan uses pleasure—which is closely linked to desire—to tempt us. Then in chapter fourteen, we will explore how Satan uses pain to evoke powerful desires. Pain and desire are not always separate. For example, if your child should die, think about the desire you would have for her return. The pain of loss would create overwhelming craving for the child, and that desire would be stronger than any pleasurable temptation you ever faced. You see, the desire to regain something or someone lost can be just as strong as the desire to gain someone or something never had. Pain of loss is a form of desire or longing; we crave the person or thing taken from us. By whipping that hurt and longing into spiritual agitation, evil forces use it to confuse our understanding, leading us into sin.

In chapter fifteen, we will explore how Satan's army uses even our desires for spiritual matters to tempt us into sin. Sound like a crazy concept? Not at all—and your own experience has shown it to be true. As long as a person's craving is for God, Jesus, and the Spirit, it is a good and holy desire. With only a slight shift in focus, evil ones gradually steer one away from God and focus her on religion in His place. How many Christians begin their walk with a desire to please and serve God but later corrupt that desire? Some replace their wanting for God with a wanting for power or prestige. Others replace Jesus with a doctrine or with more loyalty to their church than to Him. Some worship the Bible, others worship the denomination, and yet others worship the act of worship itself. Some are more interested in having the gifts of the Spirit than having the Spirit Himself. All of these are sinful cravings, but they do not appear to be sin because they occur within the context of religion. They are sin just the same. You may think those kinds of misdirection could never happen to you; my response is that they may have already.

In chapter sixteen, we will examine one of the most prolific and profitable areas of Satan's current assault—the family. The family was the first institution founded by God. Destroying it destroys God's very framework for genial society. You may think your family spiritually strong. I suggest you withhold judgment until you read chapter sixteen.

Why do Christians sin? Because Satan tempts us through desires that confuse us. Want to know more? Read on.

CHAPTER THIRTEEN

How Can Pleasure Be Bad?

"You're the guy on the radio, right?"

"Right." Each week I hosted a live call-in show on the top-rated radio station in the city, so I figured this wasn't a wrong number.

"You don't know me, but I'm calling to ask you to pray for something. I've asked my preacher, but he won't do it." He paused for a moment as if he expected me to interrupt. When I didn't, he stumbled on, nervously tripping over his words. He rambled for a couple of minutes, then, hesitantly, got to the point of his call, "I know you believe in prayer; I've heard you talk about it on the radio…and it seems like you care about people. Will you help us?"

"What is it you want me to help you with?"

"See…I know this is going to sound bizarre…but, ah, but I'm in love with my best friend's wife, and she's in love with me. You've gotta believe me when I tell you we both know in our hearts God wants us to be together. I'm sorry that some people don't understand…but it was God who brought us together, and now we desperately want to be married to each other. Will you pray that God will give us to each other and that our church can accept us?"

Hearing his words, my mind swirled with conflicting emotions. The counselor in me wanted to know how he got into such a situation; the preacher in me didn't care. A spiritual rebuke raced toward my lips, shoving aside the counselor's questions forming in my mind. My biblical training demanded I tell this man to end this ungodly relationship and to end it right now. Just in time I caught myself. If his preacher couldn't bring him to his senses, what were my chances of accomplishing that in a blind phone conversation? I didn't need to chastise; I needed to pray for God to intervene.

"Oh, God," I prayed silently, "Please bring this couple to conviction. Use me to lead these people to spiritual sanity. Please do it now." Having no time to pray longer or to meditate on what I should do, I trusted God's guidance and plunged into the battle.

"Sure, I'll be glad to pray for you. Let's do it right now. All I need are your first names."

He replied hesitantly, "My name is Gene. My best friend is Mark. Her name is Gloria."

"Okay, Gene. Bow your head and I'll pray." I waited a couple of moments to let it sink in that I was going to ask for their union, giving him time to drop his guard and lunge wholeheartedly into the prayer. Then I started quietly: "God, you know Gene's heart and his desire. You also know the desire of Gloria who wants him in place of Mark, her husband. Almighty God, I ask you to kill Mark immediately—"

"What are you doing!" he shrieked into my ear.

I answered calmly, acting as if I prayed for this kind of thing every day. "I'm asking God to make it possible for you to have Gloria as your wife. I'm just doing what you wanted me to do."

"But Mark's my best friend! We don't want him dead. Don't you have any compassion?"

"Me? Compassion? Brother, I just *prayed* a compassionate prayer for your buddy. At least it's more compassionate than what you want for him. You want him hurt—you want his wife to leave him and marry his best friend. Do you have any idea how deeply that will wound him? Can you even imagine that kind of pain? It will take years—maybe a lifetime—to get over. I'm the *only* one showing compassion here. If he's dead he won't hurt, he'll just be in heaven—"

I didn't get a chance to finish; he shouted, "You're weird!" and slammed the phone down.

Replacing my receiver gently, I thanked God for using me. I felt sure I'd given Gene plenty to think about.

THE DECEPTION OF EMOTIONS

I wanted Gene to think, because thinking and sinning don't go together—at least not logical thinking. By my "prayer" for his friend's death, I hoped to make him see the logical conclusion of his request. I struggled to bring his mind to awareness, so that the spiritual in him could overrule his emotions.

Remember the template from Ephesians 4? Satan *confuses the understanding* so he can tempt the emotions. When the tempted person sins enough, his emotions become twisted, *hardening his heart* and causing him to *lose his sensitivity.* That leads him into the ultimate state of sinfulness, *immersion in sensuality.*

Satan doesn't like logic or reason, avoiding debate unless he feels he can manipulate it to his own ends. Truth and logic lead people from evil. When Satan's forces use their own twisted form of reasoning or logic, they always attempt to confuse and create doubt. Truth being his enemy, Satan casts doubt on the truth of anything that contradicts his goals. Using philosophers, pseudoscientists, corrupt theologians, or lust-deluded people, he sows discord and doubt. He uses just enough argument to confuse, not to persuade. He doesn't have to persuade; confusion gives strength to selfish emotions, which need no persuasion.

Think about it: Which temptations come to a person through logical, intellectual thinking or reasoning?

Few, if any.

Temptations come to us through our feelings, especially if those feelings have the strength to overpower our reasoning. The reason is simple: Intellect guides us; emotions drive us. When aroused emotions become strong enough to confuse the guiding intellect, the emotions take control of the person, leaving him or her without spiritual direction. That's just what the evil forces want. Emotions unguided by reason are selfish and subjective; they twist truth and perceptions to fit their own wants. They throw a veil over the mind, blinding the individual to the error of his thinking, incapacitating the mind's power to stop the sin.

That's why Satan seldom makes a frontal assault. He comes from the least-guarded flank, infiltrating skillfully, careful not to alert the defenses. Once selfish emotions are aroused, the mind becomes more susceptible to deceit, diminishing the person's ability to fight away the attack. Reasoning and understanding lose their capability to defend.

Gene's call illustrates this method of attack. Gene is a Christian. Before he became involved with Gloria, what do you think he would have said if asked, "Is it right for a Christian to want another man's wife?" He probably would have said something like, "You shall not covet your neighbor's house. You shall not covet your neighbor's wife, or his manservant or maidservant, his ox or donkey, or anything that belongs to your neighbor" (Exodus 20:17).

Through an unusual circumstance, I met Gene later. From visits with him and his preacher, I can tell you that before he became involved with Gloria, Gene would have quickly quoted that scripture in answer to such a question. After becoming involved with her, he wasn't quoting that passage—or even remembering it was there. He even felt justified in asking other Christians to pray that God would give him his best friend's wife.

How can a person change that much?

There is an answer; Freud called it the "pleasure principle."

THE PLEASURE PRINCIPLE

Freud's psychological model illustrates how a person can be deceived by his own sinful desire. He described three concepts to explain his model: the *id,* the *ego,* and the *superego.* I know these as the *sinful nature,* the *consciousness,* and the *conscience.*

Freud's id corresponds well to the Greek word *sarx,* which is translated in the King James Version as "flesh" and the New International Version as "sinful nature." The Greek word means having a body, but Paul gave it a deeper meaning. "In Paul's thought especially, the *flesh* is the willing instrument of sin, and is subject to sin to such a degree that wherever flesh is, all forms of sin are likewise present, and no good thing can live in the *sarx.*"[1]

Other Greek literature of the era understood the word the same way, "for Epicurus the *sarx* is the bearer of sinful feelings and desires as well as the means of sensual enjoyment." Plutarch, Philo, and other writers used *sarx* with the same meaning.[2]

In explaining how the id works, Freud said it is driven by the "pleasure principle": It wants what it thinks will give it pleasure, and it isn't concerned with or controlled by anything other than its drive for pleasure. Inherently selfish, it has strong motivation and great power.

Freud saw the superego as the conscience that attempts to govern the person and as constantly at odds with the id. He believed that the superego is programmed by the beliefs and values of the people who influence the person.

The ego, or consciousness, deals with the real world around it and guides the individual through life. It is constantly bombarded by the id's desires and the superego's warnings. Ultimately, the ego makes the choices and decides what courses of behavior to follow. (My apologies to all psychologists and psychiatrists who are reading this book and wincing at my simplistic explanation. Remember, this is an illustration, not a textbook on Freudian psychology.)

Many years ago, my psychology professor illustrated the relationship among the id, ego, and superego this way: A person walks by a cart containing fresh, juicy apples but lacks the money to buy one. The id, wanting the apple, begins to clamor for it. The superego reminds the ego that there isn't any money and that stealing is wrong. The ego looks around, notices that no one is watching, and then makes the decision whether to walk past the cart or to steal the apple. Either action will set up conflict with one part of his being. Stealing the apple will bring on guilt from the superego. Passing it by will bring on craving and longing from the id.

Now, go beyond Freud and think about the same idea in biblical terms. The Christian wants her Spirit-guided mind (Romans 8:5–6) to be her conscience (superego). But no matter how completely she yields her mind to the Spirit of God, the fleshly part of her (id, sinful nature, *sarx*) is always driven by its own pleasure principle. It feels. It wants. It craves. And it sends strong messages to her consciousness (ego) that often conflict with the messages sent by the Spirit-controlled mind or conscience. When her consciousness allows itself to be directed by the godly conscience, she does right. When she allows herself to be overwhelmed by the strong emotions of the sinful nature, she does evil.

The basic human part of us, called the flesh, desires what it thinks will give it pleasure. It isn't logical or reasoning. It just wants. It continually attempts to overpower the consciousness to get what it wants without restraint.

UNPERCEIVED DANGER

When evil beings use pleasure to seduce you into sin, they usually aim the temptation at some unprotected area of your life. Frontal attacks are too easily seen for what they are. Sneaking in through an unguarded gate works better. Unprotected areas are the parts of your life where you don't *feel* weak but in reality are.

Consider the process that led Gene to call me with his bizarre prayer request.

In becoming best friends with Mark, Gene spent time with him and, naturally, with Gloria. While he found her attractive, his conscience didn't warn him to avoid her. Gloria posed no threat to his spirituality; he enjoyed her company but only thought of her as Mark's wife. Similarly, Gloria enjoyed his company but didn't fear the developing relationship with Gene because she loved Mark. Gene never made any advances or implied in any way that he wanted her. She felt herself strong, needing no protection or wariness. But in reality, she did need protection, because Satan aimed his attack at a weakness she didn't acknowledge. Her marriage to Mark, though enjoyable, didn't fulfill her needs as a woman.

Mark loved to hunt and fish, spending much of his leisure time with his friends in the woods. Gloria, loving him, never complained. She wanted him to enjoy himself. She searched for things to fill her time while he was gone but often found herself longing for someone to talk with, to share life with. Her lack of fulfillment didn't scare her or Mark because she never admitted to herself how lonely she had become. But over time, Gene and Gloria discovered more about each other and found a mutual attraction based on mutual interests, driven by unrecognized mutual needs. Gene had time to sit and talk with Gloria about nothing at all; he had the time for Gloria that Mark didn't.

The attraction grew slowly, so slowly that neither of them perceived the danger. Eventually they began to talk more, hiding their extra time spent with each other from Mark. If they had done that kind of thing at the outset, guilt from their Spirit-controlled consciences would have warned them, stopping them. But it happened slowly, giving the sinful nature time to grow stronger than the Spirit-controlled conscience. Gradually, she realized her life focused more on Gene than Mark. She still loved Mark, but now she loved Gene more. Neither she nor Gene wanted to hurt Mark, but neither were they willing to sacrifice the pleasure they found in each other.

Now it was too late for them to see the sinfulness of their actions. Through master manipulation from evil forces, they had allowed their sinful natures to slowly take over their consciousness without their consciences being alerted. Desire won over Spirit.

Gradually they slipped into the pleasure principle, until their minds were set on the things of the sinful nature and not on the things of the Spirit (Romans 8:5). Now their consciousness couldn't admit the sinfulness of the relationship. To do that meant stopping the relationship, yielding to the Spirit's control of the conscience. They wanted each other too much to let that happen. So they shut out the voice of their consciences, not allowing them to operate fully. Pleasure became its own justification.

They thought, "Surely, this is what love is. Since God is love, this must be God's hand bringing us together. He wanted us to experience this and gave us to each other." They even got to the point where they decided to ask godly people to pray that God would bless their union.

Gene and Gloria followed the path already tread by so many others. The consciousness bought the lie because buying the lie continues the pleasure. The flesh controlled. The Spirit was shut out. With intellect confused, emotions reigned. Both Gene and Gloria were on the edge of complete submersion into sensuality. Only vestiges of the spiritual conscience remained, motivating them to call to ask for a prayer for God's blessing.

When I "prayed" for Mark's death, it was a daring ploy to bring Gene to his senses—to shake his mind loose from the control of his flesh.

Unfortunately, that's difficult to do once the flesh focuses on pleasure.

THE PLEASURE OF SIN

Before the wonderfully wise Dr. Dudley Chancey began his work with Oklahoma Christian University, he served for many years as a youth minister. Years ago he found himself being questioned by another youth minister. "Why do these young people have so much trouble with sexual temptation?" the minister asked. It appeared he really didn't know.

Dudley decided to educate the young minister through the direct approach. "Because sex is fun," he replied. Then, seeing the minister pale, he added, "At least that's what many teens have told me in counseling sessions."

Don't think Dudley impertinent. He's right. Sex is fun. It's fun in marriage, and it's fun out of marriage. For those who are married, the fun continues afterward. For those who aren't, the fun ends quickly, negative emotions and consequences replacing it.

Do you think I'm wrong to say that sin is fun? The Hebrew writer said it long before I. Concerning Moses he wrote, "He chose to be mistreated along with the people of God rather than to enjoy the pleasures of sin for a short time" (Hebrews 11:25). Note that phrase, "pleasures of sin." The Bible says sin is fun.

Righteousness is fun too. Most Christians experience wonderful pleasure when they serve God. I know from experience that teaching an eager learner the truth of God is a pleasurable experience. So is meaningful worship. Paul indicated that the "high" of being filled with the Spirit and singing is better than the artificial highs of drunkenness. He wrote, "Do not get drunk on wine, which leads to debauchery. Instead, be filled with the Spirit. Speak to one another with psalms, hymns and spiritual songs. Sing and make music in your heart to the Lord" (Ephesians 5:18–19).

The things of God are just as much fun, if not more so, as the pleasures of the flesh.

Just because something is pleasurable or fun doesn't mean it's wrong. But it does mean that it can be used to deceive people into sin. When your drive for fun or pleasure takes control, the pleasure principle is at work. That means you seek what *you* want above what *God* wants. Even the most spiritual activity may become a work of the flesh when your drive for pleasure directs it, ignoring the Spirit of God.

For example, some people so enjoy worship that they worship the worship experience. Savoring emotions and exalting God's name with their lips, they focus on their feelings instead of the God they exalt. His Word and His way take second place to the warmth and joy in their hearts. They run rampant over any Christian who worships less emotionally, looking down their spiritual noses at them in pity. Their joy of God mutates into spiritual snobbery. The principles of mutual edification and submissiveness taught by the Spirit (Romans 14–15) disappear behind a veil of worship ecstasy. The glorious act of worshiping God degenerates into sin.

Please don't misunderstand; I'm not implying that all pleasure is bad and self-serving. Neither am I saying there shouldn't be great pleasure in worship. Pleasure is good; it was made by God for our enjoyment. It's the pleasure principle that's bad. When it is at work, the sinful nature is struggling to get its way. It even corrupts spiritual actions.

I'm not trying to make you paranoid, questioning every pleasurable sensation you have. I am trying to convince you that satanic forces can use pleasure to deceive you into buying a lie. They can use it to confuse your understanding, harden your heart, desensitize your conscience, and, if not stopped, immerse you into sensuality. Sometimes they even cloak it in the robes of righteousness, disguising the real principle at work until it is too late to care.

THE PLEASURE PRINCIPLE PROCESS

If there are any unprotected areas of your life, you are susceptible to the insidious infiltration of evil. Evil beings watch you and learn you, waiting for their chance to attack. They likely won't come at you head-on, giving you a chance to prepare your defenses. They bide their time, looking for just the right weakness, creating just the right opportunity.

If there is another person nearby with a similar weakness, they will arrange an introduction.

If you overextend your credit, becoming desperate for cash, they will offer you an ungodly opportunity to get it. They may provide a chance to steal it; they may con you into working night and day, ignoring the important people or proper priorities in your life. They focus you on the pleasure that getting more money would bring.

They like to bring pressures and stress. Producing undue anxiety in you works well for them. Anything that causes you to misfocus and misdirect can be used to confuse your mind. Once your mind is no longer clear, they slyly exploit the least protected, unfulfilled emotion in you. You won't admit it's happening, but you will find ways to explain and justify. One day you'll find yourself completely embroiled in an ungodly situation, refusing to acknowledge it as ungodly and unwilling to stop. The pressures drive you to seek pleasure and encourage you to ignore the rules of right and wrong.

They play dirty. Too often they win.

Somewhere in the process, you will experience guilt, but it won't be enough to stop you. It comes too late with too little power. Sweeping emotions enthrall you, covering and smothering the guilt with waves of pleasure.

Satanic forces deceive you until your sinful nature gains more power than your Spirit-controlled mind. You consciously decide to sin. The process evolves like this:

- *Deceiving*—The sneak attack begins, but the temptation is disguised so that your defenses won't engage. Blithely, you walk into a battle you don't know is going on.

- *Wanting*—Emotions gain strength, battling the Spirit-controlled mind. Your desire overpowers your godliness. Negative emotions, such as fear, stress, anxiety, or pressure, make your desire for pleasure even stronger.
- *Doing*—The sinful nature wins. The sin existing in the mind takes life. You do the wrongful deed. Thought translates into action.
- *Repeating*—Guilt races to your consciousness, but pleasure shoves it to its holy knees. Each time it rises, you try to stop. Each time pleasure pummels it down again, it becomes weaker. Unless you find the spiritual strength to stop now, the pattern is set. Soon your emotions gain unrestrained strength, taking them beyond your ability to control.
- *Justifying*—Guilt loses power as you explain to yourself why the sin isn't sin. Wanting inner peace, you buy the lie, accepting the sin as innocence in the eyes of God and man. The lie absorbs you, but you still have days of spiritual lucidity when you acknowledge you are sinning and try to stop.
- *Craving*—You no longer have the power within you to stop the sin. Any attempt to call on God is feeble and ineffective. Without the intervention of godly people doing battle for you, you face spiritual destruction. The sin can be stopped, and you can be delivered, but that will only happen if you cry out for godly warriors to fight with and for you. Any personal thoughts of abandoning sin are vestiges of spirituality, not the powerful faith that connects with God's power.
- *Dying*—Sin reaches "full-grown" maturity. You die spiritually. You may even die physically (James 1:15; Romans 6:23).

DON'T LET IT HAPPEN TO YOU

Let this chapter serve as a warning to all, no matter how spiritual you may think you are. There is no Christian so strong she cannot be tempted. Every person, except Jesus, sometimes loses to his sinful nature. I have lived long enough, counseled enough people, and sinned enough to know that any person is capable of sin. If you think yourself beyond that, I leave you with the words of Paul: "So, if you think you are standing firm, be careful that you don't fall!" (1 Corinthians 10:12).

Wait! There is another message for a special few.

I never know what God is going to do or how He is going to reach someone. Maybe you are reading this chapter because God is trying to convict you. As you read the steps listed in the last section, you saw yourself—if only for a moment. But now, already past the words that convicted you, you are again applying these truths to others and not to yourself.

Don't do that.

Let God speak to your heart. Are you continuing in a sinful activity? Be honest. Have you justified it, losing your ability to feel guilt? Hear me. I once did that too. I know how desensitized I became to God's leading, so I know how desensitized you may be now. Just for a moment, let God in. Face the truth and let it free you.

You know that what you're doing is sin. You also know that you can't stop. You have already lost the power of God to deliver you. Put down this book and pick up the phone or get in your car, but make contact right now with the most godly, most mature Christian you know. Confess your sin. Cry out for help. Have that person read this chapter; then have him or her call for other godly people to come pray for you (James 5:13–16). Tell them that they must make you accountable and that they must check with you regularly to support you in this spiritual war. Have them call on God's power for your deliverance and make them promise to continually pray for your deliverance and protection.

Scary?

Sure. No one wants to admit sin. Most of us don't want to appear weak. But you know what has happened to you as you faced this on your own. They've deceived you and will deceive you again. You must have godly help from other Christians to be freed.

Ask for it.

Accept it.

Enjoy the salvation of God and the freedom of a forgiven, Spirit-guided person again.

Do it now.

CHAPTER FOURTEEN

How Does Satan Use Pain?

"You ask questions, and she'll blink her response. One blink means no; two blinks mean yes. It's the only way she can communicate."

Nancy smiled gently as she taught me to talk with Allie, the lady she sat with during the day shift. Allie required special attention beyond that normally given in her nursing home. She needed twenty-four-hour observation, as her life ebbed from her during the final stages of Amyotrophic Lateral Sclerosis—sometimes known as Lou Gehrig's disease—the incurable illness that cripples its hosts before killing them. It had crippled Allie, causing her great pain, robbing her of almost all movement other than breathing—and blinking. Everything about her eyes still functioned; she used them as her sole communication with the world.

Sensing that Allie needed spiritual counsel, Nancy had invited me to visit her. Meeting her for the first time, I stumbled through the cumbersome process of offering various options for her to accept or decline. A single blink meant "No, you're off the mark." After each single blink I'd think of another possible option, offer it, and watch her answer. Within minutes I began to understand how she thought and learned to communicate more easily.

I wanted to understand her because there was something I wanted to know. From the moment I walked into the room, I saw rage staring through the pain in her eyes. After learning the communication system and feeling more comfortable understanding her, I asked about it.

"Are you mad at God for letting this happen to you?"

If the question caught her by surprise, her eyes didn't show it. Her response came quickly—blink, blink.

"Do you feel guilty about being angry with Him?"

A solid, steady, defiant single blink.

Then, her gaze faltering momentarily, she blinked again. Twice.

"You're so angry that you don't feel guilty about the rage you feel toward God. Then, when you think about it, you do feel guilty. Is that right?"

Her eyelids answered yes.

"It's okay to be mad at God. I would be too. He understands our human anger, and He doesn't hold it against us. He's not mad at you for being mad at Him."

Seeing the skepticism in her eyes, I related the Bible story that proved my point. I took time to explain God's reaction to our anger, sharing appropriate verses. As I talked, I watched her. The rage remained in her eyes throughout my discourse. When I finished, I waited, watching her watch me, looking for any change in those eyes. There was none; the rage continued unabated.

"Nancy tells me you're a Christian. In spite of all you're going through, do you still place your trust and faith in Jesus?"

Slowly, she blinked. And blinked again. Her steady glaze broke as a tear formed in the corner of one eye.

I talked softly. "I'm glad you still have your faith, Allie. The good news for you is that you are near death. You know that. I know you hurt; Nancy told me that the morphine no longer cuts even the edge of the pain. But soon you'll be free. Free from the pain. Free from the prison this body has become. Free from the anger and rage you feel. In just a few days, God will meet you as you enter heaven. He Himself will wipe the tears from your eyes. Yes, you'll likely be crying when you see Him. Tears like you have now. Tears of anger. Tears of frustration. Tears of release. The devil took his best shot at you and lost. He didn't defeat you, Allie. You still have Jesus; you didn't let go. You still have heaven. It won't be long after you're there that you'll forget all about this pain. I'm sorry for the pain you feel right now. I'm glad you've won your battle."

Unable to make any sound, she let her eyes flow freely, dripping pent-up emotion onto the starched sheets. I had put into words the emotions she felt, giving her a way to release them. I had also given her the reassurance she needed that her anger in no way jeopardized her salvation.

The rage was gone. In its place I saw peace. And hope. My mission done, I gently kissed her cheek and left her to die.

As I walked to my car, I thought again about how Satan uses pain to misfocus God's people. It isn't a new tactic; he's done it as long as mankind has served God.

SATAN USED PAIN AGAINST JOB

Remember the attack by Satan's forces on the righteous man Job? Satan's challenge to God was, "Strike everything he has, and he will surely curse you to your face" (Job 1:11). Satan obviously believed that if enough pain came into Job's life, he would curse God.

Satan's angels brought pain to Job by taking his herds, killing his servants, and murdering his children—all in one day. Job had awakened that morning the richest man in his part of the world (v. 3); he went to bed that night broke and childless. "In all this, Job did not sin by charging God with wrongdoing" (v. 22).

With the next wave of attack, Satan "afflicted Job with painful sores from the soles of his feet to the top of his head" (2:7). His wife finally broke under the pressure, showing her weakness and anger at God. But "in all this, Job did not sin in what he said" (v. 10).

Finally, Satan's brilliance brought three of Job's friends to finish him off. They attacked Job's righteousness, leading him to become proud and defensive. When nothing else worked, this almost did, bringing God's chastisement upon Job for his questioning (chapters 38–41).

Those same avenues of attack that the evil forces used on Job so long ago still work quite well today. Take away a person's financial security or kill his long-term associates or touch his children, and you'll bring great pain to him. Afflict him with disease or put a weaker person in his life whose faith isn't as strong as his, and you'll stagger him spiritually. Have his religious "brothers" attack him, and you'll find that any vestige of pride and arrogance existing in him will surge to the surface of his character. Satanic forces use those and similar tactics every day. They do it with the same goal they had for Job: "Maybe he'll curse God to His face."

SATAN USES PAIN TO MAKE US ANGRY WITH GOD

If you were Job, what would you have thought when all those bad things happened? Would you have questioned why God let them occur? Would you have been angry with Him?

I would have.

When I was a young preacher just out of college, I received a call from an official in a nearby city asking me to inform a family in my church that their daughter, Jan, had been killed in an automobile accident. I refused, telling the official that I had no education or training in how to do that. I insisted that she find someone else more qualified for the task. She patiently persisted, telling me there was no one else she could call, until my sense of responsibility made me agree.

Praying for wisdom, I drove my car toward the section of town where Jan's mother lived. As I drove, I decided to first tell Jan's sister, Judy, the sorrowful news. I hoped Judy would then help me tell her mother. I didn't want to further burden Judy by adding that responsibility to her hurt, but I didn't know what else to do.

Arriving at Judy's house, I found a note on the door that deepened my dread of the task before me. The note said, "Jan, come on in. I'll be home soon." Knowing that Jan would never come, I slipped the note into my pocket, sat on the porch, and waited. In a few minutes Judy returned, her car loaded with bags of groceries. Thankful for the temporary diversion, I helped her gather all the bags into the kitchen, postponing the terrible news for a moment. As we worked, Judy excitedly informed me, "Today's Mom's birthday. Jan's coming into town to help me prepare the surprise birthday party. She'll be here any minute."

My heart sank deeper into my gut. I couldn't wait any longer. Gently taking Judy's arm, I led her to the sofa and haltingly told her about Jan's accident. When I told her Jan was dead, she just sat there, stunned, opening and closing her mouth as if to say something but never making a sound. After a few moments of helplessly watching her misery, I asked if she would go with me to her mother. I felt that the sooner they were together, the better they could face this tragic shock.

Driving carefully toward her mother's house, I glanced at Judy every few seconds. Sitting in the passenger seat of my car, she looked straight ahead, silent, her face contorted. Thinking of her agony, I suddenly remembered that Jan and Judy's father had also been killed in an auto accident a few years before I moved to the community. I knew him by reputation. Though dead for years, he lived on in the hearts of his family and friends. He'd been a wonderful, loving Christian man who had died much too young.

Now a second family member, Jan, had died in another wreck. I began to think how I would feel if I were Judy. In my imagination, I saw the devil filter into my car and sit between us. I heard him whisper sarcastically into Judy's ear, "Your father was the best Christian man you ever knew. He died in a terrible car wreck. God really took good care of him, didn't He? Your sister was the best Christian woman you knew. Now she's dead. Another terrible crash. God really took good care of her, didn't He? Your God has no power…or He doesn't love your family…or He isn't there at all. Why do you still trust Him?" Then in my mind I heard him begin a repetitive, hypnotizing chant, "Doubt God. Doubt God. Doubt God."

My imagination must have been on target; Judy began to moan. The haunting sound began slowly, barely loud enough to hear. Gradually it escalated into a wail. Tears cascaded down Judy's ashen face. Then, suddenly, she began shouting, "Why, God? Why…God…why? Why do You keep letting this happen to us? Why have You done this?"

I found myself asking Him the same thing.

Of course, God didn't kill Judy's father or sister. Maybe Satan's henchmen didn't either, though I wouldn't put it beyond their twisted minds. Jan may have died just because she didn't look before she turned into the path of an oncoming truck. But there was no doubt that Satan used the resulting pain to attack the faith and hope of Jan's family. Satan uses pain to make us angry with God. He enjoys it when we yell and scream our pain at God—even when we refuse to admit to ourselves that's what we're doing.

Once I asked a Bible class if any of them had ever been mad at God. One brother intoned, "If I were, I'd never tell Him." Another person said, "You're not supposed to be mad at God." Of course, that wasn't the question I asked; we do a lot of things we aren't supposed to do. The question is whether God's people ever become angry with God.

What about you? Have you ever been angry with God? I have. Most Christians have. Sometimes it's because He let someone die, though you begged Him for her life. Maybe He allowed someone to walk out your door, never to return, though your love screamed at God not to let him go. Sometimes people get angry because He doesn't stop child abuse or prevent children from dying or getting sick. I know one man who became furious with God because he lost all he had in bankruptcy. There are as many reasons to be angry with God as there are painful situations His children face. If you've been mad at Him, you've joined a large group.

Would you like to know how He reacts when you are angry with Him?

There is a Bible story that shows clearly how He feels about our anger, doubt, and questioning. John 11 gives us a glimpse into God's reactions to our human weaknesses.

HOW JESUS RESPONDS TO OUR ANGER

You probably know the story, but I ask you to think it through with me again.

Jesus loved Lazarus of Bethany and his two sisters, Mary and Martha. Now Lazarus, His dear friend, lay dying, and the sisters sent for His help. Their faith strong; they knew He would heal Lazarus when He arrived. Patiently they waited…and waited…but Jesus didn't come. Lazarus tried to linger until His arrival. His sisters urged him to hang on, fight, just make it one more day until Jesus arrived. With His coming all would be made well.

But Lazarus couldn't do it. Overcome by his illness, Lazarus could cling to life no longer. In a final struggle with death, he closed his eyes, slipping into the sleep of the ages.

Though miles away, Jesus knew exactly when it happened. Turning to His apostles, He said, "Our friend Lazarus has fallen asleep; but I am going there to wake him up" (John 11:11).

True to form, the apostles didn't get it. "Lord, if he sleeps, he will get better." Patiently He explained, "Lazarus is dead, and for your sake I am glad I was not there, so that you may believe. But let us go to him" (v. 14). Jesus believed in these men, even though they struggled with their belief in Him. He continued to believe in the faith of Mary and Martha, though He knew they struggled with their feelings about Him too.

By now, the sisters had mourned for four days, and they couldn't understand where Jesus was and why He hadn't come. When they sent the message to Him, they made it clear this wasn't just another beggar pleading for a miracle. "Lord, the one you love is sick" (v. 3). What could be more important to Jesus than to come to the aid of the ones He loved? He'd made it clear how special they were, how important they were to Him.

Then the message came: Jesus was nearing the city. When Martha, the "do-what-needs-to-be-done" sister, heard He was coming, she rushed out to meet Him. She didn't greet Him with thankfulness, happy He had made it safely, she didn't reach for a hug of reassurance and sympathy. No, the practical Martha got right to the point. Her first words to the tardy Savior were, "Lord, if you had been here, my brother would not have died." As far as Martha was concerned, it was Jesus' fault that Lazarus was dead, and she wanted Him to know it. Then, quickly, she added, "But I know that even now God will give you whatever you ask" (vv. 21–22).

Sitting in my office, reading those verses from a distance of thousands of years, and having no pain for a dead brother fogging my judgment, I think she should have used a different approach. She should have skipped the chastisement and gone straight for the miracle. You don't castigate God and then ask Him to give you what you want through a miracle.

But Martha did. She hurt, and she didn't like hurting. She lashed out at the God who could heal the hurt because He had let the hurt happen in the first place. If He truly was God and really did love them as much as they thought He did, Lazarus wouldn't be in that grave. The sisters wouldn't have this pain in their hearts. They wouldn't have been asking over and over, "Where is Jesus? Why hasn't He come? Why is He abandoning us?"

Martha, after all, was human. What more human thing is there than to lash out at the one who let you down? She loved Him still. She knew He held enormous power. But her pain was only there because He let it be, and she didn't appreciate it.

Neither did Mary.

Falling at His feet, she said "Lord, if you had been here, my bother would not have died" (v. 32).

When Martha rebuked Him, He gently tried to teach her about His power over death and resurrection. When Mary reproved Him, He was deeply moved in spirit and troubled (v. 33). Experiencing firsthand the inconsolable spirits of the sisters and their friends, He showed His divine reaction to human anger, doubt, and questioning.

"Jesus wept" (v. 35).

And so we see into the mind of God. When those He loves—and those who love Him—rail against Him in their hearts, He cries. He doesn't chastise. He doesn't punish. He feels the pain Himself and takes the burden of the pain into His own heart.

Just as He dealt with those sisters, He deals with you—and with me. When Judy wailed her pain and anger at God, I knew how God responded. He sat in heaven watching, and Jesus sat at His right hand watching with Him. The Spirit lingered nearby, explaining what He found deep in her heart (Romans 8:26–27).

And They all cried with her.

SATAN USES PAIN TO WEAKEN FAITH

By using the pain and hurt in our lives to get us to be angry with God, Satan wins a minor victory. He temporarily weakens our faith. He shifts all blame from himself to God, maintaining his low profile to keep us from seeing who it is that really hurts us. His deception prevents us from looking to God for strength and healing. At the very time when we most need to hold His hand, we turn from Him in petulant anger, accusing Him of not loving us. We recognize His power with our lips; we doubt it in our hearts.

That's what happened to Martha. She told Jesus she knew He could still raise Lazarus, but she didn't believe it. When Jesus questioned her, measuring her faith, He said, "I am the resurrection and the life. He who believes in me will live, even though he dies; and whoever lives and believes in me will never die. Do you believe this?" (John 11:25–26).

Notice her answer. It gives lip service to His power and position but evades the heart of His question. She replied, "Yes, Lord, I believe that you are the Christ, the Son of God, who was to come into the world" (v. 27). Sounds good, doesn't it? It wasn't. She mouthed a stronger faith than she felt.

How do I know?

When Jesus commanded, "Take away the stone," Martha, the sister who said she knew Jesus could bring Lazarus back, objected. Reminding Jesus that Lazarus had been dead four days, she begged Him not to bring the stench of his death into her nostrils. Jesus couldn't bring Lazarus from the grave without removing the stone, but she begged Him not to move it. What does that tell you about her faith in an impending resurrection? She didn't believe that Lazarus was coming back, and she abhorred the thought of experiencing his death through the foul odor of his decay.

Her lack of faith didn't surprise Jesus. He'd known it all along. He understood that her pain had pushed her faith into a little corner of her mind where it could still talk but could not lead. Turning to her, He said,

"Did I not tell you that if you believed, you would see the glory of God?" (v. 40). Then, waiting only long enough for the stone to be removed, He brought Lazarus back into the realm of the living.

John doesn't tell us if Lazarus wanted to come. Summoned by Jesus, he had no choice. But we do know that the sisters rejoiced whether Lazarus was happy or not.

Satan weakened Martha and Mary for a while, but he couldn't destroy them. Though their faith retreated into mourning, it didn't die. Jesus showed them again the power of God, strengthening their faith, the apostles' faith, and the faith of all gathered there whose hearts were open.

Ultimately, He does the same for us when we hurt. If we just continue to look, we will again see Him bringing His wonderful blessings into our lives. He doesn't always answer our requests—He loves us too much for that—but He always stays faithful to us.

Stay with Him. Don't let go of His hand. He nurtures you through your hurt and brings joy in the morning.

SATAN USES PAIN TO REMOVE CHRISTIANS FROM BATTLE

Because he is evil, Satan enjoys hurting the children of God. He hurt God's children in Eden; he hurts them today. Inflicting pain on God's children inflicts pain on God.

When churches invite me to present my "Have Mercy" series on overcoming guilt, I always point out that Satan uses a threefold plan of attack for every person. The *first phase* of that plan is to keep the person from ever becoming a Christian. He's extremely effective with that one. Most of the people on earth aren't Christians.

If a person survives that attack and becomes a Christian, evil beings move to the *second phase* of the plan—deceiving him into abandoning his Christianity. Some churches call this "falling from grace." Peter wrote about it when he referred to those who return to the world after being saved from it:

> If they have escaped the corruption of the world by knowing our Lord and Savior Jesus Christ and are again entangled in it and overcome, they are worse off at the end than they were at the beginning. It would have been better for them not to have known the way of righteousness, than to have known it and then to turn their backs on the sacred command that was passed on to them. (2 Peter 2:20–21)

Fortunately, few Christians lose their salvation. Most never step from

God's grace from the day they become a Christian until the day they enter heaven. If you doubt the truth of the preceding statement, you probably live in misery and spiritual insecurity. While I don't have the space in this book to show you the scriptures that prove my point, I discuss it in my book *Forgiven Forever.*[1]

In *phase three,* satanic beings attack those Christians they can't lure away from God. If Satan can't steal a person's salvation, he attempts to steal her effectiveness. The reason is simple: If he can't keep this person from heaven, at least he can keep her from taking anyone else with her. He can keep a person so focused on healing her wounds that she never fights on the front line for those who don't know Jesus.

So, one reason Satan enjoys hurting God's people is that it takes them out of battle. Not only does it take the wounded person out of battle, it takes other Christians out as well. I learned that lesson many years ago when an army sergeant told me he preferred seriously wounding an enemy soldier to killing him. I immediately asked him why, thinking his Christianity had softened his heart. He replied that when one soldier receives a debilitating wound, *three* soldiers actually leave the battle. It takes two soldiers to transport a seriously wounded comrade away from the line of battle to the field hospital. A dead soldier might be left until the heat of battle lessens. A seriously wounded soldier needs help immediately.

In the twenty-five years of my Christian experience, I've seen the wisdom of that tactic many times. When Satan's forces seriously wound a soldier of Christ, many other soldiers of the cross spend multiple hours and great effort trying to save him. Sometimes the wounds inflicted by the evil ones are physical. Most often they are spiritual and emotional. When a debilitating wound fells a Christian warrior, loving Christians surround him, transporting him to safety.

Sometimes it seems that most of our time is spent healing the wounded, leaving precious little time to fight on the front lines, saving the lost. Maybe that's one of the reasons so few people are saved.

Surely we need to heal the wounded. Nothing I'm writing here suggests anything different. But we spend so much time working with the wounded that we fall short of our responsibility to seek and save the lost. By brilliant use of this third phase of his plan, Satan makes his army dramatically more effective in their use of the first phase. Focusing us on our own wounds or focusing us on nursing the wounds of others prevents us from concentrating on the lost souls of nonbelievers. That makes it easier for the evil beings to lure those unbelievers away from Jesus—away from God's salvation.

Now, don't let these words make you feel guilty about needing help when you are wearied or wounded by Satan's forces. You will sometimes need healing time for yourself; frontline soldiers need rest or recuperation occasionally. *Just don't stay in recuperation too long.* Jesus needs you. When Satan weakens your faith through exhaustion, remember that he does it purposely. When Satan deceives you into resenting God, into feeling angry because He let some catastrophe overtake you, remember who is at work. Satanic forces bring the pain. They want to turn you from God—destroying your faith if possible, making you ineffective in battle at least. They use your weariness and pain not only to remove you from the battle, but also to remove those who focus on ministering to you.

You and the Christians ministering to you are in the hospital, a good place to heal the hurting. But while there, none of you is on the front line, winning the lost from the world. Precious opportunities are lost, some never to reoccur.

Satan's forces will lose their battle to destroy you if you will hang on to your faith, allowing it to rebuild and control you again. But they will win the battle for any other souls you would have led to Jesus during the "hospital" time of your healing. Don't feel guilty about that, or they'll use that guilt to weaken you even more, taking you further from the battle. Just understand what they're doing and heal as rapidly as possible.

We *must* strengthen ourselves and others spiritually, so we will be tougher to seriously wound, so that our healing time will be shorter when we are wounded.

The questions that come from pain show how spiritually debilitating pain is to those who aren't spiritually strong.

The angry and frustrated cry, "Why should I serve you, God? You didn't protect me or the one I loved."

The discouraged and despairing moan, "What difference does it make? The more good you do, the more harm comes to us. No good deed goes unpunished."

The misfocused and misdirected plead, "God, will You just do this for me? Then everything will be wonderful."

Each leads to the same place—doubt. And in that state of weakened faith, we drop the shield that protects us from "the flaming arrows of the evil one" (Ephesians 6:16). We become more susceptible to their attacks, less effective in the battle for the souls of the world.

Don't fight God. Fight them. They're the evil ones who hate you.

NO SOLDIER IS MORE IMPORTANT THAN THE BATTLE

Just after the Gulf War, I visited with a member of Naval Intelligence who had recently returned to his family. He fascinated me with stories of behind-the-lines commando work that occurred as the land battle began in Kuwait. He went behind Iraqi lines with a British commando group who had the responsibility of destroying vital communications gear, giving our soldiers a much better chance for survival in their attack. As he shared the story, he told of one commando who fell before enemy fire. As the other commandos ran past their fallen comrade, they didn't stop to pick him up. Instead, they dropped their extra ammunition as they scurried by him.

Appalled, I asked why they didn't rescue him. The answer startled me, opening my mind to the gist of war. Stopping to rescue the wounded would have possibly prevented the team from accomplishing their mission. Failing in their mission would have cost hundreds of lives of Allied soldiers who depended on these commandos to destroy the enemy's communications equipment. In the balance of things, the decision was simple—one life for hundreds of lives. Dropping the wounded soldier extra ammunition made it possible for him to hold the enemy off longer, ensuring the success of the team's mission.

He died fulfilling his duty.

I'm not suggesting that we abandon every wounded believer, dropping off extra Bibles for him to throw at the pursuing enemy. Often we do have time to nurse and heal. But the soldier isn't more important than the battle, and it's time each of us who has spiritual strength realizes that. God may sacrifice any of us for the good of His army and those we seek to save. We're soldiers, not civilians. Soldiers at war in the most important battle of all.

Jesus decided to let Lazarus die because his death and resurrection would strengthen the faith of others who needed stronger faith, including the apostles (John 11:14–15). Though his sisters found it painful, the good that resulted more than equaled their sacrifice. Even to this day, followers of Jesus learn and grow from their experience. Jesus could have prevented Lazarus from dying, but the battle superseded the importance of the soldier.

Jesus may allow you similar honor.

Oh, God, give us greater faith so we can tolerate larger wounds. God, keep us in the battle. Heal us quickly when we fall. Please don't let our "hospitals" become the only battlefield on which we fight.

Forgive us, our Commander, for not following Your marching orders to bring the world to You.

CHAPTER FIFTEEN

How Does Satan Use Religion?

Larry's sermon swirled through the auditorium, touching hearts and convicting minds, leading the hearers to conviction. He argued from Scripture, illustrated convincingly from life, and eased anticipated tensions with well-placed humor. Larry knew he was in good form this morning. He relished those Sundays when everything went just right.

As he spoke, he thought to himself that this presentation would be a great addition to those he sold on cassette tape. Why let such a powerful sermon bless only the thousand souls present? It needed to be heard around the nation.

Jerry and Carol, sitting on the fourth row, didn't feel the same way Larry did about this morning's sermon. They listened in shock. Larry's sermon today contradicted the counsel he'd given them just last Friday in his office. Because they had feared they were living in sin, they had gone to him for guidance, asking what they should do. That day he had opened his Bible and had shown them verses that absolved them from guilt. Today he used different verses, convincing them once again that they were two of the most evil people on earth.

They knew they should wait and talk to Larry later, but their fear drove them directly to him as soon as the final amen wafted through the hall. Larry stood in his position by the back door, smiling grandly, ready to shake the hands and listen to the compliments of the flock. The majestic smile faded when he saw Jerry and Carol making a beeline for him. It disappeared abruptly when they challenged him, seemingly unaware of the hundreds lining up behind them for the traditional farewell blessing earned by shaking the preacher's hand.

"Brother Larry, did we misunderstand what you taught us in your office? You told us we weren't sinning and that God accepted our marriage. Today you preached about a situation just like ours and came to the totally opposite conclusion. You said the couple in your story live in adultery and should separate for the salvation of their souls. Have you changed your mind about what adultery is?"

Larry nearly whispered his response. "No, I haven't changed my mind. Let's talk later." Already looking past them, he redrew his smile, preparing to go on with his back-door duties.

Too concerned to realize her breach of church etiquette, Carol persisted, "Brother Larry, if you haven't changed your mind, why did you preach what you did today? It's not what you believe. I don't understand; why did you preach something you don't believe?"

"Look," he responded quietly, "What I told you in my office in counseling is what I believe. What I preached today is what this church believes. Understand? Now, don't worry about a thing. Your marriage is quite all right with God. I need to move on now; people are waiting." He quickly took Carol by the elbow and guided her past him. Before she could recover, he was smiling benevolently at Sister Smith as she told him what a wonderful sermon he had preached and how the church needed to hear the *truth* preached like that more often.

Sister Smith could smile; her spiritual security was intact. Carol and Jerry's spiritual security gurgled down a whirlpool of doubt and confusion. They didn't know whether or not they were sinning. They loved each other, but they also loved God. Within months their undeserved guilt would drive them apart—and away from church. They couldn't live with each other without guilt, but they couldn't attend the church that drove them from each other.

Satan used Larry, their preacher and spiritual counselor, to defeat them.

SATAN USES RELIGION TO MISDIRECT CHRISTIANS

Satanic forces use religion effectively in their battle against the forces of God. Some of their best work has been done at church.

We all know the power let loose in a church when hypocrites run rampant. Their witness to the world negates the witness of ten faithful believers. Their gossip and innuendo within the body of Christ keep critics buzzing, sects arguing, and weak Christians stumbling. If one of these hypocrites worms his way into a position of church leadership, the church suffers his arrogance and spiritual dwarfism in everything it attempts. If his hypocrisy eventually leads him into public scandal, the entire church suffers embarrassment and shame as the community laughs and scorns.

Many Christians also know the power of satanic attack that uses good brothers to battle other good brothers. Satan doesn't use just hypocrites. He can blind good folks to the effects of their actions and use them powerfully to wreck havoc within the army of God.

Less obvious is the religious attack of legalistic self-righteousness. It may be the most effective use of religion accomplished by evil beings. Hypocrisy and church disputes are damaging, leading Christians and churches into long recovery periods of healing. But with self-righteousness, recovery periods don't last long periods of time; they don't happen at all.

Self-righteousness is an insidious spiritual disease that doesn't reveal itself to its victim. It sneaks past spiritual defenses because it appears to be from God. It masquerades as deep spirituality, masking its true origin. The self-righteous person believes that everyone else is sick but that she is doing just fine. In that way she is similar to the hypocrite. The difference is that while other Christians usually avoid an exposed hypocrite, they tolerate and encourage the self-righteous.

Hypocrisy, fratricide, and self-righteousness: Each of these avenues of attack seeks the same goal—to misdirect and misfocus the Christian so that he fights anyone but the true enemy. Satan is skilled in tricking believers into fighting each other or into seeing no need to fight any spiritual battle at all. He usually accomplishes this without revealing himself as the true spiritual enemy, as he manipulates from the realm of the unseen.

The bad news is that each attack works well. The good news is that each can be defended against when recognized for what it is.

RELIGIOUS HYPOCRITES

No one likes to be called a hypocrite. And for good reason. The *Reader's Digest Great Encyclopedic Dictionary* defines hypocrisy as "the pretense of having feelings or characteristics one does not possess; especially, the deceitful assumption of praiseworthy qualities." This definition is similar to the way the New Testament uses the word. In koine Greek the word referred to an actor playing a part. Hypocrites aren't real. They pretend to be something they aren't.

That's why nobody likes being called a hypocrite.

Jesus didn't hesitate to use the slur when appropriate. He told the Pharisees, "you appear to people as righteous but on the inside you are full of hypocrisy and wickedness" (Matthew 23:28). He didn't speak to other sinners as harshly as He spoke to the hypocrites. Thieves and prostitutes received His compassion; hypocrites received His scorn. He had no tolerance for people who pretended to be what they weren't.

For example, when Jesus taught in a synagogue one Saturday, He saw a woman bent over, unable to straighten up because she had been crippled by a spirit for eighteen years. He immediately called her forward and healed her. The synagogue ruler and others among the religious leaders were indignant. How dare Jesus heal on the Sabbath day? If He wanted to heal this woman, He should have waited until Sunday morning. Jesus fired back, "You hypocrites! Doesn't each of you on the Sabbath untie his ox or donkey from the stall and lead it out to give it water? Then should not this woman, a daughter of Abraham, whom Satan has kept bound for eighteen long years, be set free on the Sabbath day from what bound her?" (Luke 13:15–16).

He humiliated them publicly, much to the delight of the gathered people.

I wish He would come back and do the same today.

Hypocrites are people like Larry—the preacher I told you about in the beginning of this chapter. They play their Christian part artfully but have little of it in their inner beings. Larry preaches for a large, urban church and enjoys the prestige of his position. When his own study leads him to a different biblical conclusion than his congregation, he simply buries his new understanding so no one in power will be offended. He preaches what the church believes, even when he no longer believes that the church's creed is godly. He's an actor, playing a part. Actors learn their lines and deliver them with great conviction. That's what makes them good actors.

When the actor is a professional, we applaud the talent. Anthony Hopkins convincingly played a depraved, cannibalistic killer in the movie *The Silence of the Lambs,* earning an Oscar for his performance. A couple of years later, he played C. S. Lewis, the profound Christian writer, in *Shadowlands.* The two characters had nothing in common, but

Hopkins's skillful acting made each character real and believable. Yet, none of us mistakes him for either the killer or the writer. He's an actor, making himself seem to be the person he plays. We admire such talent, amazed that anyone can hide so effectively behind an assumed role.

Without realizing it, many of us witness a greater level of acting talent each Sunday. Many preachers, elders, deacons, teachers, worship leaders, and others make Anthony Hopkins look like an amateur. He plays his role on the screen; they play theirs in life. They play their parts so convincingly that we believe they are whom they pretend to be. We don't erect defenses against them because they are on our side. We even follow these actors into spiritual battle, believing that their faith and wisdom will lead us to victory.

Instead, their treachery and shallowness lead us to one defeat after another. Because they play their roles so well, it is not apparent that they are the cause of the defeat. No one blames them. We love them, forgive their lapses in judgment, and charge into the next battle behind them.

Maybe I've become cynical throughout my years of Christian service, but I believe that one reason so many churches don't reach the lost is that hypocrites in well-placed positions stop them. They use their acting skills to gain responsibility in the church then take advantage of that power to keep the church from operating by faith. Like the Pharisees Jesus publicly humiliated, they watch for anything that doesn't meet their approval and, finding it, soundly criticize it. They don't care that a woman has been bound eighteen years by an evil spirit; they want the rules obeyed by *their* interpretations. And their interpretations always defeat God's intended purpose.

They control the church, making it their own domain. They are just like the brother John faced.

> I wrote to the church, but Diotrephes, who loves to be first, will have nothing to do with us. So if I come, I will call attention to what he is doing, gossiping maliciously about us. Not satisfied with that, he refuses to welcome the brothers. He also stops those who want to do so and puts them out of the church.
>
> Dear friend, do not imitate what is evil but what is good. Anyone who does what is good is from God. Anyone who does what is evil has not seen God. (3 John 9–11)

They bring constricting rules into the church, telling people they can't have or do certain things. They restrict God's people from the blessings He made for them.

> The Spirit clearly says that in later times some will abandon the faith and follow deceiving spirits and things taught by demons. Such teachings come through hypocritical liars, whose consciences have been seared as with a hot iron. They forbid people to marry and order them to abstain from certain foods, which God created to be received with thanksgiving by those who believe and who know the truth. (1 Timothy 4:1–3)

That's what Larry did to Jerry and Carol. In his sermon on that day, he forbade them to be married, just as Timothy warned. They had every biblical right to be married to each other, but that right was taken away by a hypocrite, an actor, playing a part so he could have the power that came with it. His "seared conscience" forced a lie into the lives of two people who sought Jesus as he preached "what this church believes." That hypocritical lie, taught by demons through the mouth of Larry, drove Jerry and Carol from the God who united them in marriage.

You may be asking yourself, "Why did he tell them in private they could be married?" The answer is simple. Hypocrites do and say whatever will gain the most power with the most people. Larry studied himself into believing that Carol and Jerry were justified in their marriage. Sharing his conclusion with them gave him more power in their lives. But telling the church his theological position would have eroded his personal power base in that church. And his personal power was more important to him than the fact that the church held a legalistic, nonbiblical view of marriage. The hypocrite, Larry, protected his power base by telling the church what it wanted to hear. To the couple in private, he blessed their union. To the church in public, he condemned any similar union.

Everyone lost.

The church lost by having a man-made doctrine supported when it should have been questioned. The couple lost by having so much confusion thrown into their lives they couldn't find God any longer. Larry lost because he slipped further from God in his hypocrisy. When that hypocrisy was pointed out to him by a friend who called him to accountability, he rejected the admonition. To this day he defends himself and stands justified in his own sight.

For those in that church who see through Larry's hypocrisy, deliverance comes with a price. They love their church. They love their friends there and enjoy the relationships they have established. But when they no longer can tolerate the hypocrisy of the preacher, they have no choice but to move on to another congregation. Until a majority of the church or its leaders see what the hypocrisy of their pulpit minister does to destroy the army of God, the church will never be what God intends it to be. Their battles continue to be internal, aimed at solving problems that arise from political bickering. Larry's unchecked, unchallenged hypocrisy diminishes the spiritual growth of all.

Only when churches remove the hypocrisy—in the pulpit and everywhere else it exists—will they finally join the battle to win the world from Satan. No church can fight Satan effectively when its leaders work for his cause. And hypocrites do work for his cause, whether they are personally aware of it or not.

FRATRICIDE—THE GOOD AGAINST THE GOOD

Satan also uses sincere, nonhypocritical Christians to keep the church from the front lines of battle.

Remember Job? When Satan couldn't break him by taking his money, killing his children, and striking him with a terrible disease, he brought in the "big guns." He used Job's pious religious friends.

They were good men who came to help a brother in trouble.

> When Job's three friends, Eliphaz the Temanite, Bildad the Shuhite and Zophar the Naamathite, heard about all the troubles that had come upon him, they set out from their homes and met together by agreement to go and sympathize with him and comfort him. When they saw him from a distance, they could hardly recognize him; they began to weep aloud, and they tore their robes and sprinkled dust on their heads. Then they sat on the ground with him for seven days and seven nights. No one said a word to him, because they saw how great his suffering was. (Job 2:11–13)

These were good men with good hearts—sent by Satan to defeat Job.

These righteous men came to save Job from his sin. They were convinced he had sinned because they believed that bad things only happen to bad people. Bad things happened to Job; therefore; Job must have done something bad. Arguing from the circumstances in Job's life, they concluded Job was a sinner in need of repentance.

In chapter after chapter (written in beautiful Hebrew poetry), they debated Job about his sin. He declared and maintained his innocence; they declared and maintained his guilt. While they weren't sure *what* he'd done, they were sure he *had* done it.

Of course, we know they had reached an inaccurate conclusion. From the first chapter of Job, we know that God declared him "blameless and upright, a man who fears God and shuns evil" (v. 8). But they didn't have the advantage of reading the script. They simply argued from their strongly held belief. And that belief—that bad things happen to punish the wicked—persists in the minds of some today. It is just as wrong now as it was then. Satan wants us to believe that lie because it pits brother against brother in an internal battle. Wrong theological conclusions often push believers into unwarranted battles with their brothers.

When nothing else worked in Satan's attack against Job, this approach did. When Satan took Job's riches, he kept his faith. He clung to God as he buried his children. He chastised his wife for her lack of faith, and he continued to look to heaven. But while defending himself to his brothers, he became proud. He finally became so exasperated that he asked God to come down from heaven and explain all that had happened to him.

God came. He scolded Job for questioning Him, saying that if Job could do all the things He could do, He'd be glad to explain Job's misfortune. God made it clear to Job that unless he had God's level of intelligence and power, he couldn't understand the explanation, even if God gave it.

The point to remember is that when nothing else made Job question God, the attack by his brothers did. Good men with good hearts who had come to save their brother nearly drove him to defeat.

It happens today. Often.

There are many good Christian people who sincerely love God with all their hearts. These Christians are the salt of the earth, preserving it for Him. Yet these loving Christians often rush into battle with each other, leaving the front lines of the war with Satan to fight a battle of fratricide.

Satan must be very proud of himself. Not only does he keep the Christian army from winning any people in the world from him, he brings great harm into the camp of God. Christians who murmur and complain and who judge and condemn each other bring great pleasure to those evil forces camped on the other side. Believers fight each other valiantly, slaughtering hip and thigh. If we fought nearly as viciously, tenaciously, and effectively against Satan, we'd win the lost by the thousands.

Attacks from outside our ranks force us together, making us stronger by forcing us to depend on each other. Attacks from inside our ranks wrench unity from us, making us vulnerable to the outside attacks that inevitably follow.

A Misdirected Army

Sometimes I wonder if anyone remembers the lost, dying, sin-sick world that Jesus told us to bring to Him. No church can effectively reach the lost while arguing and fighting among themselves. While the first-century church initially resisted all attacks of Satan, modern-day Christendom seems unaware of the attacks altogether. No one stops to notice the *real* enemy, who stands among them—cheering. Everyone seems too intent on defeating their brethren, thinking that's the mission Jesus left for the church.

It isn't.

He made it clear: "All authority in heaven and on earth has been given to me. Therefore go and make disciples of all nations, baptizing them in the name of the Father and of the Son and of the Holy Spirit, and teaching them to obey everything I have commanded you. And surely I am with you always, to the very end of the age" (Matthew 28:18–20).

Sometimes I picture Jesus sitting in heaven—chin in hand, as He leans on the arm of His throne—watching His followers war against each other. Long past frustration, He just waits, knowing that someday one of us will look up. When one day a Christian warrior, stopping to wipe the blood from his eyes, looks toward heaven, He stands up and signals. Pointing and gesturing, He calls that warrior's attention to something just beyond the dust of our battle with each other. When the warrior turns to see what Jesus is pointing at, he notices Satan and his army, slaughtering the people of the earth, undeterred, no longer even looking to see if we're coming against them. In my mind, I see this Christian warrior snapping a sharp salute, nodding his head to communicate his understanding of what Jesus wants, then rejoining the battle to kill his brothers. He'll get to Satan's army, just as soon as he wins his battle within the church.

Cynical?

You tell me.

Where are all the primary efforts of Christendom directed? At Satan? Or at ourselves? For the most part, the children of God can't tell Satan from a brother who doesn't agree with him on some fine point of doctrine or practice. Crying out for the destruction of the false teachers, these brothers attack any and all who don't believe just as they do, believing they are attacking one of Satan's own. In reality, they wouldn't know a false teacher if he bit them.

Their interpretations of Scripture and their analysis of the church's direction supersede the will of God. Declaring themselves His only army, they invade other battalions of His army, engaging them in a battle of words, innuendos, and slander. Determined to be God's good soldiers, they wound—and sometimes spiritually kill—the soldiers of God who don't look or act the same as they. They do so gleefully, looking forward to meeting God, so they can recount to Him their many victories.

I'm quite sure that in death these brothers will discover that their victories were real; it was their cause that was fantasy. They will find that they defeated God's own people, stopping God's own work. Having done many "good works" in Jesus' name, they will find they never knew Him. Of them, Jesus said, "Many will say to me on that day, 'Lord, Lord, did we not prophesy in your name, and in your name drive out demons and perform many miracles?' Then I will tell them plainly, 'I never knew you. Away from me, you evildoers!'" (Matthew 7:22–23).

Modern-Day Examples

When I speak across the continent, I often ask audiences, "How many of you have attended a church that has gone through some kind of church fight? How many of you have been part of a church that has split?" In every audience, people raise their hands. I don't remember asking the question anywhere and receiving only negative responses.

Just read the newspapers, and you'll know this happens regularly. The Southern Baptists fight among themselves, making headlines with their conflict-filled conventions. So do the Presbyterians. Methodists argue over issues such as accepting homosexuals and ordaining women ministers. Catholics have more dissidents than some Protestant denominations have members. Churches of Christ take out full-page newspaper ads to condemn other Churches of Christ they don't agree with.

I've seen Christians fight over which translation of the Bible one may use, how long a man's hair can be, and whether a man's wife may pray aloud in his presence. I've watched churches run people away who sang different worship songs, held their hands up when they prayed, or wouldn't wear a tie to Sunday morning services. I've witnessed intense arguments over who is a Christian, how perfect someone has to be to be saved, and what name a church building must have over the door for the members to go to heaven. I've been castigated and dissociated because I openly befriended a brother whose theological views were questioned, because I said I'll let God make His own decisions about whom to take to heaven, and because I spent social time with preachers from different religious fellowships than mine. I've watched Christians treat others like dirt for things like being baptized in a different church's baptistery because the one at their church was broken at the time, not regularly coming to Wednesday night Bible classes, or being guilty of a publicly known sin that "the church shouldn't forgive." I've heard leaders of churches excuse their lack of Christian activity because blacks might want to be part of it, because another religious group once did it, or because they need to keep a few hundred thousand dollars in the bank "just in case we need it."

And I'm only fifty-one years old.

None of the items I listed above sprang from my imagination; I'm not that creative. I didn't list the worst examples because allowing myself to think about these matters depresses me. You know more examples without my listing them. If I were to encourage every reader of this book to send examples of church "fusses" they've experienced, I could use the stories to publish another book immediately on the heels of this one that would discourage us all. There may be no limit to the range of issues over which a group of Christians can fight.

THE SELF-RIGHTEOUS FALLACY

A major reason these fraternal battles flourish is that so many saints of God feel an utter sense of self-righteousness. They feel that their standing before God is secure because of their own, "humble" obedience. They obeyed; God owes them salvation because of their obedience. While they give lip service to the inequity of their obedience to God's grace, they truly believe they have raised themselves above the wicked by their observance of the law of God. Submissive they may be; humble they aren't.

Self-righteousness contrasts dramatically with the righteousness given by God. God offers to count us as righteous because of our faith in Jesus. Righteousness is not and can never be given in reward for our own actions, even our own obedience. Paul made it clear: "Now when a man works, his wages are not credited to him as a gift, but as an obligation.

However, to the man who does not work but trusts God who justifies the wicked, his faith is credited as righteousness" (Romans 4:4–5).

God has no obligation to me at all, though I serve Him with all my heart. I can't keep every command of law perfectly. Because I can't, He doesn't have to reward me for the ones I do get right. The penalty for the broken commands overpowers any blessings "owed" for the kept ones (Romans 6:23). Therefore, God looks for my faith, not my obedience; and He rewards my faith by counting me as righteous. If He looked only for my obedience, I would have no hope of heaven at all. Thinking I have earned righteousness by my obedience makes me self-righteous.

This plague of self-righteousness is well used by Satan in his attack on the church. Self-righteous people have little compassion for those who do not read and interpret the Bible the same way they do. They prohibit or expel from their fellowship any who do not come to the same deductive or inductive conclusions, labeling those who differ rebellious and unyielding. Unfortunately for them, these self-righteous saints not only force from their fellowship all who reason *less* effectively than they, they also force from their fellowship all who reason *more* effectively than they. They lock themselves away from all the blessings meant to be enjoyed by the army of God in its wholeness. Becoming a sect, they retreat from the battle against Satan and engage lustily in their battle with all saints outside their sect.

Spiritual Egotism

In a seminar I conducted a few year ago, a lovely Christian woman made a startling confession, crying softly:

> I grew up believing that those in my kind of church were the only ones going to heaven. I was taught that people who went to other kinds of churches weren't Christians—no matter how much they claimed to love Jesus. I was taught from childhood that we are *the* church. We even referred to ourselves that way—I'm a member of *the* church. Only after reaching adulthood did I discover why that teaching so appealed to me. I wasn't the most beautiful or popular girl in school. I didn't excel at sports like some other kids. There was nothing to set me apart, make me special. Except for one thing. I was going to heaven, and the other kids at school weren't. They went to their parents' churches every Sunday and thought Jesus was going to save them on the last day. But I knew better. They were lost. And that thought gave me the superiority—the specialness—I needed to give

> me identity. Only now, as an adult, can I admit that to myself, and I am so terribly ashamed. I am ashamed before God. How could I have been so self-righteous?

You may be wondering the same thing: "How could a person be so self-righteous?"

It's easy. Base your relationship with God on your own actions—whatever those actions are—and self-righteousness naturally follows. You easily look down on all people who don't do the same actions on which you base your righteousness. For example, if you pick out just one of the biblical reasons for being baptized and base your immersion on it, believing that your understanding of that one thing validates your baptism, you will discount anyone who was baptized for any of the other biblical reasons. You won't even recognize them as Christians and will demand their reimmersion before you offer them Christian fellowship.

Or if you believe that having a certain name over the door of your church building earns you God's acceptance, you will sit in judgment on all churches who use any other name over their door.

Inevitably, people look to their own acts of obedience and judge all others who don't do them just the same way or for just the same reasons. To the self-righteous, obedience to a specific, chosen set of commands becomes the basis for relationship with God. Any commands outside the chosen set become matters of opinion—even when they deal with strong moral issues like war. Commands within the chosen set become matters of faith—even when they deal with such trivial things as which translation of the Bible you read.

Jesus' Reaction to Self-Righteousness

How does God view us when we act self-righteously? Jesus made His thinking clear in the following illustration:

> The Pharisee stood up and prayed about himself: "God, I thank you that I am not like other men—robbers, evildoers, adulterers—or even like this tax collector. I fast twice a week and give a tenth of all I get."
>
> But the tax collector stood at a distance. He would not even look up to heaven, but beat his breast and said, "God, have mercy on me, a sinner."
>
> I tell you that this man, rather than the other, went home justified before God. For everyone who exalts himself will be humbled, and he who humbles himself will be exalted. (Luke 18:11–14)

Self-righteousness is arrogance—brash, snobbish, spiritual arrogance. It treats others with disdain when they can't live up to the perfect standards chosen by the group. It's an arrogance that forgets that no one can perfectly live up to the standards of God.

Satan uses it to keep people apart and to keep the saints misdirected and misfocused. It keeps us in battle with each other. It keeps us from helping each other with warmth and compassion.

For example, Christians could deal with temptation and sin much more effectively if they could share their struggles with other Christians. James told us to "confess your sins to each other and pray for each other so that you may be healed. The prayer of a righteous man is powerful and effective" (James 5:16). Self-righteousness so saturates some churches that the saints live in fear of other Christians discovering their weaknesses and sins. No one confesses openly, without pressure, asking for the prayers of the believers. The only confession made comes when someone sins publicly and has no choice but to "come clean." Gathering a group, or even a single person, to confess to and seek spiritual strength from would be nearly blasphemous.

Self-righteousness perpetuates all the attacks that Satan exploits through religion: It is the avenue that sustains the inner attacks that come from other Christians; it is the avenue that weakens us for the outside attacks that come from the world.

When we all realize that none of us is good enough to go to heaven, no matter *what* commands we obey, we will begin to shed this deceptive blindfold. When we realize that God loves us, looks for true faith in us, and *grants* us righteousness because of that living faith, we will find a true humility before Him and before each other.

We then will understand, intellectually and emotionally, the great gift we have been given. We also will find ourselves *unable* to bicker, quarrel, and fight with others who have been granted the same wonderful gift. The insurmountable love of such a God will become too much good news to hold inside. We'll rush into the streets, telling the lost about what we've found and about the wonderful God who gave it.

SATAN'S ATTACK PATTERN

We must not let Satan use us in any way in his attacks on the church. Satanic forces work inside and outside God's church to destroy individuals, to disrupt unity, and to deter the people of God from the battleground of lost souls. Never doubt that the church is under attack. Satan attacks cyclicly—first from the inside, then from the outside—first weakening, then crushing. He attacks from the inside through the three patterns we've discussed: hypocrisy, fratricide, and self-righteousness; and he attacks from the outside through debilitating persecution or circumstances.

If you'll read through the first few chapters of Acts, you'll see Satan's attack pattern at work as he sought to destroy the infant church, and you'll also see that Satan's persistence finally paid off. Before the close of the New Testament, he was dividing and conquering, causing churches to fight among themselves and weaken. Just read 1 Corinthians to see how well it worked—or Galatians—or 3 John—or...well, you get the idea.

THE SOLUTION IS IN THE VOICE OF GOD

Our defense against the attacks of Satan is the same defense revealed in the Book of Acts. If you read closely the chronology of Satan's attacks against the first-century church, you will notice that the Holy Spirit led the apostles to thwart every battle tactic Satan used. Instead of listening to their own wisdom or direction, they listened to God. They didn't turn on and slaughter each other. They fought the enemy.

When we begin listening to the directions of the Holy Spirit, we, too, will begin to fight the true enemy. When we finally quit listening to the Diotrepheses, the philosophers, the theologians, and the hypocrites, we may again hear the voice of God.

Promoting and defending denominational dogma or personal interpretations filters God's voice so effectively that when we hear our own prejudices, we think we hear God. But those disuniting, destroying messages we follow can't be from God. The voice of God places love above legalism (Matthew 22:37–40). It places mercy above sacrifice, preventing ungodly condemnation of the innocent (Matthew 12:7). It looks beyond the boundaries of the saved, longing to reach and convert the unsaved (Luke 19:10). It doesn't lie in wait, hoping to catch someone saying something wrong (Mark 12:13). It doesn't look down its long, snooty, spiritual nose at sinners (Luke 15:1–2). It holds no record of wrongs done (1 Corinthians 13:5). Any voice that shows contrasting characteristics to these divine characteristics isn't the voice of God. It may be Satan, pretending to be God. "And no wonder, for Satan himself masquerades as an angel of light" (2 Corinthians 11:14).

The Holy Spirit of God still has the wisdom and power to lead us in our battle with the forces of Satan. When we finally listen to Him again, we will fight the true enemy and cease destroying each other. We will again be as victorious as the church in Acts, and thousands and thousands of lost humans will find their way to God through our battle efforts. But until we open ourselves to the Spirit, they have little chance.

Only when our ears are truly attuned to the voice of God will we be effective in the battle for lost souls. Then Satan won't be able to use our religion against us. He and his army will flee the power of it.

CHAPTER SIXTEEN

How Does Satan Use Families against Themselves?

She couldn't look at me as she asked the question, afraid of the answer she might see in my eyes. Instead she pretended to watch a bright orange butterfly meticulously dust the panes of our French doors. I pretended to watch it, too, glad to have the distraction. It gave me time to contemplate the hurt behind her question and carefully choose the phrasing of my answer. I knew I was too often dull in my communication with her, missing altogether the feelings behind her words. I was determined to understand her this day. It was I who pried open this emotional powder keg, and it was my duty to gently defuse it. Forever, if I could.

My question had come first, before hers that now hung heavily in the air between us. Maybe I should have asked it differently or at another time, but I didn't. It bothered me that she cried each time I packed for another speaking trip. Her tears weren't those of a little girl hating to see her daddy leave for a few days; they were tears of mourning.

So I asked. Finally. "Joanna, why do you cry every time I leave? Why does it upset you so much?"

She didn't answer immediately. Looking away, she discovered the butterfly and locked her eyes on it. After a few moments, she quietly uttered the words that brought everything into perspective.

"Are you coming back?"

Ah, now I understood. A part of me knew it all along, but the rest of me didn't want to believe it, always finding other reasons for her misery. I didn't want her to be holding on to the pain. I wanted her well, healed of the hurt I had brought into her life. I wanted her already to have forgiven me—completely—and to have forgotten what I'd done. She knew how sorry I was and how much I'd tried to make it up to her and to everyone else. It hurt into the deepest caverns of my heart that she still carried pain because of me.

When Joanna was six, I left her mother. Moving to a city one hundred miles away, I filed for divorce and began a new life. Until that time I'd been the minister of a succession of growing churches. After leaving my family, I had little use for God or His people. It's funny that I never quit going to church; some habits die hard. But I don't need to tell the story here; I tell some of that story in my book *Forgiven Forever.* I'll just tell you that I lived a godless and sinful lifestyle for a couple of years, hurting myself and all who loved me.

I did do one thing right. Deeply loving both my daughters, Angela and Joanna, I saw them every month and poured all the affection on them I could. Angela, my firstborn, is educably mentally retarded. Unable to breathe for the first eight minutes of her life, she suffered brain damage at birth. Joanna came along seven years later. Of the two, she had the tougher time dealing with my leaving. She cried for my return, unable to understand why I left. A six-year-old shouldn't have to watch a major part of her world walk out her door.

I don't mean to leave you curious, wondering what happened to make me go and what happened to make me come back, but I can't tell that story now. All that's important here is that after living apart for three years, I came to my spiritual and family senses and asked Alice to remarry me.

Of course, she refused.

She asked her church friends what she should do about taking me back. Without exception they counseled her to have nothing to do with me. I continued to pray and continued to court her, wanting her again as my wife. Eventually she believed my love and my intent. We remarried a few months before Joanna's tenth birthday. This time we *will* be married "till death do us part."

When Alice and I remarried, I never expected to be asked to speak for churches again. It never entered my mind to try to bargain with God, "I'll come back to You and to my family if You'll give me opportunity to preach again." A prodigal returned, I knew I had nothing to bargain with. I only wanted my relationship with God and my family. That was enough for me.

When churches began to invite me to speak, I reeled in shock. Why would anyone want to listen to a sinner like me? At first I refused, then I realized that my gift for speaking hadn't been developed by me. It wasn't a natural gift, but a spiritual gift; the ability to speak publicly never evidenced itself in any way until I became a Christian. Since God gave that gift to me, it was His. If He wanted to use it again, I would be arrogant and ungrateful to deny Him. With true humility and great trepidation, I began to accept the invitations to speak.

And Joanna began to cry.

Every time I left.

I reassured her of my safety, told her exactly when I'd be back, and called to speak with Alice, Angela, and her every day. I wanted to believe she just worried about me traveling in those airplanes and autos, but I was afraid to seek out the real reason.

When my reassurances failed to soothe her, I had to ask her why she cried. That led to her revealing question: "Are you coming back?" As she asked the question, she wasn't ten anymore; she was the sad, confused little six-year-old who had watched her father walk out of her life. Frightened. Angry. But afraid to show the anger because she wanted me to stay. Now I knew what she felt every time I walked out the door: "You left once and were gone for three years. You didn't want Mom or Angel or me. You saw us once a month and then drove back to your other life where we didn't fit. How do I know you won't do it again? Why should I trust you? Every time you leave, I have this tremendous fear that you won't be coming back."

Unlike her father, Joanna is a person of few words. She felt all these things but could couch them only into four excruciatingly painful words, "Are you coming back?"

Continuing to watch the butterfly, she waited quietly for my answer. I knew she would capture my every word, along with every nuance of emotion behind my words. I knew that when I finished my answer, she would turn to look at me to see whether my eyes believed my voice.

Carefully, prayerfully, I spoke from my heart to hers. "Joanna, I'll always come back. I love your mother. I love your sister. I love you. I'm terribly sorry for all I did to hurt all of you. Maybe I haven't said that enough yet...but I am. If I could take it all back and keep it from ever having happened, for your sake I would. I did wrong. I hurt the people I love most in the world. Please believe me; I'll never hurt you like that again. Every time I walk out that door, you can know in your heart I'm coming back. The only thing that can keep me away is dying; and if I die, I'll be waiting for you in heaven. And I will be watching. Thinking of you. I love you, baby. I'm sorry. I pray that you can find it in your heart to completely forgive me and to trust me again."

The words were as honest as any I've ever spoken. They didn't work magic, but they did help. I had to repeat them again, several times, over the next couple of years. That was okay; I didn't mind. I hurt her for the three years I lived in sin. I would continue to speak healing words and give healing comfort for as long as it took to make her heart well.

Gradually she learned to forgive me—and trust me again.

As I write this, she's a beautiful twenty-two-year-old Christian. Of course, she endures all the struggles of any young adult, feeling her way through the confusing maze called life. But there is one thing Joanna knows without doubt—Daddy always comes back. He loves her too much to do anything else.

Never will I hurt her or any of my children—nor my wife—again. Not if I have any say-so about it.

My own odyssey and the pain in the hearts of my family members showed me clearly how Satan uses families against themselves. It happens constantly. He delights in hurting people within the boundaries of their safe haven, convincing them that no secure and happy place exists for them.

He attacks families of believers. He just as viciously attacks the families of all people. God has two institutions on earth—the church and the family. Since the family reaches broader and farther than the church, Satan knows that attacking and destroying it gives him an edge in his battle against God.

When satanic forces destroy a family, they destroy a hundred other good things that come from that family. Attacking families opens the door for unfaithfulness, addictions, and loss of identity. It breeds gangs, abuse, and utter lack of sensitivity. It diminishes respect for authority, self, and mankind in general.

In his battle against God, Satan uses people in both of God's institutions. He uses people in churches, and he uses people in families. Since these are the two places people feel safest and are least guarded, the infiltration works well.

Satan attacks families in the same three ways he attacks churches. He uses the sin and hypocrisy of family members, he uses any conflict he can create within the family, and he uses self-righteousness and aberration of religion.

When he can combine any of these approaches, his attack takes on inordinate power to deceive and destroy.

SATAN USES SIN AND HYPOCRISY

Several years ago, Jody came to me with an unusual request. She wanted to know if I'd perform a marriage ceremony for her and her lover. Her lover was also a woman.

Of course, I refused, showing her the passages upon which I based my belief that homosexuality is unacceptable to God. Jody responded by telling me she wasn't homosexual; she knew homosexuality was sin, and she wouldn't do anything sinful. I asked, "If you aren't homosexual, why do you want to marry Wilma? And why are you having sex with her? Don't you think these actions show that you are homosexual?"

That question led to counseling sessions over the next several weeks in which Jody revealed her sad story. She had grown up in a Christian home where every person in the family attended every church service. Her father had served as a deacon and had taught an adult Bible class for years.

He also taught his daughter about sex.

Sometime in her sixth year of life, he entered her bedroom late at night and performed oral sex on her. For six years he persisted regularly in this hideous molestation. As she got older, he tried to make her perform oral sex on him. Repulsed, she refused adamantly enough that she dissuaded him from consummation of that act. When she was twelve, he walked into her room one day and asked her to forgive him of what he'd done. He never molested her again. Neither did he ever mention anything about it again. He selfishly pushed six years of continual molestation deep into the core of her being by pretending it never happened. Maybe he feared prison. Maybe he was just ashamed. But the damage he did in the end was worse than that of the beginning. She had no help, no one to talk to, and no way to heal. Her shame, fear, and love bottled everything inside her, seething, until it mutated into a perversion.

Now, at eighteen, Jody sat before me convinced she wasn't homosexual—homosexuality is a sin. She found men repulsive; the only people she could trust enough to love were other women. She loved her current "friend" so much she wanted to spend the rest of her life with her in a marriage bond.

Of course, Jody's refusal to admit to herself that she was homosexual was pure denial. Her actions belied her pious words. But the course of events that led her to this point clearly showed that she could overcome her chosen homosexuality with time and proper therapy. My job as a Christian minister was to convince her to cease the practice of homosexual union immediately and to seek the proper help to relearn her natural heterosexuality.

I'm not telling her story to begin a debate on homosexuality. I'm sharing it to show how Satan used one family member's sin to bring sin and harm to another. The sin might last an hour or a decade; the resulting harm may last a lifetime.

The Sin of Abuse

Churches today pretend that child abuse doesn't happen in the Christian ranks. I've read articles where Christian writers claim that the evil of child abuse exists only among nonbelievers!

But the truth is quite different.

I used to speak to a gathering of a couple of thousand teenagers in the Southeast each year. Several years ago while I was speaking to them, a thought popped into my head. Any person who speaks or teaches knows the phenomenon—an idea, not in the outline, comes to you in the middle of a presentation. The thought led me to mention child abuse and to encourage any teens who were being abused to *tell* someone, so the abuse could stop. I pointed out to them that "protecting the person who is abusing you harms everyone. It continues your pain. It keeps the person abusing you from receiving the help they need. For the sake of yourself, the person doing the abuse, and anyone else they may be tempted to abuse in the future, please tell someone responsible what's going on and ask for help."

After making that point, I went on with the lecture I'd prepared. The response at the conclusion of the sermon was overwhelming. Hundreds of teenagers swarmed to the front, sharing their pain, begging for deliverance.

I'll never forget what one sixteen-year-old girl said: "Please pray for me that I can forgive my father for taking my virginity." She and the other teens who responded that night broke my heart. I never had a clue until that moment what was going on in so many "Christian" homes. The honesty and pain of those teens changed my life. They changed my level of courage in confronting sin.

I rolled the sixteen-year-old girl's words in my mind all the way to my hotel room. I pictured the tortured young faces of the other teens who asked us to help them stop their abuse. I found myself thinking, "Surely this kind of thing isn't happening in the church. The response from that audience must be a fluke." To find out, I brought it up again when I next spoke to teens—and again after that—until now I mention it at least once to almost every Christian teenage group I am invited to speak to. The consistent response tells me clearly that the reaction from that first audience wasn't a fluke. Many Christian teenagers are being systematically abused—many by other Christians. Sometimes fathers, sometimes uncles, sometimes others. It isn't just Christian girls; Christian boys are enduring the same harm.

Recently an organizer of a youth gathering decided to prepare the youth workers, before I spoke, to help the kids who would reveal their abuse. He knew I would mention abuse in my speech. His workshop brought together a couple of thousand teens from several states. After the first morning's equipping sessions, the person teaching the class to the youth workers came out of the meeting pale and shaken. When I asked him what was wrong, he replied, "More than half the youth workers just told me they were abused as teens. Most of them haven't dealt with their own hurt. Just thinking of how to deal with the kids in their youth group who have this problem is throwing them into emotional turmoil. They need help as badly as the kids."

That night, when the hundreds of teens responded, we realized we couldn't read their response cards to the audience. Why? We'd be sued. These kids were naming names and listing dates. We turned the cards over to the youth leaders from each group and asked them to take them home to their elders.

Two months later, a lady pulled me aside as I spoke for a weekend church meeting in another part of the country. She reminded me of the presentation I had made to the youth gathering, informed me that the teens from her church had been there, and thanked me. "We had no idea our teenage son was being abused by one of the men who works with the kids in our church. After hearing you speak, our son came back from the youth gathering and told us. The authorities are dealing with the man. My son is in therapy. He'll learn to deal with his horror now rather than suffering from it for years before seeking help. Thank you…thank you."

I deserve no thanks. I didn't stop the abuse; the courage of that teenage boy did. I'm glad he asked for help, telling the people who needed to know what was happening.

I wish that every church had the courage to talk about this plague and to ask their kids to seek help if it's happening to them.

Don't misunderstand my point. Child abuse isn't the only sin destroying families. Drunkenness, lying, unfaithfulness, materialism, and dozens more are being used by Satan to destroy families. The sin isn't always directed at a family member. Any sin committed by any family member anywhere can be used by Satan to destroy the family.

Even sins that we wouldn't normally think of as being so "bad" are destructive.

The Sin of Weakness

The sin of a family member doesn't have to be a great immorality to be used by Satan. Mrs. Job illustrates this principle well.

Teachers sometimes make Mrs. Job sound like a wicked, sinful woman. When Job lay sick and dying, she urged him to curse God and die (Job 2:9). Obviously, she should not have encouraged him to do such a sinful thing, but those words don't necessarily make her evil.

She was very likely a godly woman. Perhaps the severity of the tragedy surfaced her human weakness. Put yourself in her life to see how you would respond: During your married life you carry ten children in your womb, delivering each in the mixture of love and pain known as birth. You suckle each of the ten at your breast. You raise them, giving your life to them as only a mother can. You watch each become an adult, proud of who they are and what they have become. Now, on one day, you bury all ten of them. You pull their broken, mangled bodies from the wreckage of the house destroyed in a tornado. You carefully prepare each one for burial, washing away the dirt and the blood, anointing them with oils and spices before wrapping them in their shrouds. Then you stand weeping as the last words are said and they are laid to rest, one after the other, until all ten are in the earth. Reeling from a broken heart, you ask yourself what worse thing could happen. It doesn't take long to find out. Your husband, the man you love and have given your life to, is dying. He develops hideous sores from the top of his head to the bottom of his feet. The pain surges through him, and there isn't a thing you can do. The stench of his rotting flesh fills your nostrils with death, even while life ebbs feebly through his body.

Now, how strong do you think you would be? Do you think you would say something like, "Job, it's okay. God loves us and is caring for us in all that has happened." Or do you think your hurt, confusion, and anger might lead you to bitterness: "Are you still holding on to your integrity? Curse God and die!" (Job 2:9).

I don't justify her words. I do understand them.

Satan used brilliant strategy in leaving Mrs. Job alive as he killed the rest of Job's family. He used her weakness to attack Job's faith. She wasn't evil, but she was weaker than Job. Her weakness became an avenue of potential defeat for the man Satan wanted to destroy.

He still uses that tactic. How many times have you seen evil forces use the weakness of a family member to defeat the stronger members of the family?

The family member through whom the attack comes may be a nonbeliever. I have personally witnessed the pain and misdirection that comes to a believer married to a nonbeliever. The nonbeliever constantly erodes the faith of the believer, pulling him or her away from God. Constant care and concern for the nonbeliever weakens the believer, sapping spiritual strength.

But the less obvious and often more effective attack comes through family members who are believers. Satanic soldiers work through the spiritually weakest member of the family to spiritually misdirect the rest of the family. Because they all believe, the family doesn't suspect that the weak member is actually a pawn of Satan. They think the battle is *for* the weak person rather than *through* him. The battle strategy is to divert the family from the actual attack. When the major attack comes against the unguarded flank, all defenses are focused on the initial, diversionary thrust, and many families are defeated.

Every teenager reading this book should ask him- or herself such probing questions as, "Are evil beings using my spiritual weakness to hurt my parents? Am I being used to destroy the faith of my brother or sister? What am I doing that could be used by these bad beings to destroy my family?"

Every mother should ask, "Are my weaknesses being exploited to hurt my husband? My children? How can Satan use my doubt and lack of faith? How can he use my temper? What bad qualities are showing up in my children that are replicas of my less than godly behavior? Is my husband being fulfilled by our union, or am I helping satanic forces set him up for temptation?"

Every husband should ask himself questions such as, "How can Satan attack my wife or children through me? Are the hours I spend at work teaching my children materialism and denying them love and attention? Does my wife stand spiritually strong without my help? Have I let down my family in my responsibility to be the spiritual head of the family? Where are my wife and children headed spiritually, and how have I affected that?"

Satanic hordes need only one family member to infiltrate the family unit. Once inside, they work tirelessly to erode everything that is good and holy.

SATAN USES FAMILY CONFLICT

When Satan deceives family members into fighting each other, rather than fighting him, he carries his attack to a deeper level.

For example, about twenty-five years ago I listened as a dedicated church leader detailed the problems he faced with his son. The son, a Christian, fell into the wrong crowd and began living in a decidedly non-Christian way. My friend, convinced that Satan was trying to steal his son, joined the battle with all the fierceness of a loving father.

You may be thinking, "Who could fault that? Any loving parent will fight for his children." I thought the same thing at the time. I was wrong.

While the attack on the son was real, it wasn't the major thrust of the evil attack. Destroying the son would accomplish a minor victory. Destroying the entire family would accomplish a much greater one, wider than just the family itself. This family projected great influence for good in the community and in their church. Nonbelievers and believers alike looked up to them, using them as great examples for strong moral behavior.

Chronicling the events that destroyed the family would take a book of its own. Without explaining all the details, I'll share the results. Focusing on the young man absorbed the father, causing him to neglect his wife and daughters. While they, too, loved the prodigal, they continued to have needs that only a husband and father can fulfill. They didn't make the pursuit of the son the total focus of their lives, as the father did. The family drifted apart. The wife decided she couldn't live with the fanatic her husband had become. The daughters wanted out of the unhappy home. The son dreaded seeing his father, fearing the verbal attacks that intensified with each encounter. The once strong, vibrant Christian family dissolved, each member scarred spiritually and emotionally.

The defeat of the son apparently wasn't Satan's ultimate goal; the destruction of the family and its great influence for good was. The son's weakness pulled the father away from the real focus of the battle, and the battle was lost.

While everyone who sins bears personal responsibility for his actions, how would you like to be the weak person in the family through whom Satan destroys others in your family?

If you are a teenager flirting with temptation, driving your parents to distraction with worry and concern, the evil ones are using you. If you are a father, so focused on making money or making your mark on the world that you have little time for your wife and children, the attack is coming through you. If you are a wife, devoting your life to your social activities or placing your children before your responsibility to God and husband, the battle is coming through you. You see, the battle sometimes doesn't appear to be an attack at all. It doesn't have to be overt sin. It may be an effort to misfocus you enough to remove you from the primary role God designed for you in your home. While you're supposed to be at your post, serving your family, you leave them unguarded by your misfocus, open to spiritual attack that may destroy them.

Member against Member

The words you will read in this section may be among the most controversial in this book. I pray that you read them carefully, hearing what I say instead of some imagined message your emotions conjure.

You read earlier of my hatred of child abuse and my feelings about how Satan uses it to destroy so many families. I hold to those convictions with all my heart. But knowing how Satan operates, I also know how he uses every nuance of an attack to get the most from it. Child abuse is real, and it must be stopped. But there is also another battle flank that must be examined: the *false* claim of abuse used by Satan to pit family member against family member and bring utter chaos to a family.

I watched a teenager, we'll call Claudia, bring great pain to her family when she reported to the authorities that her father had sexually abused her. You know that I encourage teens to seek help to stop any abuse inflicted on them. The trouble with Claudia's report was that it wasn't true. Her father had never abused her in any way. His "sin" was that he forbade her to live a lifestyle inconsistent with his Christian beliefs. When she couldn't stay out as long as she wanted, smoke in his house, or hang out with the local "toughs" she found so attractive, she got her way by using the legal system to get her out of her parents' home.

How do I know?

Claudia is a Christian—obviously, a struggling one. She continued to come to church through the ordeal, and one day she finally confessed her sin of lying about the abuse. She told us her father had done none of the things she accused him of. She made the claim that he did them only because she wanted to punish him, while working the system to her benefit.

Professional Helpers Used by Satan

Since experiencing this awful accusation of a Christian brother, I've seen it several more times with other teens. The system, in its zeal to protect, contributes to their lying. Some social workers, and others in helping professions, actually "help" the child become more creative in his lies by their strong desire to prosecute the "offender." Please don't misunderstand, I'm not attacking social workers. I very much appreciate what they do and the great sacrifices they make. But I have no doubt that some of them, in their belief of any sordid story they're told, bring unearned harm to families who have done no wrong.

And never doubt that just as Satan has preachers and elders in churches who work for him, he has social workers, psychologists, lawyers, and judges working for him too.

There are many good Christian social workers, psychologists, lawyers, and judges who give their lives ministering to people in the name of Jesus. I in no way am attacking or maligning them. Yet my counsel to them is: "Satan attacks you just like he attacks the rest of us. Because you are in a position to bring great penalty to people while protecting those that need to be protected, evil beings try everything they can to deceive you about who is guilty and who is innocent—about who is the predator and who is the victim. I admire you for sifting through all the lies and deceptions and for looking for the truth. But, please, listen to the Holy Spirit of God so satanic beings won't use you to punish the godly through the ungodly. Let God guide you."

Since I'm speaking boldly, let me continue. I confess that I am skeptical about the stories of some adults who suddenly "remember" the abuse done to them as a child. Do I doubt that such an event can happen? No. I don't doubt that it can or that it sometimes does. But I have peripheral knowledge of a counselor who led almost every person who saw her to this conclusion. Oh, not enough knowledge to make a case for malpractice. But enough knowledge to wonder if she is somehow helping people "remember" things that never happened. Satan uses people in the helping professions—both inside and outside churches.

If you are in one of the helping professions and find yourself angry at the words of this section, I have a question for you: "Why?" I'm only warning and encouraging you to be spiritually discerning. If my words cut deeply, maybe you should look within yourself to see why.

I know that satanic forces try to bring as much conflict, anger, and fighting into the home as possible. Every family member should be on guard against being used in such a dastardly fashion. Every Christian in the helping professions should be alert against being used by Satan.

Satan and his henchmen are brilliant. They use child abuse. Then they turn around and use false allegations of child abuse. They know what they're doing, and they do it well. Confusion leads to misdirection and misfocus. That leads to deception and sin.

Are they using it on you?

Don't let them use you to hurt any family—especially your own. Tell the truth. Seek help if you're being abused. Seek God in all that you do.

SATAN USES ABERRATION OF RELIGION

Beyond all the attacks mentioned to this point, Satan also uses aberration of religion to destroy families. His forces use religion against families in several ways.

For example, do you remember how the Pharisees used religion to direct people away from their family responsibilities? Jesus pointed out to them that religion doesn't free one from his duty to his family.

> And why do you break the command of God for the sake of your tradition? For God said, "Honor your father and mother" and "Anyone who curses his father or mother must be put to death." But you say that if a man says to his father or mother, "Whatever help you might otherwise have received from me is a gift devoted to God," he is not to "honor his father" with it. Thus you nullify the word of God for the sake of your tradition. You hypocrites! (Matthew 15:3–7)

When Doing Good Can Be Bad

One way satanic forces use religion today to destroy families is by focusing too much of a Christian's time on his religion, leading him to ignore his other God-given responsibilities. Many church leaders spend so much time on church duties that they neglect their spouses and children. How many times has it been said of some preacher, "He spent so much time saving other people's children, he lost his own"? An ex-elder once stood in a class I taught and said, "The young man is right. I spent so much time and energy being an elder in my church that I neglected my wife and children. I thought that because I was doing good, God would fill in the gaps where I didn't give my family what they needed. The gaps were filled, but it wasn't God who filled them. My total absorption in church destroyed my family. Now, I'm alone. I lost them to the world."

If you are a "superactive" church member, maybe you should slow down and count the cost. Is Satan using your religion to direct you away from your God-given family responsibility? Justifying your absorption by saying that God gets the glory is exactly the reasoning used by the Pharisees in Matthew 15. Jesus will condemn your twisted religious logic just as He condemned theirs.

Punishing the Sinner

A less obvious way Satan uses religion to destroy families is the harshness shown toward family members who sin.

A few years ago, I watched in horror as an elder in a church resigned his position of leadership because his grown son had an extramarital affair. I loved the son and was doing my best to restore him spiritually. The young man struggled, seeking to regain his faith and his love for God. The elder's resignation shouted to the world that his son's actions proved him an inadequate father who shouldn't be an elder.

The spiritual impact on the young man was devastating.

It didn't help him become stronger; it heaped extra guilt on him, making him easier prey for satanic attack. His father's action told him he couldn't win the spiritual battle, convincing him he was evil and no good. Reeling in guilt and frustration, he became an easy target for another affair. At least in that relationship he felt love and acceptance. No, I don't justify his behavior, nor do I say it's all the father's fault. But I do believe the father's action showed a religious harshness that the evil beings used to full effect. If anyone had asked the father if his actions were designed to punish his son, I'm sure he would have said no. I believe that in his mind he did what he thought was the right thing to do spiritually. But he was wrong. His son's sin wasn't his sin. When he made his son's guilt his own guilt, he magnified tenfold the guilt the son felt. He played right into the hands of the attacking evil ones. The father's misuse of religion worked to bring spiritual harm into his son's life.

Shortly after that I watched the same thing happen in a different church with another elder. This time it was a daughter who sinned.

Years later, I ended up counseling her. Though several years had passed since her sin, she still felt that her father hadn't forgiven her. He had resigned his position when the affair occurred, heaping unbearable, extra guilt on her. Even years later, he continually reminded her of her sin and guilt. He did it by avoiding certain subjects and by the manner in which he treated her husband. Interestingly, in years past I had heard this man teach that we should be tolerant and forgiving of penitent people who had sinned against their spouses. He had often referred to David and Bathsheba as a biblical guide for how we are to treat people who sin and later marry the one they sinned with. While he taught us to treat others with godly love and compassion, he couldn't do it with his own daughter.

And she hurt.

Badly.

She misses the love and acceptance of her father. She's done everything she knows to find the forgiveness of God and the church where she lives. God forgave her long ago. The church, locked into its traditions, took longer. But they, too, finally forgave and accepted her. There is one thing that keeps her from total spiritual restitution. Satanic forces still use the weakness of the father—his inability to forgive what his precious daughter did—to bring spiritual harm to her soul. Though forgiven by her heavenly Father, she won't find true spiritual peace again until she experiences her earthly father's forgiveness. Using her need for a father's forgiveness and acceptance, Satan keeps her from focusing clearly on God. She loves God and gives herself to Him the best she can. But without peace, she can't always see Him clearly. Unable to steal her salvation, Satan stole her joy. Only her father can take that tool from him and give her what she needs.

And deserves.

In case you think I'm writing about you, I am.

Whoever you are.

By the grace of God, I beg you to come to your spiritual senses and stop. Get back where you belong; do what God designed for you to do. Be for your family what you are supposed to be. Quit letting your ego, wants, drives, or hurts take you from your post.

Satan has used you to damage others long enough. It's time to repent and open yourself to the power and use of God.

THE FIGHT FOR THE FAMILY

Remember that Satan's most effective tool is deception. Misfocusing, misdirecting, and misleading, he guides you as far from the truth of God as possible.

God intended a man and woman to marry for life. He designed the marriage relationship to be one of companionship and mutual support. He wants each mate to be a support for the other. He made marriage commitment a prerequisite to raising children in a way that will give them all they need.

Return to a personal commitment to every member of your family, beginning with your spouse. Dedicate yourself to a lifelong relationship of mutual respect, caring, trust, compassion, and love. Be for your children all that they need you to be. Don't ever be too busy making a living to be the father or mother they deserve.

Be strong. Not just for yourself but for all who love you.

And, above all, never let your interpretation of Scripture lead you to believe that you should treat any member of your family with anything other than pure, unconditional love. While drastic actions are sometimes necessary to make a person realize she is headed toward a path of destruction, those drastic actions must never communicate a lack of parental or spousal warmth and caring. Coolness, harshness, and continual reminders of sin are damnable. It makes little difference whether you continue the rebuke by harsh words or by being cool and distant in your actions. Either is wrong. Actions speak as eloquently and forcefully as the greatest vocabulary.

Love as God does. Act as God acts. He, as our heavenly Father, portrays perfect family love.

SECTION

4

FORCES AT WORK FOR US

CHAPTER SEVENTEEN

Why Does God Let Satan Hurt Us?

Working the late shift that spring night in 1985 at the Days Inn just south of Montgomery, Alabama, Julie Lindsey never imagined that her life was about to change through a most horrible experience. A fine, young Christian, she loved God and served Him willingly. Earlier in her life she'd enjoyed working as a church secretary. She'd recently moved to Montgomery to finish college and start a professional career. The hotel job helped pay the bills as she finished school.

Just after 11 P.M., two men came to the registration desk where she worked alone. They asked about a room for the night. As she turned to look at the motel diagram for a vacancy, one of them produced a pistol and pointed it at her head.

Julie is one of my dearest friends. She's consented to sharing her story in this chapter, and she wants to tell it in her own words, first published in an article she wrote at the request of the *Alabama Journal.*[1]

> I wanted to scream but I couldn't. I couldn't move. I was paralyzed with fear. I could hardly breathe I was so frightened. The one holding the gun told me to act natural and do as he told me.
>
> They both walked behind the counter and cleaned out the cash register. I felt the gun pressed into my spine. He was standing so close

behind me I could feel his breath on my neck. He grabbed my arm and told me we were going for a ride.

I begged him not to hurt me. He told me I wouldn't get hurt as long as I did what I was told, but that if I didn't, he'd use his gun on me.

The three of us walked to their car. One man got into the back, while the gunman forced me into the passenger side. He never took his eyes off me as he walked around to the driver's side and got in.

He pulled onto the interstate and proceeded south at a high rate of speed. I remember the radio was on, and they were singing. They kept asking me if I knew where more money was. I finally convinced them I didn't. I assured them they had gotten all the money there was.

The man in the back seat leaned up and put his hand down my shirt. He then pulled me into the back seat and forced me to perform oral sex. He kept asking me if I thought I was too good, and he kept calling me names. I prayed I wouldn't be sick.

The driver kept threatening me with the gun if I didn't do what they told me. Finally, he let me up and pushed me back into the front seat.

The driver then demanded oral sex. It was all I could do not to throw up.

He pushed me over to the passenger side of the car. He pulled off the road and told me to get out of the car. He threatened to shoot me if I didn't. I got out and he followed. He grabbed my arm and led me into the woods while the other man stayed in the car.

He stopped me in front of a tree and handcuffed me. He walked around behind me and raped me. I kept praying for it to be over. He was brutal and he delighted in hurting me. I began to think about what it was going to be like when he killed me. I really believed he was going to shoot me.

I prayed to live. I thought about my family and friends and how they would feel knowing I had died such a horrible death. I thought of all the things I hadn't said or done. I didn't want to die this way.

When he finally finished raping me, I closed my eyes and waited for him to kill me. He took my jewelry and began walking away from me. He turned and told me he would call someone and tell them where I was. Then he left.

My whole body sagged in relief. I couldn't believe he'd left me alive. I heard him get in the car and drive away. I fell to the ground and just lay there. I couldn't think. I didn't know what to do. I kept telling myself to think.

Finally, it came to me that he probably wasn't going to call anyone

> to tell them where I was. I also thought he might think twice about letting me live and come back after me.
>
> I found my way to the highway. At two in the morning there's not much traffic. I tried to flag down a couple of cars. They wouldn't stop. Thinking back on it, I can't really blame them.
>
> Eventually a truck driver stopped and called for a state trooper over the radio.

Arriving policemen took Julie to the hospital and then to the police station. In shock, she endured the examinations, the confiscation of her tattered clothes for evidence, and the repetitive barrage of questions. It was after daylight before the police allowed her sister to take her back to Montgomery.

Though her nightmare began suddenly, it dragged on for months. The hotel fired her. She dropped out of school. She says, "I couldn't function. Everything I did was a major effort and every decision monumental. I was shattered, lost, and bewildered."

A few weeks after the assault, I sat with Julie just outside the meeting room of the Grand Jury of Montgomery County, Alabama. The police had caught the rapists a few days earlier, and Julie had picked them out of a lineup, signing warrants for their arrests. The Grand Jury was meeting to decide whether to indict them. Before testifying, Julie paced the worn floor tiles nervously, afraid and distraught. The two robber/rapists committed a crime spree while traveling down an interstate through the southeastern United States. She kept wondering aloud, "Why did they come back here? They'd gone hundreds of miles and had committed many more crimes before they came back. Of all the people they've assaulted, why do I have to be the one to face them in a courtroom? I'm scared. Why do I have to live this awful thing all over again?"

The two detectives working her case assured her she wouldn't see the rapists that day; she would go before the jury alone. The detectives also predicted that Julie wouldn't have to face the rapists in a courtroom and endure the pain of telling her story as they sat watching her with hatred and threats in their eyes. They felt the pair would seek the best possible deal with the court through a plea bargain. For Julie's sake, I'm glad they predicted correctly. Both criminals now serve sentences in Holman Prison in Atmore, Alabama.

Obviously, these men brought great pain and harm into the life of an innocent Christian, Julie Lindsey. As you read her story, did you find yourself asking, "How does she feel about what happened to her?"

I thought you might, so I asked her to write her perspective on this terrible event.

Nearly nine years after that tragic night, Julie wrote:

> After this experience, I spent a great deal of time thinking about God, my relationship with Him, and what I believed about Him. I searched and I prayed for understanding. I longed to be healed, and I wanted desperately to feel the power of God's presence. My spirit and my faith were sorely tested; my spiritual journey in the months that followed was painful—and also wonderful.
>
> It seemed to me this event was a classic case of good versus evil—an event that led to the infamous question of why bad things happen to good people. But it finally occurred to me that the question was not "why me" as much as "why not me?" God didn't promise me that nothing bad would ever happen to me. His own Son was crucified, suffering the cruelest death known to man.
>
> Do I believe God could have stopped this tragedy from happening to me? Absolutely. The question is: Why didn't He? I believe God wants me to love, honor, and serve Him because I *choose* to. God has never forced Himself on me or made me serve Him. He certainly has the power to do so. But the Almighty God, who could annihilate the universe with a mere thought, gave His creation free will. I have the gift of choosing. But as I have choices, so do others. Choices have consequences. Choices have blessings. If I accept the concept that I have free will, I must also accept that the two men who raped me have free will as well.
>
> God wants a real and honest relationship with me. In order for that kind of relationship to exist, I must choose it. God gave us the choices from the very beginning. I had often wondered why God placed the tree of knowledge of good and evil right in the middle of the Garden and then told Adam and Eve not to eat from it. Now I understand that God was giving them a choice about whether to obey Him and believe Him.
>
> The two men who raped me made a different choice than I, and our choices came into conflict. It would appear that I had been overcome and that Satan had triumphed by inflicting great pain and damage into my life. And for a while, that's how I felt.
>
> But then the blessings of *choosing God* came! God allowed me to profit from an awful and devastating event. So many good things are in my life now. I have wonderful friends—most of whom I would never have met or known were it not for this experience. I have a job that allows me to work with and serve crime victims. I have a deeper relationship with God. I am spiritually wiser and

> more mature. I have been blessed beyond what I can tell in these pages, and I am very grateful. Romans 8:28 came alive in my life: "All things work together for good for those who love God and are called according to His purpose."
>
> I chose God and He did not fail me. I continue to recover, and God continues to teach me. The two men who raped me did not choose God and were a vessel of Satan to do harm. They are both serving lengthy prison terms in a maximum security facility. They and their families suffer as a result.

Now I ask you—who won?

Indeed.

Julie now heads a nonprofit agency that works with victims of crime. She also serves as a volunteer rape counselor. Many people find the help they need through her compassion and her deep understanding of the emotions they feel.

Beyond that, because of this ordeal Julie discovered a wonderful gift from God she hadn't known about earlier in her life. God has endowed her with the talent of being an effective speaker who dramatically affects the lives of those who hear her. Because of her experience, many groups invite her to speak to them, giving them a closeup and personal picture of crime and its effect on victims. She touches audiences in ways that change their perspectives on life and their views of themselves. At first, only police organizations and other people-helping groups asked her to share her story. But her reputation and influence soon spread beyond those borders. Her powerful speaking touches an audience in ways far beyond the simple sharing of a victim's story; civic organizations and churches also invite her to speak. Even street-weary, cynical career cops have approached her after her speeches to tell her how moved they were by her words.

If your church or organization invites her to speak, her story and her understanding of God will inspire you and give you strength to face any trial. Her faith and endurance will strengthen your own faith, giving you greater spiritual stamina when attacked by the evil ones.

The evil attack of satanic beings frightened and hurt her, but God has used that experience to bring great good to hundreds and thousands of people.

Julie doesn't have a single fond memory of her terrible ordeal. But the blessings brought from it to her and to those she touches far outweigh the evil that the satanic beings inflicted on her.

GOD'S WAYS ARE BEYOND UNDERSTANDING

There are reasons God allows the evil ones to harm us. I can't explain them to your full satisfaction, but I can give a few insights that might give you peace. The only way anyone—even God—could explain the problem of human suffering to your complete satisfaction would be if *you* possessed divine knowledge, wisdom, and power. When Job questioned God about the harm in his life, God replied by pointing out Job's lack of divine knowledge. He made it clear that if He explained why He let Satan attack him, Job wouldn't be able to understand it.

> Who is this that darkens my counsel with words without knowledge? Brace yourself like a man; I will question you, and you shall answer me. Where were you when I laid the earth's foundation? Tell me, if you understand. Who marked off its dimensions? Surely you know! Who stretched a measuring line across it? On what were its footings set, or who laid its cornerstone—while the morning stars sang together and all the angels shouted for joy? (Job 38:2–7)

God told Job he had no right to question a Being so superior that He is beyond human comprehension. He pointedly reminded Job of His sovereignty: "Who has a claim against me that I must pay? Everything under heaven belongs to me" (Job 41:11).

I read those words spoken by God and know I have no right to question His judgment or doubt His love. I can no more explain Him or His decisions than I can create a new world. Therefore, I accept God's sovereignty and trust that He knows everything that happens. He intervenes as necessary to accomplish His holy will. He assures us He watches and that we should not be afraid. Jesus comforts us saying, "Are not two sparrows sold for a penny? Yet not one of them will fall to the ground apart from the will of your Father. And even the very hairs of your head are all numbered. So don't be afraid; you are worth more than many sparrows" (Matthew 10:29–31).

That's the most important thing to remember. God watches over us and never abandons us—even when it sometimes appears He isn't there.

Having made clear my lack of divine knowledge and my keen faith in the Father, I still believe I can give you some insight into why bad things happen to good people. The scriptures and principles that follow give me peace and hope.

May they do the same for you.

MORE PRECIOUS THAN GOLD

Sometimes God allows satanic forces to attack us because we need to grow or change or learn some important lesson. He doesn't let them defeat us, but He does permit them to cause us great struggle. He allows it because we need it.

Read carefully the words of Peter:

> Praise be to the God and Father of our Lord Jesus Christ! In his great mercy he has given us new birth into a living hope through the resurrection of Jesus Christ from the dead, and into an inheritance that can never perish, spoil or fade—kept in heaven for you, who through faith are shielded by God's power until the coming of the salvation that is ready to be revealed in the last time. In this you greatly rejoice, though now for a little while you may have had to suffer grief in all kinds of trials. These have come so that your faith—of greater worth than gold, which perishes even though refined by fire—may be proved genuine and may result in praise, glory and honor when Jesus Christ is revealed. Though you have not seen him, you love him; and even though you do not see him now, you believe in him and are filled with an inexpressible and glorious joy, for you are receiving the goal of your faith, the salvation of your souls. (1 Peter 1:3–9)

Reminding us that we have a living hope and that we are shielded through our faith by God's power, Peter writes that we should rejoice when we suffer grief in all kinds of trials. He doesn't say that our living hope and God's shield will protect us from grief—he makes it quite clear that those shielded by God's power *will* suffer grief. But he explains the reason for our grief—so that our faith may be proved genuine and so that we will give praise to Jesus.

Peter uses a most interesting illustration in describing the trials a Christian faces. He compares the trial process to the process gold endures when it is refined by fire. That analogy intrigued me enough that I consulted a good friend of mine who is an expert on gold. I wanted to know what Peter meant by the illustration.

When I first met Herbert Ledbetter, he served as Director of Merchandise for the A. A. Friedman Company, Inc., the largest privately owned jewelry chain in America. Their stores, Friedman's Jewelers, spanned the Southeast. I approached Herbert because of his extensive knowledge of jewels, gold, and precious stones. He is a graduate gemologist and a goldsmith. He's also a believer who seeks to follow Jesus.

We read the verses from 1 Peter together and then I asked, "Herbert, why is Peter comparing faith to refined gold? What can I learn from his illustration?"

For the next half-hour I scribbled rapidly as Herbert taught me about refining gold. I'm aware of the principle that no one should dig too deeply into any biblical illustration or he'll miss the point of the passage. But the things Herbert told me about refining gold shed greater meaning on many of my personal trials. I can't say that Peter stopped to think of all the intricacies of the comparison, but they fascinate me. Herbert pointed out several areas where the characteristics of tried faith and refined gold blend into a perfect analogy, giving insight into suffering.

According to Herbert, the purpose of the first-century process of putting gold through intense fire was to:

- burn away impurities (to make the rough ore into a precious metal)
- bring the gold to such a high gloss that the goldsmith could see his reflection in it
- make the gold malleable enough that the goldsmith could shape it however he chose
- increase the strength of the gold (the strength increased with each refining)
- increase the value of the gold (the value increased with each refining)

As the goldsmith worked the gold through the process, he had to be careful to prevent two things:

- He could never let the gold become too heated, or it would bubble and ruin, becoming less valuable.
- He could not let the gold cool too quickly from the fire, or it would become brittle and useless.

After explaining gold refining, Herbert reflected on how these same principles work in the life of a Christian. He said, "Joe, have you noticed that the people most mightily used by God have always been through some tragedy? God puts them through the fire, just like gold."

That's true.

I know from firsthand experience.

My guess is that you do too. Any person serving Jesus knows that trials come. In earlier chapters of this book, I cited several biblical passages that said we should expect them. This passage in 1 Peter inarguably states that followers of Jesus will suffer grief in all kinds of trials.

But isn't it wonderful to know that as God allows Satan to attack us, He uses Satan's attacks to bless us? Just as the goldsmith works the gold, God allows our faith to be made more precious by the trials satanic beings bring to us. *God uses Satan against himself.*

Point by point, let's examine the comparison of refining gold and refining faith.

Burning Away Impurities

Untried, unproven faith may not be faith at all. Many people who think they have faith in Jesus actually follow an idea rather than a Master. Jesus spoke of these kinds of people in the parable of the soils. He told about seed being sown on rocky soil, then He explained what He meant. "The one who received the seed that fell on rocky places is the man who hears the word and at once receives it with joy. But since he has no root, he lasts only a short time. When trouble or persecution comes because of the word, he quickly falls away" (Matthew 13:20–21).

God allows Satan to bring trials into our lives to enable our faith to grow roots—so that our faith will last. The trials that prove the reality and substance of our faith also make the faith precious. If you've experienced a great tragedy, trial, or persecution, you know that the attack drives you to your knees. As you pray, seeking God's power and deliverance, you come to rely solely on Him. Money, prestige, personal power, and all those other things that so allure humanity lose their appeal. They can't give us the things most precious to us.

A couple of years ago, a very wealthy Christian stood in a hospital intensive care room looking at the mangled body of his daughter. Speaking to a close minister friend, he said, "Just last night she called and told us how happy she'd be when she got home for spring break. A drunk on the wrong side of the interstate demolished her car, and now she's lying here, unconscious. The doctor said that even if she lives, she may never have the mental and physical functions of a normal twenty-year-old. You know, I've always gotten my way in most everything. I can charm or bully my way through any deal. I have millions of dollars and a lot of power. But now there's nothing I can do. I'm totally helpless. I have nothing but God."

All of us who have come to the realization that we have nothing but God cling to our faith as our most precious possession. The trials and griefs we suffer burn the impurities from our faith, making it more precious than gold. Faith is our link to the power of God.

Reflecting the Goldsmith

Goldsmiths today have methods to measure the purity levels of gold. The price of gold is determined by its level of purity—you pay more for 24K gold than 10K gold. Goldsmiths in the first century used a simpler method: When the gold reached such a level of gloss that the goldsmith could see his reflection clearly in it, it was deemed a precious and valuable product.

The same is true of the people of God. When they reflect Him, they are more valuable in His cause. When satanic forces attack the people of God, those who cling to their faith become more like God. God wants us to be participants in His divine nature (2 Peter 1:4). It shouldn't surprise us that He uses Satan to make us partakers of that nature.

"Grief in all kinds of trials" burns away our doubts, fears, and sinful desires. Those impurities in a Christian distort God's reflection, keeping those around us from seeing Him clearly. As we endure the trials of life, our faith becomes stronger, destroying lingering doubt and removing limiting fears. We become stronger in our ability to resist temptation. We become more like God. We reflect him clearly, revealing Him to those who interact with us.

Any Christian not yet reflecting God to the world may discover that God will use Satan to change her. If she is plagued by fear or doubt, trials may come to drive her to Him, proving Him true and trustworthy. If a Christian persists in some weakness or sin, trials may come to refocus him on the important, turning him from those things that fade into emptiness.

God wants us to be like Him. He wants those with whom we interact to see Him in us.

Becoming Malleable

Like gold, Christians are best shaped when malleable.

To be malleable is to be capable of being shaped or molded. It requires being flexible and pliable. Since gold is a metal, heat must be applied to make it malleable. The process of designing it into jewelry requires hammering and shaping. Hammering a cold gold nugget would only damage it, achieving no intricate and valuable shape. Intense heat makes it soft enough to hammer and shape at will, creating beauty and worth.

I've learned that I'm much more malleable—pliable—when I suffer trials. When things are going well and life seems a breeze, I continue on course. I have little regard for any interruption or redirection. That changes when trials come. Then I find myself seeking God and being completely open to the direction He sends.

Maybe you're a lot like me.

And we're both a lot like the apostle Paul.

The apostle Paul had what may be called a strong personality. That personality drove him, leading him to success in life. Well educated, he had many things going for him that set him apart from the crowd. He listed some of them in Philippians 3:4b–6: "If anyone else thinks he has reasons to put confidence in the flesh, I have more: circumcised on the eighth day, of the people of Israel, of the tribe of Benjamin, a Hebrew of Hebrews; in regard to the law, a Pharisee; as for zeal, persecuting the church; as for legalistic righteousness, faultless."

Because of Paul's intensity and ego, God continually used trials to keep him listening to His direction. When Jesus first approached Paul to convert him, He struck him blind for three days, making him reflect on his behavior and his misguided zeal. After making him an apostle, God kept Paul in the fire that kept him pliable. Paul wrote about it:

> To keep me from becoming conceited because of these surpassingly great revelations, there was given me a thorn in my flesh, a messenger of Satan, to torment me. Three times I pleaded with the Lord to take it away from me. But he said to me, "My grace is sufficient for you, for my power is made perfect in weakness." Therefore I will boast all the more gladly about my weaknesses, so that Christ's power may rest on me. That is why, for Christ's sake, I delight in weaknesses, in insults, in hardships, in persecutions, in difficulties. For when I am weak, then I am strong. (2 Corinthians 12:7–10)

To keep Paul pliable, God allowed Satan to torment him through the "thorn in the flesh." Paul doesn't tell us what the thorn was, but my opinion is that God continued to allow a problem with his vision (see Galatians 6:11). I think God started Paul's conversion experience by making him blind and continued his submission by keeping his vision imperfect.

Did Paul resent his suffering? You read his answer: "For when I am weak, then I am strong." What effect did it have on his view of God and his service to Him? Read his own words.

> But whatever was to my profit I now consider loss for the sake of Christ. What is more, I consider everything a loss compared to the surpassing greatness of knowing Christ Jesus my Lord, for whose sake I have lost all things. I consider them rubbish, that I may gain Christ and be found in him, not having a righteousness of my own that comes from the law, but that which is through faith in Christ—the righteousness that comes from God and is by faith. I want to know Christ and the power of his resurrection and the fellowship of sharing in his sufferings, becoming like him in his death. (Philippians 3:7–10)

Paul didn't want only to know Christ and the power of His resurrection. He also wanted to know "the fellowship of sharing in his sufferings." Paul learned that suffering kept him open to the leading and direction of God. He didn't resent it; he appreciated it.

Suffering keeps me open to the leading and direction of God. What about you?

Increasing Strength

Goldsmiths make gold stronger each time they put it through the annealing process. It appears that the same happens to Christians.

Annealing is the process of heating, hammering, shaping, and cooling gold. Because gold can be ruined by too much heat, the annealing process isn't a single step but a series of steps. The goldsmith knows what design and shape the finished product will have. He also knows that only simple, relatively invaluable results can be gained by a single annealing. He must take it one step further in each phase, getting the most from that heating, but never ruining the gold by heating it too high or cooling it too quickly.

Think about it: multiple steps to become what the goldsmith wants; strength through a series of fires. Sounds familiar, doesn't it?

When I was young, I thought that any lesson God needed to teach me could be accomplished by simple instruction. I approached my spiritual life blithely: "Just tell me what You want, God, and I'll do it. Tell me how You want me to be, and I'll be it." That view definitely showed my spiritual naiveté. My own humanity often kept me from hearing God's voice.

Even when I heard it, I usually twisted it until it said what I wanted to hear. On those occasions when I did hear it clearly, I still sometimes fell short of what He wanted.

God's major lessons to me didn't come from earning a college degree in Bible or from studying to preach. They came from experiences in life that produced at least some pain and a lot of struggling. He turned up the "fire" to make me malleable.

Beyond the learning and changing that came from those periods, I noticed something else: Each experience made me stronger spiritually and emotionally than I was before.

Someone told me that a when a broken bone mends, the place of the healed break becomes stronger than the rest of the bone. I mentally picture it like a weld on a broken piece of metal. The added strength of the weld makes that part of the metal stronger than the rest. It seems the same thing occurs when a tragedy comes into a Christian's life.

Unless, of course, the Christian gives up his faith, abandoning God because of the difficulty.

None of us enjoys hurting. We all avoid it if we can. Yet every Christian who has suffered gained strength she didn't have before. The place in our faith that endured the trial is stronger after it heals than it was before. We don't like the learning process, but we do like the strength and the value it brings to our lives.

Imparting Value

When Herbert taught me about refining and shaping gold, he pointed out the importance of continuing the refining process rather than stopping at an intermediate point. He said, "Think about steel for a moment. From a pound of steel you can make many different products. You can go through a short series of annealings and make horseshoes. Or you can go through more annealings and make hypodermic needles. Which is more valuable: a pound of horseshoes or a pound of needles? The more designed and better shaped the metal, the greater the value."

Then, smiling and gently looking into my eyes, he made his point: "Don't you think the same is true of people?"

He continued, "Joe, no matter what I've done to the gold to refine, shape, and design it, I must reheat it to take it to the next step. I have to put it into the fire again. Here's something I've learned about Christian living that is parallel to refining gold: If God wants again to change your shape or design to make you more valuable to His work, He must put you through another fire, no matter what you've already been through. Each stage makes you more useful than the one before, but each one requires you to go through the refining trial again."

While I understand that principle, I don't always enjoy it.

Often I've heard Christians say they want to continue to grow, but they don't want any more pain. I heard one person pray, "God, make me grow. Use me in your service. Prepare me as you will…just don't hurt me again!"

If Herbert's analogy is correct—and my own experience convinces me it is—God can't continue our growth without putting us through additional trials. Enduring them purifies us, making us more valuable for what He wants from us.

Understanding this makes me realize how much God loves me and what confidence He has in me. Those of us who suffer should *thank* Him for His confidence. Then, in anticipation, we should look with joy for the great thing He's preparing us for.

Of course, that's much easier said than done. It's also easier to do looking back than looking forward. As my wise spiritual counselor, Larry Brannan, likes to say, "I have no problem seeing God in my taillights. It's finding Him in my headlights that's difficult."

Me, too.

But wouldn't it be encouraging if we could see Him in the headlights more often? Maybe a familiar story from the Scriptures will help us see Him in the headlights.

A VALUABLE EXAMPLE

A wonderful example of how God uses the annealing process is found in the life of Joseph.

At age seventeen, Joseph angered his brothers so much that they sold him into slavery to an Egyptian named Potiphar (Genesis 37). For a while, Joseph prospered, but soon he was subjected to more suffering. Potiphar's wife, finding him "well-built and handsome," flagrantly invited him into her bed. When he refused because of his righteousness, she accused him of trying to rape her. Because of her lie, Potiphar threw Joseph into prison (Genesis 39).

If we could have interviewed Joseph during his ordeal, what do you think he would have answered to our questions? "Joseph, is God preparing you for something? Why has He let these terrible things happen to you?"

Obviously, we can only guess what he would have said, but I do find one clue to his view of that time. When finally delivered from prison and married, he named his firstborn son Manasseh, saying, "It is because God has made me forget all my trouble and all my father's household" (Genesis 41:51). His statement leads me to believe that Joseph didn't have a great outlook on his predicament at the time. He called it his "trouble" and only "forgot" it after being released from prison and marrying. He missed his simple life as a shepherd boy, apparently still hurting from the rejection and hatred of his brothers.

When he was seventeen, Joseph knew only one thing: shepherding. God, looking into the future, knew that Joseph needed to understand farming and politics—things beyond his opportunity to learn as a shepherd boy. God saw clearly where Joseph could learn these things. God planned to use Joseph to save the Egyptians and Israelites from starvation in just a few years. To accomplish this, Joseph would need a good knowledge of farming and a better knowledge of the Egyptian government. He needed to know all the back-room workings of the government that would assist him in completing his assignment.

Cleverly, God allowed Satan to deceive Joseph's brothers into selling him into slavery. There, in Potiphar's household, Joseph learned farming. Gaining Potiphar's respect and trust, he took control of all Potiphar's possessions.

> From the time he put him in charge of his household and of all that he owned, the LORD blessed the household of the Egyptian because of Joseph. The blessing of the LORD was on everything Potiphar had, both in the house and *in the field.* So he left in Joseph's care everything he had; with Joseph in charge, he did not concern himself with anything except the food he ate. (Genesis 39:5–6)

The sheepherder learned about grain as a slave in Potiphar's household.

Joseph still didn't know how to deal with the politicians that controlled Egypt. As in every government, he needed to know which politicians to make allies and which to avoid. God outsmarted Satan again as Satan used Mrs. Potiphar to have Joseph thrown into prison. Evil forces must have gloated over Joseph's imprisonment. They thought that since he was now in a dungeon, he would suffer. Instead, he learned.

Because Potiphar locked Joseph in *Pharaoh's* prison, instead of a regular prison, Joseph was in free and regular contact with anyone Pharaoh cast into prison. You may recall from the story in Genesis that whenever the capricious Pharaoh was upset with anyone—baker or butler or anyone else—he would cast them into prison. Some he restored to position; some he executed.

From these political insiders rotating through Pharaoh's jail, Joseph learned the intricacies and inner workings of the Egyptian government. So impressive was Joseph's ability to deal with the other prisoners that "the warden put Joseph in charge of all those held in the prison, and he was made responsible for all that was done there" (Genesis 39:22).

Before ever meeting Pharaoh, he learned what to avoid and what to pursue when working with him.

God prepared Joseph for the greatest task of his life by selling him into slavery and sentencing him to prison. These two annealings put him at the right place at the right time to gain the right knowledge to save Egypt from starvation.

Just think, God prepared Joseph to save a whole nation.

But God's preparation of Joseph accomplished something even greater than the salvation of a single nation: through the lineage of the Israelites, the Messiah entered the world and offered salvation to all mankind.

When Joseph was able to look back on his life, he could finally see God in his "taillights" and understand the reason for all his troubles. He explained it to his brothers this way:

> And now, do not be distressed and do not be angry with yourselves for selling me here, because it was to save lives that God sent me ahead of you.... But God sent me ahead of you to preserve for you a remnant on earth and to save your lives by a great deliverance.
>
> So then, it was not you who sent me here, but God. He made me father to Pharaoh, lord of his entire household and ruler of all Egypt. (Genesis 45:5–8)

Joseph now understood, without doubt, that all the annealings were intentional: God had chosen Joseph for His cause. God had taken advantage of evil to bring about His good. Joseph told his brothers later, "You intended to harm me, but God intended it for good to accomplish what is now being done, the saving of many lives" (Genesis 50:20).

God's preparation of Joseph required a series of annealings, not just one. When his brothers sold him into slavery, it must have hurt him deeply. But Joseph didn't despair; he kept growing and prospered in his pain. When he did the right thing and refused the advances of his owner's wife, he found himself facing pain again. It must have crossed his mind that if he had sinned with her, he wouldn't have suffered the injury of being thrown into a prison. Again, he didn't despair. Maintaining his faith, he grew and prospered once more.

All the pain and hurt of slavery didn't rule out Joseph's need for further preparation by prison. As Herbert said, "If God wants to change your shape or design again, to make you more valuable to His work, He has to put you through another fire, no matter what you've already been through. Each stage makes you more useful than the one before, but each one requires you to go through the refining trial again."

How long? How many annealings? How painful?

The answers to those questions depend on the task God prepares you for. Just remember that Joseph was sold into slavery at age seventeen and didn't become second to Pharaoh until he was age thirty. His series of annealings took thirteen years.

To put that into perspective: How long is thirteen years to a seventeen-year-old? A lifetime.

All suffering seems to last that long, doesn't it?

THE CAREFUL GOLDSMITH

Remember what Herbert said about a careful goldsmith never letting the gold become too hot? There is a biblical parallel to that principle. Though God allows Satan to bring pain and temptation into our lives, He will not allow the fire to get too hot. We have His word on this: "No temptation has seized you except what is common to man. And God is faithful; *he will not let you be tempted beyond what you can bear.* But when you are tempted, he will also provide a way out so that you can stand up under it" (1 Corinthians 10:13).

We can trust God never to let the pain of any trial be more than we can bear. Sometimes the pain may seem unbearable—even Paul felt the weight of it. He said,

> We do not want you to be uninformed, brothers, about the hardships we suffered in the province of Asia. We were under great pressure, far beyond our ability to endure, so that we despaired even of life. Indeed, in our hearts we felt the sentence of death. But this happened that we might not rely on ourselves but on God, who raises the dead. He has delivered us from such a deadly peril, and he will deliver us.

> On him we have set our hope that he will continue to deliver us, as you help us by your prayers. (2 Corinthians 1:8–11)

Notice his words, "under great pressure, far beyond our ability to endure," and "so that we despaired even of life." Have you ever felt that way? I can assure you I have. But notice the reassuring words that follow those emotions: "this happened that we might not rely on ourselves but on God, and he will deliver us."

God will never let the heat get so high that it ruins us or destroys us. The heat of trial and suffering can only destroy false gold, never real gold. Since we are more precious to God than any gold could ever be to a goldsmith, He protects us from anything that would ruin us.

When persecuted, faith strengthens and endures. Pseudofaith fails.

The second part of a goldsmith's care is the cooling process. To prevent brittleness and uselessness, the goldsmith must let the gold cool gradually. Cooling too quickly undoes all the good done by the annealing process. I think there is a comparison here, too, between faith and gold.

When under pressure, I often ask for complete and immediate deliverance. Sometimes God grants that request; often He doesn't. I believe I see a pattern in His actions. When God has nothing to gain from Satan's attack on me, He intervenes with His forces, quickly ending my trial. When He wants me to learn something, He allows time for me to absorb it and learn all the lessons from it. Ending the trial too quickly teaches me nothing. In those cases, He answers my prayer by standing by me, but He does not stop the procedure until He gains all He wants from it.

TWO REASONS FOR SUFFERING

If you've read this chapter carefully, you've seen there are at least two reasons for a Christian to "suffer grief in all sorts of trials." The first is for his own growth and spiritual good. The second is for the good of others.

In my seminars, I phrase it this way: "Sometimes *I* need to suffer; sometimes *you* need for me to suffer."

When my impurities of doubt, fear, and sinfulness are burned away by suffering, I needed to face the trial for my own spiritual good. When I learn a lesson—like Joseph—that prepares me for some work of ministry, I needed to face the trial for the good of those I will minister to.

Looking back on my life, I discovered that during the toughest trials of my life, I needed the suffering for both myself and those I minister to.

I so often need refining for my own spiritual good that when faced with any difficulty I find myself thinking, "What could God be wanting me to learn from this? What spiritual lesson is there here for me? What could God be telling me about my life or my actions?"

Finding any lesson I can, I don't settle into a session of self-pity or debilitating self-analysis. I then ask the next question, "What might God be preparing me for? What can I learn from this that I may use for His ministry?"

Notice the order. First ask what God may be trying to get you to learn or do differently. Then ask how God may be preparing you to minister to others. If you miss the lesson God is teaching you by prematurely making application to others, God will just have to allow more trials until you learn the lesson He wants you to get.

Personally, I want to learn them the first time.

THE EXCITEMENT OF SUFFERING

"And we know that in all things God works for the good of those who love him, who have been called according to his purpose" (Romans 8:28). God didn't promise to make everything *work* good; just to make everything *work out* good.

Several years ago I watched a friend of mine suffer mightily at the hands of angry brothers who attack him ferociously. Similar to the mob that gnashed their teeth at Stephen (Acts 7), these people do nasty, evil things in the name of Christianity. They don't like this brother because he questions their status-quo beliefs. He challenges them to rethink and openly study the Word instead of defending their long-held dogmas. As I watch his suffering, I know him well enough to know that some of it is for his own good. His strong personality is much like the apostle Paul's, and he needs some thorn to keep him from trusting his own education and intelligence. Strong personalities can sometimes be very dominating, preventing those who have them from reflecting God clearly. Attacks keep the strong-personality person humble if he relies on God rather than his own ability and self-righteousness. I believe one reason God allows the attacks on this brother is to keep him humble and God-focused.

But I also know that much of what this brother is suffering, he suffers for me and all those like me—Christians who want to learn and grow, who want to put God above our heritage and inherited doctrines. His suffering doesn't deter him from delivering his message and his spiritual challenges. His faithfulness in the face of persecution gives courage to the rest of us to have the stamina to continue to learn and grow ourselves. We watch how the attackers treat him and decide from the actions of each who more clearly represents the spirit of Christ. His suffering through this trial is similar to Joseph's in slavery and prison. He suffers so others will benefit from God's blessing.

I don't know if he understands this or not.

I also don't know if you understand why you face the things you do. But I can assure you that if you endure, hanging on to God with all your faith, you will prosper spiritually. You will become purer, more godlike. And you will be prepared for greater ministry.

Sickness, divorce, death of a loved one, jail, slandered reputations, financial ruin, abuse, and many other evil things may be used against you by evil beings. Whatever their attack—whatever their harm—you will survive if you hold on to God.

And you will grow.

And you will be used by God for some wonderful ministry.

Look through the pain. See God. Isn't it exciting?

CHAPTER EIGHTEEN

How Does the Cross Defeat Satan?

The sun went dark the day God left the earth. He had no choice but to leave; His heart demanded it. As He retreated from the battlefield, a different god advanced, menacingly moving in with his legions as the army of heaven backed slowly away.

A murmuring mob of humans stood fascinated by the cruel spectacle played out before them, echoing mockeries and ignorant insults at a Being they didn't understand. Though they couldn't see the dark god or his gathering forces, perhaps they sensed his powerful, evil presence. Or maybe they were so immersed in hypnotic, mindless bloodlust that they sensed only the malevolence haunting their own souls, incredibly unaware of the spiritual transformation occurring around them. If ever a place and time demanded darkness, that one did. Light didn't belong there. Evil filled the air, permeating the assembly of death worshipers—human and angelic, living and dead.

It was the day they crucified Jesus.

Closing my eyes to live that day with Him, I picture what it must have been like. Blend your imagination with mine as we live it with Him, grasping to comprehend the price He paid.

...As darkness settles on the earth, Satan filters slowly from the air to the front of the cross. He's in no hurry; he's here to gloat. Pleasure this fine is meant to be sipped, savoring every drop. Gradually making himself visible to the Son of Man hanging from hammered nails, Lucifer's emergence from the gloom is breathtaking. The darkness cloaking the earth works to his advantage, magnifying his appearance. He stands taller than the cross, shimmering like a diamond caressed with black lace. Satan wants the Son to remember him as He created him, wise and beautiful—unequaled by any other angel. He relishes his utter contrast to the dying, bleeding human body the Son now occupies.

They've known each other for a long time. Thousands of years by human reckoning—longer than that beyond the boundaries of mortal time. They've met and talked many times—but never like this—never with the devil in control.

Satan looks curiously into the contorted face of the suffering carpenter, moving slightly to find the best angle for assessing the God-man's eyes. He's seen many men die by crucifixion, but it intrigues him that Jesus seems to suffer it differently. His pain is considerably more than the thieves dying on either side of Him. Lucifer feels no pity, just curiosity and, of course, elation. Whatever Jesus had come to do, He had failed. Satan had turned the people against Him. The Son came to be their king; they made Him their sport.

"Look at You, *Logos.*" Satan curls his lip in disdain and loathing. "You could have had everything this world offers. I made it a gift to You…remember? All You had to do was bow down and worship me. These angels and demons surrounding You, laughing at Your failure, would have followed Your every command. You would have been second only to me.

"But, no, You rejected me and my power here in the world. And for what? For *these?*" Satan pauses, slowly sweeping his arm toward the gathered crowd relishing the macabre sight of three crucified criminals—one claiming to be a king. "You came for them? You actually thought they'd sacrifice their pleasures to follow You? How foolish. It seems You would know them better.

"Now they've killed You. They listen to me, not You. They love my ways, not Yours. You have no place here. I rule here."

Then slowly, caressing each syllable of his final line, giving just the right sarcasm to the last word, Lucifer hisses, "You lose, *King.*"

The raucous laughter of evil beings, applauding their leader, heckling their victim, drowns the droning of the humans who see only three dying men.

In heaven God watches, Michael standing near. As Satan berates Jesus,

Michael can stand it no more. He shouts the command calling his angels to readiness, "Army!"

"No, Michael." God says quietly, not taking His eyes from the heart-breaking scene on earth.

"But, God, they're hurting Him. You gave me the duty to—"

"No."

"But, Mighty One, see what—"

"No!" God turns to Michael, speaking sharply, making it clear there will be no more talk of rescuing the Son. Even Michael has no right to question Him or to disagree. God knows what is happening at Golgotha and, though it hurts Him, wants it to continue.

Just then, Jesus makes it hurt more. From earth He begins to scream, "My God, My God, why have You forsaken Me?"

Jesus shouts these words from a wounded, writhing heart. God doesn't answer. He doesn't have to. Jesus, too, knows what is happening and why it must happen. His question from the cross doesn't seek an answer; it is indescribable pain shouting its inexpressible agony.

Michael doesn't understand why God doesn't answer—why He doesn't do something to stop this travesty. But he knows he can't do a thing; he won't question God again.

Satan doesn't understand either. If he did, he would be trembling in terror instead of smirking in sublime satisfaction.

THE PURPOSE OF THE CROSS

When Jesus came to earth, Satan wasn't sure why He came, but he knew he didn't want Him here. No angel, good or bad, understood completely what He had come to do. God cleverly cloaked all the prophecies about Jesus in mysterious language that angels couldn't clearly interpret (1 Peter 1:12).

When Jesus came to earth, Satan incredulously watched Him enter the body of a teenage girl, becoming a baby in her womb. He must have thought that attacking and destroying Him would be easy, since the Son of God had become a helpless, human child. It turned out not to be so easy because of the incessant intervention of Michael and his angelic army. From the time Mary conceived Him, angels protected Him, keeping Satan from killing the God-child. Satan tried. He killed many innocent babies in the melee, but the baby Jesus survived (Matthew 2:16; Revelation 12). Satan taunted Him about His angelic protection later, trying to turn their very protection into a temptation. "'If you are the Son of God,' he said, 'throw yourself down. For it is written: "He will command his angels concerning you, and they will lift you up in their hands, so that you will not strike your foot against a stone"'" (Matthew 4:6).

During that same period of temptation, Lucifer offered all the kingdoms of the earth and their splendor to Jesus if He would just bow to him. As with each of the other temptations, Jesus refused, continuing His mission (Matthew 4:7–10).

Jesus made it clear that He had come to seek and save the lost (Luke 19:10). He also clearly dominated Satan's forces during His ministry by casting out demons, healing the sick, and raising the dead (see Luke 10:18). From these and other obvious actions of Jesus, Satan knew that He intended to deliver mankind from him, but he didn't understand the methodology God, Jesus, and the Holy Spirit planned for saving us.

Satan likely prepared for a battle for the world. God quietly sought a different, unprotected battlefront. God planned a redemption to save us from His own wrath. His mysterious plan offered a substitution that would satisfy His divine nature while giving us a home with Him in heaven. Satan's defeat wouldn't come in an immediate battle to cast him into hell; it would come when he lost his hold on mankind.

GOD'S LIMITATIONS

To save us, God had to work within the limitations of His own nature. While we don't like to think of God in terms of being limited, He is. His very nature precludes His doing certain things; there are some things He *cannot* do. For example, God cannot lie (Titus 1:2). It is impossible for Him to lie and still be God (Hebrews 6:18). A lie would violate His very nature.

God cannot sin. To be holy is to be sinless. If God were to sin, He would no longer be holy. He would no longer be the essence of His own being. Therefore, God cannot sin. God cannot violate any of His own laws. He must keep them all.

God made the punishment for violating His law clear. Anyone who violates His law must die. He stated it at the beginning: "And the LORD God commanded the man, 'You are free to eat from any tree in the garden; but you must not eat from the tree of the knowledge of good and evil, for when you eat of it you will surely *die*'" (Genesis 2:16–17).

The penalty for violating God's command is death. Through Paul He said it again in the New Testament: "For the wages of sin is *death,* but the gift of God is eternal life in Christ Jesus our Lord" (Romans 6:23).

What makes our predicament so damning is that we have *all* sinned. Not one of us has eluded the condemnation of the law. All of mankind is deserving of death. "For all have sinned and fall short of the glory of God" (Romans 3:23).

Simply defined, the word *death* means separation. Physical death is the separation of body and spirit (James 2:26). Spiritual death is worse than physical death; it is the separation of a human being from God. While there is a sense in which separation from God can take place on earth, it has its full impact in hell. When a human leaves the earth and dwells in hell, he has no access to God at all. While still on earth, he is in the general presence of God and can approach God at any time. Only in hell will a human be totally separate from her Creator. The ultimate penalty for disobeying God is to dwell without Him in eternity in the place we call hell.

God cannot violate His law. He cannot ignore our sinfulness and save us anyway. He can't pretend we didn't sin just because He loves us and wants us in heaven with Him. His law applies to every sinner, whether the person commits many sins or a single sin. It doesn't matter if it's a "big" sin or a "little" sin. Sin violates God's law and brings about the penalty of death. God's divine nature requires that he honor that law.

Honoring that law led to His plan to have Jesus die on the cross.

JESUS SUFFERED SEPARATION IN OUR PLACE

The price was a precious one.

When Jesus went to the cross, He went with great fear, begging God to find another way, if possible. "Father, if you are willing, take this cup from me; yet not my will, but yours be done" (Luke 22:42).

Jesus didn't relish going to the cross, but His fear didn't focus on the physical pain. I have heard many sermons on the cross that focus on the beating He took from the Romans, the splinters that shoved themselves into His lacerated back, and the cruel nails that dug through His flesh. I admit that I, too, would dread such a death.

But concentrating on the physical aspects of His death misses the divine point of what happened on the cross. The penalty of sin is death—separation. Jesus could only pay the penalty for you and me if He were separated from the Father. It wasn't His physical death that saves us; it was His spiritual death. The means of that death had little relevance. Since it was better for His death to be public, crucifixion proved to be a perfect choice. Crucifixion also produced symbols of paid debt that the inspired writers of the New Testament used to illustrate our forgiveness (see Colossians 2:14; Galatians 3:13). But there was no special reason or divine power in crosses, splinters, or nails. Other than the symbolism of "with his stripes we are healed" (Isaiah 53:5 KJV), there was no divine significance in the whipping He received. The important thing was not the means of death but the spiritual phenomenon that occurred as He was dying.

Jesus had to be separated from the Father in order to accomplish His goal of granting us salvation. He had to fulfill the law of Romans 6:23, "the wages of sin is death." His physical death symbolized His spiritual death that occurred while He was on the cross. For the first and only time in all eternity, He and the Father would not be one. God would leave the earth, causing Jesus to cry after Him, "Why have You left me?"

Jesus didn't go to hell after His physical death. He told the thief next to Him that on that very day He would meet him in paradise (Luke 23:43). No, He wasn't going to hell *after* His physical death; He was going to be in hell *during* His physical death. *Hell is where God isn't.* God left the earth that day to leave Jesus to fulfill the law by being separated from Him. That's why the world turned dark. God is light and in Him is no darkness at all (1 John 1:5). He is the Father of the heavenly lights (James 1:17). Darkness descending on earth showed God's departure. Jesus crying out that He was forsaken provided final proof.

The indescribable pain He suffered resulted from His one and only separation from His Father. He who is one with God suffered hell by losing union with Him. The pain of a whip or a splinter or a nail paled into insignificance. The agony of hell superseded it.

Jesus went to hell for us on the cross so we don't have to go when we depart this life. His death gives us life. Satan no longer has a hold on us.

SAVED BY THE BLOOD

When Jesus gave His spiritual life for us, He paid our penalty for us. In His physical death He accomplished the spiritual death that satisfies the divine law of Romans 6:23. To carry that idea through in graphic symbolism, the Bible speaks of our being saved by the blood of Jesus (Acts 20:28; Romans 5:9). The theological point should not be misunderstood. It gives us freedom, peace, and hope.

The symbolism is profound. Blood and life are synonymous. God says, "For the life of a creature is in the blood, and I have given it to you to make atonement for yourselves on the altar; it is the blood that makes atonement for one's life" (Leviticus 17:11).

Shedding one's lifeblood is the same as giving one's life. The emptying of the blood that sustains the life is the sacrifice of the life.

Being saved by the blood of Jesus means that He gave His spiritual life in our place when He and God were separated. Our sin separated them. On the cross He took our sin on Himself, becoming sin in the process. "God made him who had no sin to be sin for us, so that in him we might become the righteousness of God" (2 Corinthians 5:21). Bearing my sin, He bore my guilt. When He paid the price, it wasn't for Himself; it was for me. My sin demands separation from the Father. He was separated from God on my behalf.

Jesus employed the symbolism of blood equaling life to tell us we must become part of His life to have our own spiritual life. He said, "I tell you the truth, unless you eat the flesh of the Son of Man and drink his blood, you have no life in you. Whoever eats my flesh and drinks my blood has eternal life, and I will raise him up at the last day" (John 6:53–54).

He wasn't telling us to eat His *real* flesh and drink His *real* blood. He was using those ideas to speak of our lives being immersed into His.

Being saved by the blood of Jesus (Ephesians 1:7) means being saved by His separation from the Father on the cross.

HIS DEATH—OUR DEATH

For those who have faith in Jesus, the principle is clear. Jesus defeats Satan by saving all those who choose to follow Him. He offers us a way to overcome and be set free.

When our faith leads us to be baptized into Jesus, we are baptized into His death and, vicariously, into our own death. This means that when we come into contact with His separation from the Father during our baptism, we come into contact with our own separation. We go to hell for our sins through Jesus being in hell on the cross. Having paid the penalty through Him, we no longer have any penalty to pay. Our sins have already been paid for. We paid through Jesus by getting on the cross with Him. Paul said it this way: "we are convinced that one died for all, and therefore all died" (2 Corinthians 5:14).

Notice how Paul phrased it when he explained to the Romans the difference Jesus made in their lives:

> Don't you know that all of us who were baptized into Christ Jesus were baptized into his *death?* We were therefore *buried* with him through baptism into *death* in order that, just as Christ was raised from the dead through the glory of the Father, we too may live a new life.
>
> If we have been *united with him* like this in his *death,* we will certainly also be united with him in his resurrection. (Romans 6:3–5)

That freedom not only saves us from hell; it also delivers us from the power of Satan in our lives. He no longer holds the preeminent position he had while we were without God.

> For we know that our old self was crucified with him so that the body of sin might be done away with, that we should no longer be slaves to sin—because anyone who has died has been freed from sin....
>
> Therefore do not let sin reign in your mortal body so that you obey its evil desires. Do not offer the parts of your body to sin, as instruments of wickedness, but rather offer yourselves to God, as those who have been brought from death to life; and offer the parts of your body to him as instruments of righteousness. For sin shall not be your master, because you are not under law, but under grace. (Romans 6:6–14)

CROWNING VICTORY IN RESURRECTION

Jesus accomplished all this by His separation from the Father on the cross. He then validated everything by returning to His human body and resurrecting. Our forgiveness comes because of what He did on the cross. His miraculous rising from the dead proves that He actually was the Son of God.

Paul said of Jesus' resurrection: "Through the Spirit of holiness [He] was declared with power to be the Son of God by his resurrection from the dead: Jesus Christ our Lord" (Romans 1:4). His claim to be the Son of God rested in His ability to rise by the power of the Holy Spirit.

The resurrection became part of the gospel story.

> Now, brothers, I want to remind you of the gospel I preached to you, which you received and on which you have taken your stand. By this gospel you are saved, if you hold firmly to the word I preached to you. Otherwise, you have believed in vain. For what I received I passed on

> to you as of first importance: that Christ died for our sins according to the Scriptures, that he was buried, that he was raised on the third day according to the Scriptures. (1 Corinthians 15:1–4)

A PUBLIC SPECTACLE OF SATAN'S FORCES

Jesus won the battle for our souls the day He died. He removed our sins and our slavery to Satan. "He took it away, nailing it to the cross. And having disarmed the powers and authorities, he made a public spectacle of them, triumphing over them by the cross" (Colossians 2:14b–15).

If Satan had known what was about to transpire, he would not have killed Jesus on that cross. He would have protected Him, preventing Him from fulfilling the requirements of the law and taking away our sinfulness.

Satan no longer can control those who give themselves to Jesus. He loses his power to defeat us on earth. He loses his ability to keep us out of heaven. While he will never go to heaven again, we who are the saved will.

No wonder Paul says of the rulers of this age: "We speak of God's secret wisdom, a wisdom that has been hidden and that God destined for our glory before time began. None of the rulers of this age understood it, for if they had, they would not have crucified the Lord of glory"(1 Corinthians 2:7–8).

That's right. If Satan and his hordes had understood what they were doing, they wouldn't have done it.

Now we have been set free from sin and death. That victory marks the moment of decline for Satan. There will come a day when God casts him into hell forever, taking him from the world he rules. God will destroy the earth, the stars, and all the universes around us (2 Peter 3:10–13). Satan will have no place to run, no place to hide, no living humans to rule.

If God had come to destroy these things and cast Satan into hell *before* Jesus had freed us from bondage to sin, Satan would have taken all of us to hell with him. He wouldn't have done it by outmaneuvering and defeating God; God Himself would have been forced to send us there with Satan. His law would have demanded it.

So He fought the most important battle first, the one Satan didn't understand. Jesus didn't come to take the world from Satan; He came to take people from Satan's world. Satan fought a carpenter who he feared would be an earthly king. He helped the carpenter become a heavenly king—a king who extends freedom to all His subjects (Galatians 5:1). God used Satan's misunderstanding against him. We are the winners.

For each of us who is saved, Jesus defeated Satan for us by dying in our stead on the cross.

Blessed be the name of the wonderful Savior.

CHAPTER NINETEEN

Why Does the Holy Spirit Live in Me?

The line of people advanced toward me with the speed of a reluctant glacier. They remained after the service to talk with me, primed with questions or comments about the presentation I'd made that evening. I noticed a striking young lady a few people back barely tolerating the pace; her impatience spotlighted her, making her stand out from the others. Every few moments she shifted her weight to her other foot while chewing her bottom lip and glaring at the person taking longer with me than she thought appropriate. Watching her, I half-expected her to plow past the people between us and commandeer me. I couldn't decide if she was angry or just extremely worried. The intensity of her emotion made her difficult to read.

Nearly ten minutes later, she reached the head of the line. Without preamble, she blurted, "Does each person have her own guardian angel?"

"No." I answered. "While it is true that angels minister to the saved as promised in Hebrews 1:14, there is no indication that any of us has a full-time guardian angel focusing solely on us."

She immediately challenged my answer. "What about Jesus saying that children have angels? Doesn't that prove we have guardian angels?"

"You're referring to Matthew 18:10." I opened my Bible and read it to her. "See that you do not look down on one of these little ones. For I tell you that their angels in heaven always see the face of my Father in heaven."

Turning my Bible so she could see the verse, I explained the meaning, "Pay close attention to the words. Jesus says there are angels in heaven concerned with the welfare of children on earth. That makes children special. He's emphasizing a point He made earlier in verse five. See it? 'Whoever welcomes a little child like this in my name welcomes me.' Jesus taught people to treat children as precious. No one should look down on a child: Children have angels in heaven ministering before the very throne of God.

"But where are these concerned angels? Notice that Jesus said they are in *heaven*—not on earth guarding each individual child. If every child had an angel guarding him personally, there would be no child abuse. Milk cartons wouldn't carry pictures of missing children. We would see no television commercials showing haunting pictures of starving children who have been reduced to doe-eyed skeletons. No child could be hurt if an angel stood by protecting her. Yet, as we both know, many children are hurt.

"You see my point? Jesus didn't say children have guardian angels here on earth—just that they have angels in heaven who see the face of God. Children don't have specially assigned, individual guardian angels and neither do Christians."

She didn't like what she was hearing. Pressing me, she asked, "If I don't have an angel guarding me, then I'm unprotected. I can't accept that. Right now I *need* a guardian angel. Will God send angels to me if I ask?"

Looking behind her, I rapidly counted the people still in line, mentally checking time available against a spiritual counseling appointment set for later that evening. I knew I shouldn't spend too much time with one person, but I couldn't easily dismiss her. It was obvious she needed help to face whatever it was that plagued her.

Aware my answer would not be the one she wanted to hear, I bluntly answered her question, "God may send angels in answer to your prayer. Then, again, He may not. I can't speak for God, but my opinion is that there are not always enough angels to cover every follower of God at every moment. Think about it. God created angels before He made the world. As I explained in my lesson tonight, angels don't procreate; they aren't making baby angels. Whatever the number of created angels may be, that's all there is. I don't know if God made twenty thousand or twenty million. I just know that it's a finite number; there isn't an endless supply of them.

"The Bible tells of an incident in Daniel 10 when Daniel prayed for three weeks before an angel showed up to answer. The angel had tried to come sooner but was detained in battle for twenty-one days, fighting the prince of Persia. Only when Michael showed up to help the messenger angel was the angel able to fight his way through to Daniel. Where had Michael been for those twenty-one days? Neither you nor I know, but we do know this messenger angel fought *alone* for three weeks. Michael apparently was tied up someplace else and couldn't get there to help him. As important as it was for that angel to get through to give Daniel an essential prophecy, he fought without additional angelic help for days.

"See, angels aren't everywhere and there isn't an unlimited number of them. There are actually places where no angel—good or bad—is present. I don't mean to offend you, but if God took three weeks to get an angel to Daniel, my opinion is that He won't always send one to you to be at your beck and call anytime you feel you need him."

On the verge of panic, she moaned, "Then I have no hope."

"Sure you do. You're just looking in the wrong place for it. Angels are wonderful and do great things for us, but angels aren't God. Don't panic because you can't call an army of angels to your side when you need them. You have something much more powerful with you wherever you go, even when no angel is nearby. As a Christian, you have the Holy Spirit living in you. Who do you think has more power—a company of angels or the Holy Spirit? Your hope isn't in angels; it never was. Your hope and your ultimate protection are in God."

Bewildered, she stared blankly as if I'd spoken to her in Swahili. She stood there oblivious to the people waiting behind her. I didn't want to hurry her now; I enjoy watching people as truth sinks in. Gradually, understanding began to glow in her eyes and a smile crawled across her face.

"Thank you, God," she whispered.

Whirling, she strode confidently toward the door. After a few steps she turned, grinned at me, and gave me the "thumbs-up" sign.

It was my turn to whisper, "Thank you, God."

THE PROPER PERSPECTIVE

Inevitably, when I speak on the subject of angels, someone asks how Christians can be protected if angels from God don't surround them.

When I hear it, the same response always forms in my mind: "How could any believer, filled with the Holy Spirit, think our protection comes only from God's angels?"

Maybe we've talked so much about angels that we've played right into the hands of Satan himself. His primary tool is deception that misfocuses the believer, making him susceptible to further lies. Believing lies leads to destruction. Lies about angels lead people away from God. Those who think our hope is in the power of angels believe a lie that deflects them from God. Paul warned of this wrong emphasis: "Do not let anyone who delights in false humility and the worship of angels disqualify you for the prize. Such a person goes into great detail about what he has seen, and his unspiritual mind puffs him up with idle notions" (Colossians 2:18).

I believe angels do good for us. The next chapter tells some of the services they render Christians. I'm glad they exist, and I'm elated that God occasionally uses them to bless me. But, to put things in perspective, I feel the same way about my fellow Christians. They, too, are agents of God for good. Often a brother or sister ministers to me at just the right time in just the right way to deliver me. I praise God for them. But at no time do I feel I *must* have another Christian nearby to have God's presence and power. Neither do I feel I *must* have an angel nearby. Christians and angels are agents of God; they aren't God. The God who directs them is the God of the universe, the Most Holy and Most Powerful.

While I appreciate His agents, my trust is in Him. The Holy Spirit of God lives in me. I'm never alone. I'm never abandoned. Never unprotected.

It's true that sometimes the Spirit allows Satan's forces to attack me. But when that happens, He always has a purpose and a plan. Never does He abandon me; never does He leave me helpless and hopeless.

"What does the Holy Spirit do for us in this great spiritual battle?" you ask. While my personal study on this subject is ongoing, I'd like to point out a few scriptures that have encouraged me and that should encourage you.

I must remind you that this isn't a book about the Holy Spirit. The sketch shared here is brief but includes important information.

HE LIVES IN US

As Peter preached on Pentecost, he convicted his hearers of their need for salvation. Cut to the heart, the convicted crowd shouted, "What shall we do?" The Holy Spirit heard their cry for deliverance and guided Peter to an answer that gave more than hope for salvation. It gave hope for living. Through Peter's mouth the Holy Spirit promised: "Repent and be baptized, every one of you, in the name of Jesus Christ for the forgiveness of your sins. And you will receive the gift of the Holy Spirit" (Acts 2:38).

That day the disciples of Jesus baptized three thousand believing, repenting souls into Christ (Acts 2:41; Romans 6:3; Galatians 3:27).

Not only did the three thousand receive forgiveness of sins as they were added to the number of believers; they received the Holy Spirit into their lives. Sin left; God moved in.

The companionship of the Holy Spirit became integral to the hope of the apostles and all believers. All of them wanted Him in them and expected His coming with their submission to the will of God. When Peter stood before the Sanhedrin, he referred to the witness of the Holy Spirit "whom God has given to those who obey him" (Acts 5:32). Every person who obeyed God, giving her life to follow Jesus, received the Holy Spirit.

When Paul wrote Romans to encourage Christians to maintain righteousness through a life of faith, he reminded them that the Holy Spirit lived in them. He based his argument for holiness on the bedrock truth that Christians are controlled by the Spirit who lives in them (Romans 8).

That means that if your faith in Jesus led you to repent of the sinful life you once lived and to be baptized in the name of Christ, the Holy Spirit lives in you too. If you aren't aware He's there, it's time you know it and gain strength in it. The Holy Spirit lives in you, wanting to guide you. Anyone who deceives you into believing He's not there is stealing spiritual strength from you.

How important is His presence? Paul wrote, "You, however, are controlled not by the sinful nature but by the Spirit, if the Spirit of God lives in you. And if anyone does not have the Spirit of Christ, he does not belong to Christ" (Romans 8:9).

Read those words again slowly. Our Christianity depends on the Holy Spirit living in us. The Holy Spirit who represents both God and Christ brings the power of the entire Godhead into you.

Encouraging, isn't it?

HE LEADS US

We Christians must allow the Holy Spirit to lead us or we will surely lose the spiritual battle. Paul makes it clear in his theological treatise we call Romans that we must be led by the Spirit to overcome our own sinfulness. "For if you live according to the sinful nature, you will die; but if by the Spirit you put to death the misdeeds of the body, you will live, because those who are led by the Spirit of God are sons of God" (Romans 8:13–14).

Of course, the words of the Spirit given in the Scriptures are an integral part of the Spirit's leading. But there is more. The Holy Spirit guides us in ways beyond the words written in the Bible.

Doubt that?

Think about it. What Christian hasn't prayed for wisdom? Is there any mature Christian who hasn't asked God to lead him away from temptation? And how many Christians have asked for strength to face a trial? In each case, the person praying asks for something beyond what he will gain from simply reading the Bible. While truth comes clearly packaged in the Bible, the application of the truth into any individual life often comes from listening carefully to the Spirit as He answers our prayers and guides our lives. You may still be thinking that God guides you only through the words written in the Bible. But if that's true, why pray for wisdom? If the answer to your dilemma had been clearly given in Scripture, you wouldn't have asked for wisdom; you simply would have done what the Word directed. Your asking for wisdom means you have choices and you aren't sure which one to pursue. You want God to guide your life beyond the words He gave you in the Bible.

If you recall the illustration in chapter thirteen of the *id, ego,* and *superego,* you remember that part of every person wants to sin, a different part of him wants to do right, and a third part makes the daily decisions between the two. Using more biblical terms than Freud, I referred to those aspects of a person as the *flesh, consciousness,* and *spirit-controlled mind.* The flesh (called "sinful nature" in the New International Version) wants what it craves. The spirit-controlled mind wants to live in godliness and truth. The consciousness makes the decisions about how to react to the world, including choosing between doing wrong and godly service.

In this chapter, I want to emphasize how we can hear and follow the Spirit's leading instead of the flesh's craving.

Many Christians find it difficult to live by the Spirit-controlled mind. They hear the voice of the sinful nature more clearly than the voice of the Spirit. The flesh demands more loudly, often getting the attention and cooperation of the consciousness. Being led by the Spirit requires being able to hear the Spirit over the clamor of the sinful nature.

How does a believer hear the Spirit of God? Carefully. The Spirit of God isn't the only one sending messages to the consciousness. As John warned, "Dear friends, do not believe every spirit, but test the spirits to see whether they are from God, because many false prophets have gone out into the world" (1 John 4:1).

Of course, the only sure test for the message received from any spirit is the Word of God, clear and true. Anything that contradicts the Word comes from some source other than God.

When thoughts, impulses, or urges enter your mind, they may come from one of three sources: They may originate within you, they may flow from God or His forces, or of course, they may come from Satan or his forces. As I explained more thoroughly in chapter three, spiritual beings have the capability of communicating into your mind. They can project thoughts there. Some thoughts aren't yours; they've been communicated to you.

Don't panic. You don't have to prevent mind control by wearing aluminum foil on your head like a character in a situation comedy. No spiritual being but God can make you operate outside the parameters of your own will. Through our belief in what we Christians call "free moral agency," we believe that even though God *can* control us, He *doesn't*—neither does He allow any other being to control us. The only way any being, human or spiritual, can "control" your actions is through suggestion, manipulation, deception, or threat. And that isn't real control; it's seduction.

Christians want to follow urges and thoughts that lead them in righteous ways. They must avoid those that lead into sinfulness.

When a thought comes to you after you ask God for wisdom, it may be from the Holy Spirit or it may be from some evil being. When you ask God for wisdom, you ask Him to guide you to the best choice. He will. But other beings may try to confuse you by sending their own thoughts.

How, then, can we hear the Spirit of God; how can we know which thoughts are godly and which are deceptive? How can we know which are leading us to righteous actions and consequences and which are seducing to sin? The answer, like many others, resides in spiritual maturity and spiritual communion.

LEARNING TO HEAR

Those Christians who hear the voice of God have *trained* themselves to hear God. How? By learning the principle God taught to Joshua long ago. "Do not let this Book of the Law depart from your mouth; meditate on it day and night, so that you may be careful to do everything written in it. Then you will be prosperous and successful" (Joshua 1:8).

The way to hear God is to have His Word on our lips. But this must be more than simple Scripture recitation. The person wanting spiritual success must also meditate both day and night. Meditation on God and His Bible leads one to hear God clearly in every aspect of life.

Consider the following passages from Psalm 119. As you read them, look for the ways the psalmist learned to hear God more clearly. The same principles will work for you.

> I have hidden your word in my heart that I might not sin against you. Praise be to you, O LORD; teach me your decrees. With my lips I recount all the laws that come from your mouth. I rejoice in following your statutes as one rejoices in great riches. I meditate on your precepts and consider your ways. (vv. 11–15)

> Your statutes are my delight; they are my counselors. (v. 24)

> Let me understand the teaching of your precepts; then I will meditate on your wonders. (v. 27)

> I will speak of your statutes before kings and will not be put to shame, for I delight in your commands because I love them. I lift up my hands to your commands, which I love, and I meditate on your decrees. (vv. 46–48)

> Oh, how I love your law! I meditate on it all day long. Your commands make me wiser than my enemies, for they are ever with me. I have more insight than all my teachers, for I meditate on your statutes. I have more understanding than the elders, for I obey your precepts. (vv. 97–100)

> My eyes stay open through the watches of the night, that I may meditate on your promises. (v. 148)

Reading these verses from Psalm 119, I noticed a clear pattern for learning to hear God. I shudder anytime I suggest a pattern, knowing some will key on the pattern and lose the great truths behind it. But these verses show the steps for learning to listen to God. Read the entire psalm to see if you agree.

Step One: Love the Law of God

Loving God makes it easy to love the law He made. His law is holy just as He is holy. A good understanding of God's nature can be gained through understanding God's law. Those who don't know His law don't know Him or what He wants. I have little respect for those who want to tell me about God when it's obvious they don't have a clue as to God's nature or will. He is found in His revealed will.

Step Two: Obey It with Rejoicing

Halfhearted or reluctant obedience cannot lead to spiritual sensitivity. Only those who want to do His will are open to hearing it clearly. Any selfishness, private agendas, or prejudices that deter our spiritual surrender keep us from hearing the Spirit. You can't hear God clearly unless you *want* to hear Him.

Step Three: Hide It in Your Heart

Memorizing the Word makes it available for study or meditation anytime, anywhere. Jesus showed that memorization also makes Scripture handy for resisting temptation (Matthew 4:4, 7, 10). But simply memorizing the Word has little spiritual effect. Some of the most ungodly people I've met could quote verses for everything. However, memorizing Scripture for easy recollection and for meditation and understanding has great spiritual value. If I'm really thirsty for the Spirit's guidance, I must fill myself with as much of His revealed Word as possible.

Step Four: Understand What It Means

Misunderstood Scripture becomes ammunition for the evil ones. Learning what God said—rather than what someone wanted Him to have said—is essential to godliness. Tremendous harm has been done by misapplied Scripture, forcing people into slavery to those who misuse it.

I must understand the Word, or I don't have the Word—just some man's interpretation of it.

Step Five: Meditate on the Word and the Ways of God

This is where you find spiritual sensitivity. Those too busy to meditate on God, His Word, or His ways are also too busy to hear the Spirit when He speaks. They can't identify His voice within the jumble of noise permeating their fast-paced, hectic lives. Meditation tunes out that excess, useless noise, attuning us to Him. I don't meditate just on the Word, though it reveals God. I also meditate on God and His ways. I don't want to focus on the Bible so much that I lose my focus on the One who wrote it. My meditation takes me to a level of understanding and openness that makes me a spiritual antenna for the guidance of the Holy Spirit.

Step Six: Reach a Level of Wisdom and Deep Understanding

When a person learns God through the first five steps, she reaches a state of spirituality, wisdom, and understanding that gives her confidence in her ability to recognize God's direction in matters calling for spiritual perception. A person who is focused on God follows the Spirit's leading. Through growth, a person attaining this level of maturity reaches the spiritual summit where he "test[s] and approve[s] what God's will is" (Romans 12:2). He knows when he's headed in the right direction—and when he isn't. He trusts his thoughts, knowing which are ungodly and which are godly. The Spirit guides his life.

HE REPRESENTS US

As the Spirit guides our lives, we become effective soldiers in the great spiritual war being fought on earth. Soldiers who listen and obey accomplish great feats for their commander. Soldiers who don't hear can't know what the commander wants from them.

But the Spirit doesn't live in us just to direct us in this holy war. The Spirit gives blessings to us as He lives within us. He does things for us that we cannot do for ourselves.

One of the most important blessings is that the Holy Spirit communicates God to us and us to God.

Paul wrote that the Spirit brings the mind of God to us:

> As it is written: "No eye has seen, no ear has heard, no mind has conceived what God has prepared for those who love him"—but God has revealed it to us by his Spirit.
>
> The Spirit searches all things, even the deep things of God. For who among men knows the thoughts of a man except the man's spirit within him? In the same way no one knows the thoughts of God except the Spirit of God. We have not received the spirit of the world but the Spirit who is from God, that we may understand what God has freely given us. This is what we speak, not in words taught us by human wisdom but in words taught by the Spirit, expressing spiritual truths in spiritual words. The man without the Spirit does not accept the things that come from the Spirit of God, for they are foolishness to him, and he cannot understand them, because they are spiritually discerned. The spiritual man makes judgments about all things, but he himself is not subject to any man's judgment: "For who has known the mind of the Lord that he may instruct him?" But we have the mind of Christ. (1 Corinthians 2:9–16)

Just as He knows the mind of God, the Spirit knows our minds. Just as He reveals God's mind to us, He reveals our minds to God. "In the same way, the Spirit helps us in our weakness. We do not know what we ought to pray for, but the Spirit himself intercedes for us with groans that words cannot express. And he who searches our hearts knows the mind of the Spirit, because the Spirit intercedes for the saints in accordance with God's will" (Romans 8:26–27).

I like knowing that the Spirit prays for me, explaining things to God that I can't possibly express clearly.

Jane is a very godly Christian woman married to a dedicated country preacher. I'll always remember her telling me of her experience on moving day. For years, the houses they had lived in had belonged to the different churches for which her husband preached. As times changed, one church they served offered to sell their "preacher's home" and give Jane and her husband an increase in pay so they could purchase their own home. They gladly accepted.

The day came for the brothers to cart the couple's possessions from the parsonage to their newly purchased home. There was much to do. The pickups and cars couldn't carry everything in one trip. During one lull, Jane realized she was the only one in the new house; everyone else had gone for another load. The quiet, empty house offered the perfect opportunity for her to express her deep appreciation for God's wonderful blessing. At last, after all these years, she would live in her own house. No more worrying about every new hole made to hang a picture. No more asking for permission to replace a worn, faded carpet. This house belonged to them, and no deacon need be consulted about anything they did to it. She could even paint every room a different color if she liked!

I'll never forget her story.

"Joe, I tried to pray but I couldn't say anything. The only words that came from my lips were, 'God…God…God.' Nothing else got past my deeply felt emotions of love and thankfulness."

Unable to express herself, Jane needed an intercessor to explain her emotion to the God who searches our hearts. Her prayer to God was eloquent though it contained no sentences. It was a prayer of pure love, devotion, and thankfulness. The Spirit who lives within her gave the right meaning to the Father.

To those who listen to the message delivered through the Word, the Holy Spirit reveals the mind of God. To God, He reveals the innermost feelings and thoughts of the people He possesses.

God knows your heart. The Holy Spirit makes sure He does.

Why is that important? Knowing your heart, the God of heaven doesn't judge you just by a set of rules—requiring you to obey perfectly, never failing. No one can live that sinlessly. Instead God looks for the love and faith that live in your heart and judges you by their presence. Sometimes a few random actions mask your love and faith, causing you to misjudge yourself. You become too harsh and unforgiving toward yourself. The Holy Spirit makes sure God doesn't judge you on those random acts; He judges you on the faith and love in your heart. He sees beyond the deeds to the heart of the doer.

HE STRENGTHENS US

Not only does the Spirit intercede between God and me, He offers me personal strength as I live here on earth. Paul prayed, "I pray that out of his glorious riches he may strengthen you with power through his Spirit in your inner being, so that Christ may dwell in your hearts through faith" (Ephesians 3:16–17).

Just as we ask for God's leading, we also ask for strength to endure. Paul said the Spirit will give us that strength, placing it deep within us. He replaces your weakness with His strength. He does it by His power.

How else could we survive when we are "under great pressure, far beyond our ability to endure, so that we despair even of life"? (2 Corinthians 1:8b). We don't have enough strength to face life when things get that bad. Fortunately, God does. By His Spirit and by His power, He places His strength in our hearts.

Ask for it the next time you need it.

Then believe it's there. The Holy Spirit may not come with great fanfare, but He *does* come. You'll know He's there, answering your prayer, because you will endure. Thank Him for the strength He gives to get you through each day and ask Him for more for the next.

We need the strength only He can give.

Did you notice the great result of His imparted strength? "So that Christ may dwell in your hearts through faith" (Ephesians 3:17). The strength placed in us by the Holy Spirit gives us more faith. Having more faith gives Jesus a greater place in our heart.

What a wonderful gift to a soldier, battle-tired and weary on the front lines of a never-ending war. He gives strength *and* a personal visit from the Commander Himself, squeezing Himself into the battle line, fighting by my side.

DON'T LOSE HIM

Because the Spirit lives in me, there are certain things I cannot do if I want to keep Him. To win the spiritual war, I must avoid these or risk losing the Spirit who lives in me. Without Him, who will protect me from Satan's dominion?

What could make Him leave me?

Living according to my sinful nature rather than listening to the Spirit's guidance indicates that the Spirit does not live in me (Romans 8:4–15).

Participating in sinful activities that the Spirit won't be party to—like involving myself with prostitutes—violates the presence of the Spirit in my body (1 Corinthians 6:12–20).

Allowing my relationship with God to degenerate, like King Saul did, will cause the Spirit to quietly take His leave, abandoning me, leaving me vulnerable to the evil spirits ruling the world (1 Samuel 16:14).

In this great spiritual war, we cannot live like the enemy and continue in the ranks of the righteous. It is a war of commitment. The one we surrender to is the one who becomes our master (2 Peter 2:19).

PRAY FOR THE SPIRIT

For the surrendered saint, the Spirit indwells, leads, represents, and strengthens. Does He do more? I believe He does, but those words must wait for a different study.

I encourage you to pray for His leading. Thank Him for His intercession. Pray for the strength that comes from His power. Don't ignore Him. Don't doubt Him. Love Him and surrender to Him—He is the Spirit of God and the Spirit of Christ.

Thank you, God, for your Holy Spirit who guides us and fights along with us in the war that rages around us.

CHAPTER TWENTY

Are Good Angels Active in My Life?

Four of us stood at the foot of his bed, hypnotized by the labored breathing of the man in the coma, saying nothing to break the reverence of the moment. We were watching a holy man die.

Three of the four had served for many years as fellow church elders with Selton, owning a relationship with him I envied. For the few months I had been the new minister of this church, Selton's illness prevented my having much interaction with him. Mostly I knew him through his glowing reputation. It seemed everyone in the congregation had a "Selton story" that always brought a smile and a grateful word for his love. Selton Phipps loved God.

My attention drifted from the dying man on the bed to the three who stood with me. Their eyes never left him—never glancing out the window, never looking at each other. They were too busy remembering to be distracted by the present. Having heard their Selton stories, I imagined what each was remembering. Thurman was riding along with Selton, singing beautifully as they headed to some small country church where they would take turns directing the congregation in the grand old songs they loved. Willard sat in a living room with Selton, sharing the good news with the couple who lived there, teaching them the gospel that would lead them from the world to Jesus. Roy went back further in time to a time when their children were young. He sat in his backyard with Selton, cooking on the grill, watching the kids play, praying for their futures.

I felt like an intruder.

A few minutes later we rode down the elevator together, still silent. I felt a need to minister to these shepherds. Praying for wisdom, I said, "You know, if we could see with spiritual eyes, we'd see angels lingering here. If we could hear with spiritual ears, we'd hear those angels say something like, 'Selton, what are you waiting on? Quit clinging to life. We're here to take you home. Let go, and we'll go meet the Father.' " None of them responded. They looked at the floor, smiling, gently wiping their tears.

As we left, Margie, Selton's wonderful wife, and three of his daughters, Linda, Karen, and Rhonda, entered his room to take up the death watch. Though each daughter had a family of her own, none would leave the hospital for an extended period. They occasionally hurried away, attended to the needs of their families, then rushed back. They wanted to be there with their mother when the end came.

They didn't have long to wait. The next evening Selton died.

Standing outside his room at the moment of his death, I was able to offer comfort to Margie and the girls. Each daughter's husband came from the nearby waiting room, taking his wife into his arms and consoling her as best he could. They hugged and cried, feeling that confused mixture of sadness and relief that always follows lingering death.

Suddenly Rhonda raised her head from her husband's shoulder, awareness dawning in her eyes. She whispered the names of her two younger sisters, "Cheryl and Michelle." Cheryl was ten years old and Michelle eight. Too young to be allowed on this floor, they waited in the lobby on the first floor. As their mother and older sisters mourned, the younger daughters didn't even know their father was dead. They would have to be told.

Margie nodded her head when Rhonda whispered their names and started toward the elevator to tell them the end had come. I gently stopped her, wanting to know if she were up to it. "Would you prefer I tell them?" I didn't want the task; I just didn't want Margie to hurt any more than necessary. "Please." The single word spoke her appreciation eloquently.

I walked to the same elevator I had ridden with the church elders the night before, escorted by Margie, Linda, Karen, and Rhonda. I chastised myself for volunteering. Bewildered, I didn't know what to say to the children waiting a few floors below. All the way to the first floor I prayed for wisdom.

God answered.

The girls were playing a game on a table in the middle of the waiting room, kneeling beside it to better reach the pieces. They looked up, curiously observing our approach, wary at our sudden appearance. I knelt between them, wrapping my arms around them, looking into the eyes of Cheryl and then Michelle. Their mother and sisters knelt with us, holding back tears, doing their best to smile bravely for the children.

Taking a deep breath, I ended my prayer for wisdom and opened my mouth. The words that emerged surprised even me. "Have you ever seen an angel?"

The question caught their attention, eliciting a typical childlike response, "No, Silly, have you?"

That response made me smile. "Not that I know of." Pausing slightly, I changed the question, "Would you like to see an angel?"

Each responded enthusiastically, grinning, one the echo to the other, "Yeah, that would be neat. It would make us happy to see an angel!"

"Then you should be happy for your father. He saw angels just a few minutes ago."

I started to go on, explaining what I meant, but the instant recognition on their faces stopped me. They knew what I meant. Almost in slow motion, the smiles faded and tears formed in the wells of their eyes, cascading drops of instant grief onto their cheeks.

After a few moments I spoke again, explaining how angels took their father to heaven, but halfway through the teaching my words faded. There are times when hugging is much better than preaching. Their mother and older sisters wrapped them in a blanket of love, warming them, protecting them.

As I sat helplessly, watching them cry, I noticed a most unusual occurrence. Every few moments either Cheryl or Michelle would suddenly smile broadly through her tears, then just as abruptly lapse into sobbing again.

I wondered what could possibly be running through their minds, causing that reaction. Then it hit me.

They were picturing their daddy with the angels.

And they had just told me that seeing angels makes you happy.

Wouldn't it make you happy if the angels of God had just come to take your father home?

It would if you had the faith of a child.

ANGELS MINISTER TO CHRISTIANS

The angels of God do many things for God's children, including escorting them to paradise at death (Luke 16:22). The Hebrew writer made it clear that their responsibility is to minister to us. He assured us of their service by asking the rhetorical question, "Are not all angels ministering spirits sent to serve those who will inherit salvation?" (Hebrews 1:14).

They use their magnificent power to minister to us, serving us. Obviously, we humans don't have the power to command them, directing them in what they do for us. Angels obey God, doing what He sends them to do. They serve us in obedience to Him, not in obedience to us.

What kinds of things do the angels of God do for God's people? Though there are many, we'll look at only three:

- God uses angels to carry messages from Him to man.
- God uses angels to arrange blessings for humans.
- God uses angels to deliver us from harm.

Let me first list a few examples found in the Scriptures and then make applications about what they do for us today.

GOD USES ANGELS TO CARRY MESSAGES FROM HIM TO MAN

Sometimes the messages from God to us are messages of good news. Gabriel delivered the message to Mary that she would bear the Messiah (Luke 1:26–38). Angels announced the Savior's birth to shepherds in the fields (Luke 2:8–15). And angels told the women seeking Jesus' body that He had been resurrected (Matthew 28:5–7).

Sometimes the messages are warnings. Angels warned Lot to flee. "With the coming of dawn, the angels urged Lot, saying, 'Hurry! Take your wife and your two daughters who are here, or you will be swept away when the city is punished' " (Genesis 19:15). Centuries later, angels warned Joseph. "An angel of the Lord appeared to Joseph in a dream.

'Get up,' he said, 'take the child and his mother and escape to Egypt. Stay there until I tell you, for Herod is going to search for the child to kill him' " (Matthew 2:13).

Sometimes the messages contain the very law of God. Angels delivered the law to Moses to give to the people of God (Galatians 3:19).

Do angels still bring messages from God to man? If you've read the previous chapters of this book, you know I believe they do. But I *do not* believe angels are bringing any more of His law to man. The law under which we will live until the coming of Christ was given once for all (Jude 3). It came through Jesus, making it better than any law that could ever be delivered by any angel or prophet (Hebrews 1:1–4). His law replaces the one brought by angels through the prophets. Nothing they could ever say would or could supplant or replace it. As the Hebrew writer phrased it,

> For if the message spoken by angels was binding, and every violation and disobedience received its just punishment, how shall we escape if we ignore such a great salvation? This salvation, which was first announced by the Lord, was confirmed to us by those who heard him. (Hebrews 2:2–3)

Paul warned,

> But even if we or an angel from heaven should preach a gospel other than the one we preached to you, let him be eternally condemned! As we have already said, so now I say again: If anybody is preaching to you a gospel other than what you accepted, let him be eternally condemned! (Galatians 1:8–9)

Any guidance coming to you through an angel or the Holy Spirit must and will be consistent with the will of God revealed through His word. Any message beyond those boundaries isn't from God. The spirit teaching it is evil, wanting to lead people from God. Anyone listening to them will "abandon the faith and follow deceiving spirits and things taught by demons" (1 Timothy 4:1).

GOD USES ANGELS TO ARRANGE BLESSINGS FOR HUMANS

I'm intrigued by a most interesting story from the Book of Genesis that shows how God uses His angels to bring us blessings. Abraham sent a servant to go "to my country and my own relatives and get a wife for my son Isaac" (Genesis 24:4).

The servant asked a logical question when presented with such an unusual chore: "What if the woman is unwilling to come back with me to this land? Shall I then take your son back to the country you came from?" (v. 5). No doubt the servant thought Isaac ought to pick out his own wife in the first place. I would have if I were sent on such an unusual mission.

Insisting that under no circumstance was Isaac to go to that land, Abraham continued, "The LORD, the God of heaven, who brought me out of my father's household and my native land and who spoke to me and promised me on oath, saying, 'To your offspring I will give this land'—he will send his angel before you so that you can get a wife for my son from there" (v. 7).

Abraham believed that God's angels would provide a wife for his son. He was correct in that belief.

How did the angel provide a wife for Isaac? When the servant arrived at the chosen location, he waited near the well where the women came to draw evening water.

> Then he prayed, "O LORD, God of my master Abraham, give me success today, and show kindness to my master Abraham. See, I am standing beside this spring, and the daughters of the townspeople are coming out to draw water. May it be that when I say to a girl, 'Please let down your jar that I may have a drink,' and she says, 'Drink, and I'll water your camels too'—let her be the one you have chosen for your servant Isaac. By this I will know that you have shown kindness to my master."
>
> Before he had finished praying, Rebekah came out with her jar on her shoulder.… The girl was very beautiful, a virgin; no man had ever lain with her. She went down to the spring, filled her jar and came up again.
>
> The servant hurried to meet her and said, "Please give me a little water from your jar."
>
> "Drink, my lord," she said, and quickly lowered the jar to her hands and gave him a drink.
>
> After she had given him a drink, she said, "I'll draw water for your camels too, until they have finished drinking." So she quickly emptied her jar into the trough, ran back to the well to draw more water, and drew enough for all his camels. Without saying a word, the man watched her closely to learn whether or not the LORD had made his journey successful. (vv. 12–21)

God answered the prayer of the servant, keeping his promise to Abraham. How did He do it? If Abraham was correct, it was an angel who led the servant to the right place at the right time to meet the right girl. He even made sure the servant knew which of the girls drawing water was the chosen one.

That sure beats computerized dating services, doesn't it?

Now, if you're single, your eyebrows probably raised during that last Bible story. If you are a parent praying that your children will marry the right people, likely your interest intensified too.

You may be asking yourself, "Does God still use His angels to provide spouses today?" My answer is that He most certainly does.

And you believe that, too, or you wouldn't pray about it.

How could any single Christian or any concerned parent pray that God will bring the right person along and not believe that God will answer that prayer? Any prayer must be prayed in faith to be powerful. Jesus Himself said, "If you believe, you *will* receive whatever you ask for in prayer" (Matthew 21:22). He said that we *will* receive if we ask, seek, and knock (Matthew 7:7).

You know from your study of angels that God sometimes uses them to answer prayer—just as He did in the story from Genesis 24. God used an angel to get Isaac a wife, and God can use an angel to get the spouse you pray for. How? Just like He did then—by using an angel to have the right people at the right place at the right time doing the right things.

If you don't believe it, quit praying for it. Why insult God with an insincere, unbelieving request? He isn't some good-luck charm; He's the God of heaven and earth.

Now, some of you may be thinking, "Why hasn't He answered my prayer already? I've been asking for a mate, and He hasn't sent any angel to get one for me." May I suggest several possibilities for God's lack of answer to your prayer for a mate? (Or any other request you feel God hasn't answered.)

He Is Answering

The right person for you will come at the right time. Wait for Him to put everything together for the best spiritual result. Which would you rather have: a warm body now or the right person later? If you're spiritual, you'll gladly wait for the right person.

You're Not Praying in Faith

If He rewards your doubt with answered prayer, you won't thank Him for the answer, you'll think you're lucky and give the credit to coincidence.

When you believe He's listening and His power will give you what you need, He can answer. Rewarded faith grows stronger—so does rewarded doubt. He's waiting to increase your faith, not your doubt.

Your Request Is outside His Plan

He won't answer your requests for things outside the parameters of what He wants to accomplish through you or through some other person affected by your prayer. He didn't answer Jesus' prayer in the garden because He had something more important in mind. The same could be true of you; He may have a specific purpose in mind for you.

That doesn't take away any of our confidence that God answers prayer. On the contrary, John said it gives us more confidence. "This is the confidence we have in approaching God: that if we ask anything according to his will, he hears us. And if we know that he hears us—whatever we ask—we know that we have what we asked of him" (1 John 5:14– 15).

The confidence we have is that His power makes the answer to any prayer a reality. The wonderful foundation of that confidence is that He won't give us anything outside the boundaries of what He wants for us, plans for us, or plans for His cause on the earth.

The Answer Is More Important to You Than He Is

If God sees in your heart that you are so focused on a mate that you would make that mate the focus of your life, He won't give you one. Why would He give you the very thing to replace Him? He will never give you anyone or anything that you will use selfishly (James 4:2–3).

God answers prayer, bringing blessings into our lives. His blessings range from the food on our table to the spouse sitting across from us. He even gives the table. He gives health, wealth, and happiness. He loves His children, and He blesses them bountifully. Often, angels are the emissaries bringing those blessings.

Does God, then, want us all to be healthy, wealthy, and have everything we ask for? Obviously not. I don't need to discuss that here. If you've read the preceding chapters, you know that adversity and pain come to the believer. But never doubt that blessings come too. God gives them gladly. Angels bring them, probably smiling at the good fortune they deliver.

Oh, one last thing before we leave the idea of God bringing your mate into your life. God intends for you to stay with that mate as long as you live. When He gives a blessing, He intends for you to appreciate and treasure it for as long as you live.

I think that may be true of all the blessings He gives us. They aren't toys to be discarded; they are gifts from God to be cherished.

GOD USES ANGELS TO DELIVER US FROM HARM

When Jacob described what God had done for him, he referred to "the Angel who has delivered me from all harm" (Genesis 48:16). David knew about that kind of protection also. He sang about it: "The angel of the LORD encamps around those who fear him, and he delivers them" (Psalm 34:7).

When the children of Israel fled Egypt,

> The angel of God, who had been traveling in front of Israel's army, withdrew and went behind them. The pillar of cloud also moved from in front and stood behind them, coming between the armies of Egypt and Israel. Throughout the night the cloud brought darkness to the one side and light to the other side; so neither went near the other all night long. (Exodus 14:19–20)

Angels delivered the three Hebrew children from the flames of persecution in Babylon. Tied and thrown into a fire seven times hotter than any the king had ever used for punishment, they survived without even a blister.

> Then Nebuchadnezzar said, "Praise be to the God of Shadrach, Meshach and Abednego, who has sent his angel and rescued his servants! They trusted in him and defied the king's command and were willing to give up their lives rather than serve or worship any god except their own God." (Daniel 3:28)

Nebuchadnezzar believed in the protection of angels for the people of God: He watched one walk around the furnace with the three who were supposed to burn to death.

Later, a different king in Babylon, Darius, cast Daniel into a lions' den. Darius didn't want Daniel to die; his order came because he was politically trapped. Rushing to the lions' den early the next morning, he shouted to Daniel, wanting desperately to know if Daniel's God had delivered him from the lions. Daniel replied to the inquiring king, "My God sent his angel, and he shut the mouths of the lions. They have not hurt me, because I was found innocent in his sight. Nor have I ever done any wrong before you, O king" (Daniel 6:22).

If you're thinking that angels were much more active in Daniel's time than now, let me remind you that angels work beyond the borders of Babylon and outside the period of the Old Testament.

An angel delivered Peter from prison in Jerusalem in the first century. Herod had just killed the apostle James; he then arrested Peter with the same goal.

> The night before Herod was to bring him to trial, Peter was sleeping between two soldiers, bound with two chains, and sentries stood guard at the entrance. Suddenly an angel of the Lord appeared and a light shone in the cell. He struck Peter on the side and woke him up. "Quick, get up!" he said, and the chains fell off Peter's wrists.
>
> Then the angel said to him, "Put on your clothes and sandals." And Peter did so. "Wrap your cloak around you and follow me," the angel told him. Peter followed him out of the prison, but he had no idea that what the angel was doing was really happening; he thought he was seeing a vision. They passed the first and second guards and came to the iron gate leading to the city. It opened for them by itself, and they went through it. When they had walked the length of one street, suddenly the angel left him.
>
> Then Peter came to himself and said, "Now I know without a doubt that the Lord sent his angel and rescued me from Herod's clutches and from everything the Jewish people were anticipating." (Acts 12:6–11)

That story fascinates me. Obviously the angel had power over things mechanical and physical. He made the chains fall from Peter's wrists. He swung the gate open without touching it.

But he did two things that make me ponder. The first is that he could have awakened Peter in any number of ways, but he chose to do so by striking Peter on the side. Why did he punch him? Was Peter a deep sleeper? Was the angel in a hurry? It seems he was. The second thing he did was to tell Peter, "Quick, get up!"

Why be in such a hurry? Was he afraid of waking the soldiers? Did he dread having to kill or maim them if they started to raise an alarm? Surely he didn't think they could stop him; no human can defeat an angel.

Though I don't know the absolute answer to any of those questions, I do have one speculation I want you to consider. The angel's striking Peter and his quiet urging for speed obviously indicate he wanted out of that jail in a hurry. I don't think the angel feared any human intervention or that he was in a hurry to be someplace else for his next appointment. I believe it more likely he expected opposition that would challenge his level of power, making his mission more dangerous and less sure—not human opposition, but spiritual opposition. There is no doubt some bad and powerful lieutenants of Satan wanted Peter dead. They used Herod to put Peter in prison and planned to use Herod to put Peter to death. Having just used Herod to kill James, they were heady with victory, lustily anticipating another celebration when the next apostle fell.

But God wasn't ready for Peter to die. Rescuing Peter from prison would prevent the saints from wholesale fear. Reeling from James's death, the disciples needed reassurance that God still reigned in heaven and still cared for their safety. God sent an angel to rescue Peter from prison because the church needed Peter to be delivered. The angel's opposition wasn't just the humans working for Herod, it was the angels working for Satan.

Quietly, surreptitiously, he sneaked Peter from under their guard. For some unknown reason, God didn't send an army to battle Peter out; He sent a commando to slip him out.

Peter was delivered, the church rejoiced, and the Word of God spread. Later, when God was ready for Peter to come home, he wasn't rescued. Tradition tells us he was crucified upside down and that he requested that unusual posture because he felt unworthy of being crucified upright like Jesus. Whether he died that way or not, he *did* die. No one is protected to live on this earth forever.

With that reminder of reality and spiritual war, let me hasten to say that we are protected by angels who minister to us. I've made it clear in other chapters that persecution and trials will come. I've given you serious thoughts to ponder when they do. But have you yet asked yourself, "Why don't persecutions and trials come more often? Why don't the evil angels just wipe out all the Christians and assume even more influence over the rest of the people of the earth?"

The reason is that God protects us, delivering us from things that could destroy us. Yes, He sometimes lets Christians die, but most of us continue to live with only minor physical mishaps or diseases that aggravate us but don't kill us. With all the evil that humans do, all the cancer cells floating in any person's body, and all the things around us that could maim or kill, why do so many of us succeed in life? The reason is simple: God loves us and protects us.

More than just wanting us to survive, He wants us to succeed. He doesn't want us to live lives focused on worldly success, but He does want us to live abundantly. Jesus said it: "I have come that they may have life, and have it to the full" (John 10:10).

"Have it to the full." I like that, don't you?

God wants that for us, and He gives it to us. He, His Son, and His Spirit protect and bless us. They often use angels as the agents for those blessings. They use them for our protection.

I pray for God's protection from the evil one. Jesus taught me to. In the model prayer (often called the Lord's Prayer) He ended with "deliver us from the evil one" (Matthew 6:13). I ask God to protect my family and me. I ask Him for the protection of others, naming them specifically. I know that when Satan's hordes can't get to me, I am free to gain financially, to live healthily, and to work effectively. Without their interruption and with God's leading, my life is indeed one that is abundant. Full. Wonderful.

I pray for the physical health of those on my prayer list. I pray for their financial and physical needs. I pray for their effectiveness in their family roles, church activities, and employment responsibilities.

God answers those prayers. Through His mighty power, His Holy Spirit, and His loyal angels, He watches over us, granting our requests as a good Father. When He chooses to let pain or difficulty come, there is always a purpose and always a hidden blessing to come later. He promised it: "And we know that in all things God works for the good of those who love him, who have been called according to his purpose" (Romans 8:28).

THE HEAVENLY REVELATION

Sometimes I think about what it will be like when I stumble through heaven, overwhelmed at all that is around me, swiveling my head rapidly to take it all in. I'll see angels of all kinds, godly people singing, and the Loving Light streaming from the throne.

Somewhere, sometime, in that introduction to the home of God, I expect to hear an angel call my name. He'll know me, though I won't yet know him.

"Joe. Good to see you here. Welcome home."

"Thank you, I'm glad I'm here. I…I…I don't know what to say or what to ask. I'm reeling, staggered by the splendor."

"Take your time. Worship the King. You'll be here forever; there's no need to be in any hurry about anything."

"Wait. Before you leave, may I ask one thing. You know me. How? Do you angels know everything?"

"No. There is much we don't know. I know you because we've met before—at least in a manner of speaking. I was there, watching, helping, guarding. You just didn't know I was there."

"When? Can you tell me when and what was happening? I've wanted to know these things for a long time. Make them clear for me. Tell me what happened."

"Well, I wasn't always the angel sent to help you. But I remember once when..."

And so I expect it to go. I won't worship him, but I'll surely thank him. And all the others.

So will you.

CHAPTER TWENTY-ONE

How Do God's People—Living and Dead—Help Us?

The ringing grated through to my brain, refusing to go away, doggedly dragging me awake. I looked at the phone, wondering who it was this time, then slowly focused on the glowing red numbers across the room. Two o'clock. It figured; they seemed to always come between two and three in the morning.

"Hello." The word rumbled deep in my throat, vocal chords refusing to wake up, protesting the impolite intrusion into their rest. That was okay with me; I wanted the caller to know I'd been asleep. When I was younger I would try slinging the sleep from my voice when the phone rang by running "hellos" up and down a distorted musical scale before I picked up the receiver. After passing forty, I no longer felt the need to impress people with twenty-four-hour alertness. Now I've reached the age where I want them to realize they have wakened me. Maybe one of them will recognize that some night, apologize, and call back the next day. Maybe. But it hasn't happened yet.

"Are you Joe Beam?"

"Um-hmm."

"Are you the Joe Beam who spoke for a youth ministers' conference in the Northeast a few months ago?"

"Yeah, that's me. How can I help you?"

"My name's Byron. I heard you speak there. You talked about going through some tough times. I, uh, know you know what it is to face the consequences of your own sin."

He paused, waiting to see how I'd respond. By now I was awake enough to pull my spiritual senses together. If this turned out to be one of those "I'm-awake-so-I-thought-you'd-be-awake-and-we-can-chat" calls, I would rebuke him smartly. My heart told me it wasn't. I sensed I had a hurting young man on the other end of the line and that he needed help right now.

"That's right, Byron, I know what it's like to sin and pay dearly."

He started sobbing quietly into my ear from a thousand miles away.

"Can you tell me anything to keep me from using this gun in my hand? All I can think of is that I want to die. I can't face what I've done."

"Where are you, Byron?"

"In my office at church. I am…I was the youth minister here. All my things have to be out of here by tomorrow." Then, in a short burst of defiance, "Maybe I'll just let them take this stuff out themselves—and my body with it." The defiance died as quickly as it erupted. Again, a lonely young man sat crying alone, broken.

"What did you do, Byron?" I didn't know if he'd answer, but I figured we'd better get to the heart of this rapidly, before one of his mood swings thrust a blazing barrel into his mouth.

He sighed deeply, "I molested a boy in my youth group. I'm going to jail; that's what the police say. My lawyer says it too. The church here fired me. The members avoid me as if I had leprosy." He gave a bitter little laugh, "I guess I do."

I lay on my secure bed listening to a desperate man who felt no security at all. Silently I prayed, "Child abuse. Lord, you know I have trouble helping people who have hurt children. Please guide me through every word of this one. Fill my heart with love for this man." I made no comment, waiting for him to finish.

Now he talked slowly, quietly. "I have a wife and a baby daughter, just six months old. My wife can't decide whether to take my baby and get away from me or stay and help me through this. I can't let her make that decision. It isn't fair to her."

He paused again, a moan escaping him. "I won't be able to make it if she does leave. So I'm sitting here, ready to die. It's best for everybody. The church can move on. The boy can forgive me when he sees how sorry I am. My daughter won't grow up hearing how perverted her daddy is."

"If you're so convinced of that, why did you call me?"

"I don't know. Your name just came to mind and then I remembered the story you shared with us about your own sin. I know it was different from mine, but somehow I thought you might understand. Remember when you made them turn the tape recorder off and laid bare your soul to us?"

"Yes, I remember. I don't do that often, Byron. Sometimes I tell audiences a little of what happened to me but seldom as candidly as I did that day."

"Do you remember me? Can you place who I am?"

"No. There were a couple hundred of you youth ministers and your spouses. I don't know you. But I do know one thing, Byron. There was obviously a reason I stopped the recorder and spilled my guts to you guys. It must be the same reason my name came to your mind tonight. God sent me there to minister to you, and now He's given me the responsibility of keeping you alive. I didn't plan to open my heart so wide in that seminar; God must have wanted me to do it for you, Byron. You called me because God hasn't given up on you."

His voice was timid, almost childlike, "Do you really believe that?"

"Yes, Byron, with all my heart. Now listen for a few minutes while I tell you why you should live. Molesting that boy was a sin; you know that. It was wrong, and you should never do anything like that again.

"You may go to jail. That's okay. Jesus said that when you violate the law you pay the penalty. You know His reference to it in the Sermon on the Mount. But remember, Byron, God loves and leads those in jail just like He leads those in other situations. It isn't where *you* are that matters; it's where your *heart* is.

"Are you penitent about your sin?"

"Yes. Oh, God, yes. I'm so sorry. If God can forgive me, I'll never do it again."

"Good. But you'll need help not to do it again. If evil beings tempted you with it once, they can find the weakness in you to tempt you again. You need the right kind of Christian counseling to learn how to deal with that temptation. When the desire comes again, don't take it as a sign you're rotten and no good. That's what the evil ones will want you to believe; they can use your spiritual depression to defeat you. When you find yourself tempted, just remember they're hitting a weak spot in you. Don't let them use it. But don't try to fight the forces of Satan alone; find someone to cover your weakness with his or her strength.

"Now, about your daughter. Listen carefully. If you kill yourself, there is no doubt she *will* hear about why you did it. Some busybody will insist on ensuring her knowledge of her father's sin that led to his suicide. She'll bear a terrible burden—alone. She'll never know the good in you, the heart you have. All she'll know is that the man who gave her life did some terrible thing and then hurled himself headlong into eternity without so much as a thought about what she would face later.

"If you stay alive, she still may hear about your sin when she gets older. I figure she will; people can be cruel. But if she knows you, sees your heart, and knows your love, she won't be crushed by it. You'll be there to wrap her in your arms and reassure her of God's grace and forgiveness. She can forgive you then. It will be harder for her to forgive you if you abandon her.

"She will face your sin someday, Byron. The question is whether you will selfishly make her face it alone by killing yourself. Dying by your own hand is the most selfish thing you can do. It shows only concern for yourself. Where's your concern for your wife, for your baby? Don't make them face this alone.

"You face what is coming, Byron. If they put you in jail, serve God there. When you get out, keep serving God. You likely won't ever be a youth minister again, but you can always be a Christian. God uses people in other positions than youth ministry, you know. You have to live, Byron. It's the only responsible, loving, Christian thing to do.

"God will bring you blessings somewhere in the future that will make you glad you did. You know He will; you've heard my story. It's true my sin was different. Society looks at what I did differently; no one wanted to put me in jail. Leaving your wife to live a worldly life isn't a headline-making sin. Even at that, I publicly humiliated myself by what I did and lost relationships with people who were dear to me. But you know my story, Byron. You see where I am now and what God is doing for me. He'll do that for you too—if you let Him. He can't do it for you if you kill yourself.

"Now, what are you going to do?"

His sobbing had stopped sometime during my soliloquy. Byron was thinking. I was praying. I had nothing else to say until I heard his response. Time isn't important—even to a sleepy man—when spiritual matters are at stake.

"I'm going home to my wife and daughter. I…I mean, God and I…will face what is ahead together. I guess I thought God had left me and that I faced this alone. He hasn't though, has He?"

"No, Byron, committing a sin doesn't make Him leave. He only leaves when you submit to sin as your master. He leaves then because He refuses to share you. You sinned, Byron, but I can tell from your call that you haven't been overcome by sin. Sin isn't your master. God will stay with you. He's forgiven you.

"And, Byron, I forgive you too."

He cried again, but this time it was different. I no longer heard the tears of despair. Now I heard only tears of cleansing and hope.

"Go home, Byron. Whatever happens, whoever leaves you, God will be there...and so will I. Just call when you need me."

"Good night, brother."

"Good night, my young brother, I'll pray for you."

THERE FOR EACH OTHER

I never will get used to the late-night calls. Sometimes I find myself musing about how nice it would be if crises struck people around two in the afternoon. And sometimes they do. People don't call just at two in the morning; they call all hours of the day and night.

Most of the time they call for me. Sometimes they call for my wife. Alice isn't trained in counseling, but her gentle, sweet heart makes her a wonderful helper. Because of the struggles earlier in our life, some women call her to ask how to survive a marital breakup. They see us as their hope: "If God brought Joe and Alice back together, maybe He will do the same for us."

Taking time to talk is never convenient, but it's always essential. Dinners cool, the most exciting innings of ball games go unwatched, and children learn patience. Neither of us looks forward to it; hearing another person's pain makes you a participant in that pain.

We do it because God wants us to do it.

God intended that every Christian help other Christians, giving them the comfort they need. He comforts us so we can comfort others. Paul wrote about it: "Praise be to the God and Father of our Lord Jesus Christ, the Father of compassion and the God of all comfort, who comforts us in all our troubles, *so that we can comfort those in any trouble with the comfort we ourselves have received from God*" (2 Corinthians 1:3–4).

Did you notice he used the word *comfort* four times in these two verses? He definitely wants us to get the point. It is the koine Greek word that means "comfort, encourage, cheer up."[1] Those who have been comforted through some struggle or ordeal can comfort others who struggle—encouraging and cheering them. Those who have received comfort are better at giving comfort than those who haven't.

- Parents who lose children are the best comforters for parents who lose children.
- Parents of retarded or handicapped children can better understand and minister to other parents who have children born with mental or physical handicaps.
- Christians facing divorce are best comforted by those who have struggled through divorce and have found the healing and comfort of God to overcome and heal.
- Those dying graciously are the best ministers to Christians who have just been diagnosed as terminal.
- A Christian with AIDS knows how to minister to others who contract the disease, leading them into a peaceful communion with God.
- A couple whose marriage was shattered by adultery and then healed by the power of God are the ones who can help others overcome their own shattering, finding the healing they need to sustain their marriage.

You get the point.

Even when the comfort you received came as you healed of your own sin, God comforted you so that you could comfort others. I'm glad we've reached a time when Christians healed of terrible sins can preach and teach in churches. Don't misunderstand my point; sin should never be extolled or glorified. The "rob-the-bank-and-then-write-the-book" syndrome is always wrong. But truly penitent believers, ashamed of their sins, rejoicing in their forgiveness, have much to offer other Christians. They can teach and preach about sin in ways that dramatically penetrate hearts. They have been where no one should go and feel burning compassion to keep anyone else from going there. Their openness and humility communicate messages the theologians don't know.

I appreciate the theologians and scholars who are immersed in the Word. Their contribution to the church is priceless. I also appreciate the forgiven sinners, people who know God's grace from life instead of a book. Their contribution to the church is just as priceless.

No one condones my sins—certainly not I. But I continually praise God in awe and wonder that His people listen to me, a sinner, preach. I try to preach honestly and openly about where I've been and how I got there. I'm able to help Christians know where they're headed if they cease fighting valiantly in this spiritual war. I believe God spared me so I would rescue sinners.

More than fifteen years after the event, I can talk about it more openly than I could when I first returned to my spiritual senses. Why do I talk about those things in my life, dredging up my past again and again? Why not just preach like everyone else and never mention my story? Some of my friends encourage me to do just that. "When will you ever be allowed to forget it happened?" they ask.

From the viewpoint of feeling guilty, I *have* forgotten it. I'm ashamed it happened, but it isn't a current, humiliating shame. I feel completely, absolutely, positively forgiven. I rejoice too much in God's grace to sit around beating myself up for things I can't change. I don't let others beat me up about it either. They're not allowed to take God's grace from my mind or my heart. But reading 2 Corinthians 1 made me realize I have a mission. I, like you, must comfort others with the comfort with which I have been comforted. Refusing to do so would be ungrateful to the God who delivered me.

Though it does bring those 2 A.M. phone calls.

And it does drag Alice into the comforting business. But she does it willingly, honoring God who uses her to bless others. Alice will likely never stand before a vast audience to speak. The thought immobilizes her. She likes being a wife and mother, aspiring to no public position of glory or prestige. She'll be embarrassed to find her name in this chapter. Quiet and unassuming, she serves God without fanfare. I'm telling you about her so you will see that even a quiet Christian like Alice must reach out to comfort others. God expects it of her.

What about you?

Isn't there some comfort God has given you that brought you through some trial or sin? He means for you to use that same comfort to minister to others. Second Corinthians 1:3–4 was written for you. God "comforts us in all our troubles, *so that we can comfort those in any trouble with the comfort we ourselves have received.*" It doesn't matter how outgoing or how shy you are. It makes no difference whether you have great communication skills or you trip over every word. God comforted you so you may comfort others.

Don't hold back; go find someone to comfort!
We're here for each other. Don't withhold what God has given you.

HOW THE LIVING HELP EACH OTHER

Our Prayers Affect Each Other

In that same chapter in 2 Corinthians, Paul wrote:

> We do not want you to be uninformed, brothers, about the hardships we suffered in the province of Asia. We were under great pressure, far beyond our ability to endure, so that we despaired even of life. Indeed, in our hearts we felt the sentence of death. But this happened that we might not rely on ourselves but on God, who raises the dead. He has delivered us from such a deadly peril, and he will deliver us. On him we have set our hope that he will continue to deliver us, as *you help us by your prayers.* Then many will give thanks on our behalf for *the gracious favor granted us in answer to the prayers of many.* (2 Corinthians 1:8–11)

Facing great pressure, far beyond his ability to endure, Paul despaired of life. God delivered him. Did you notice the part his fellow Christians played in that deliverance? He said they helped him by their prayers, causing God to grant a gracious favor in response to those prayers. He made it clear it was the prayers of the *many* that brought about that blessing.

I don't know about you, but if I knew someone as spiritually strong as the apostle Paul, I would tend to think he didn't need my prayers. Surely anyone that close to God gets all he needs by his own prayers. Thinking that, I would have been wrong. Paul said he was helped by the prayers of those in Corinth and other cities. God granted him favor in answer to *their* prayers. Paul implies that deliverance would not have come if these brothers had not prayed.

That means that one way we help each other in this spiritual war is to pray for each other. Our combined prayers make a difference. They affect God and what He does.

Sometimes our prayers are the only spiritual defense a person has. Sometimes our prayers are the *only* prayers in her behalf, because sometimes she isn't even praying for herself.

We all have periods of weakness and spiritual lethargy. There are times when we don't pray, leaving our weapon of prayer lying neglected, collecting dust. If during those times, other good saints pray for us, we still have the power of prayer in our lives. Oh, not as strongly as when we add our prayers to the battle, but there just the same.

John wrote about it: "If anyone sees his brother commit a sin that does not lead to death, he should pray and God will give him life. I refer to those whose sin does not lead to death. There is a sin that leads to death. I am not saying that he should pray about that" (1 John 5:16).

I can't pray effectively for your forgiveness if you commit a sin that "leads to death." My prayers for you won't stop the judgment of God if you turn from Him to make sin your master. But for anything short of that, my prayers affect your relationship with Him. You read the words in the passage, didn't you? I pray for the brother, and God gives him life. My prayers affect God's blessing him, even if he isn't praying for himself.

If *my* prayers are that powerful for you, how powerful must they be when combined with your prayers and those of other Christians? When many Christians pray for the same thing, the power of God is unleashed in greater magnitude. If the faith of one opens a "transmission line" of power from God to him, how much power will be transmitted through the *many?* Paul said that even though he was under severe spiritual attack, despairing even of life, he was delivered by the prayers of the many.

Prayer is our major weapon in this spiritual war. When Paul wrote to the Ephesians, warning them of the powers we battle, he told them of the weapon of prayer.

> For our struggle is not against flesh and blood, but against the rulers, against the authorities, against the powers of this dark world and against the spiritual forces of evil in the heavenly realms....Take up the shield of faith, with which you can extinguish all the flaming arrows of the evil one. Take the helmet of salvation and the sword of the Spirit, which is the word of God. And *pray in the Spirit on all occasions* with all kinds of prayers and requests. With this in mind, be alert and *always keep on praying for all the saints.* (Ephesians 6:12, 16–18)

Faith and prayer. Those combined make a mighty arsenal.

Allow a suggestion here. Get together with some brothers and sisters who live righteous lives and hold strong faith. Put them in one room and make a prayer list. Pray for people present. Pray for struggling individuals who may have ceased praying for themselves. Keeping a log of your prayers, meet together once a week for two months to pray. At the completion of the two months, compare the answers with the requests.

When you see what power your prayers have in this spiritual war, you will never lay aside that weapon again. You will use it mightily to defend the believers and defeat the enemy.

Our Honesty Brings Healing

As powerful as our prayers are, we can make them more effective when we know specific weaknesses or sins to pray about.

But church folks often hide their weaknesses, preventing others from praying specifically. From outer observation of fellow Christians, it often appears that they have no struggles with temptation, no sins to mourn, no pains to heal. We don't want to appear to be the weakling in the bunch, so we, too, learn to smile our way through services, appearing pious and untouched by the world. The only thing wrong with that picture is that every Christian is tempted, every Christian sins, and every Christian suffers sometimes. When we learn to trust each other enough to reveal our needs, our struggles, and our weaknesses, we will find a higher dimension of spiritual protection.

What am I talking about?

Confession. Confession of weakness. Confession of sin.

> Is any one of you in trouble? He should pray. Is anyone happy? Let him sing songs of praise. Is any one of you sick? He should call the elders of the church to pray over him and anoint him with oil in the name of the Lord. And the prayer offered in faith will make the sick person well; the Lord will raise him up. If he has sinned, he will be forgiven. Therefore confess your sins to each other and pray for each other so that you may be healed. The prayer of a righteous man is powerful and effective. (James 5:13–16)

Troubled people should pray. Happy people should sing. Sick people should ask the elders of the church to anoint them with oil and pray for their healing. Why elders? Because the prayer of a righteous man is powerful and effective. Elders are supposed to be righteous. If they aren't, they shouldn't be elders.

Sometimes the prospect of physical healing overshadows another truth taught in that passage. After saying the sick person will be made well, James says his sins will be forgiven. Then he makes that often overlooked statement, "confess your sins to each other and pray for each other so that you may be healed."

Healed? Healed of what? Physical diseases? That appears to be considered in the context, but he takes it beyond that. He's writing about being healed of sin.

While some physical ailments may be hidden from other people, they usually reveal themselves eventually through the deterioration of the body. Sadly, spiritual or emotional ailments may remain hidden forever. A person could come to church for years, hiding a spiritual or emotional ailment, never letting it expose itself. She knows the right smiles to flash, the right words to say, and the right way to deflect any probing questions. Those who sit next to her think they know her well, while she makes sure they don't know her at all. Because other Christians don't know about her struggle, they can't use their powerful prayers to bring the power of God for healing. Even if she seeks professional help, she misses the great power brought down by the combined prayers of the believers.

I believe in medical doctors, but I also believe God is greater than medical science. The church I attend isn't charismatic, so we don't practice healing services like many charismatic churches. But as an elder in the church, I have been asked, along with my fellow elders, to anoint with oil and pray for healing. None of our elders hesitate a moment. As prescribed in James 5, we approach God with heartfelt petitions for healing. The difference in us and the charismatic churches is that we expect the healing to occur over time, rather than immediately, perhaps benefiting from the skills and medicines of science. But we believe in God's healing just as strongly as they—even for "hopeless" diseases. God heals—no matter what means He chooses.

Our prayers don't heal; He heals. But our prayers affect His decisions and methods of healing.

Just as I believe in medical doctors, I believe in counselors, psychologists, and psychiatrists. And just as I believe prayer can bring the power of God into physical healing, I believe it can bring His power into spiritual and emotional healing. Praying for a person to be healed of depression is no different, and no less important, than praying he be healed of cancer. The same wonderful power of the Godhead can be used to heal either.

I believe we should call on Him to heal those who seemingly can't break bondage to a specific sin. We should also pray for those who have anxiety attacks or depression. We should pray for those haunted by guilt, loneliness, or emptiness.

Trust Opens Doors to Confession

While most Christians wouldn't hesitate to ask the church to pray for the remission of cancer, many hide their depression, ashamed that it exists. A Christian will ask the church to pray for healing of his physical heart, but is too afraid to ask the church to pray for healing of his spiritual heart. He hides his sin either because he doesn't trust his brothers or because he is ashamed for them to see what he is really like.

He fights alone, though the army of God camps near.

When we learn to trust each other enough to confess our sins to each other, we will find that the combined prayers of the believers will give us power to overcome those sins. Paul said the prayer of the many brought God's gracious favor to him, delivering him from the great stress he endured. The prayer of the many can remove—or at least reduce—temptation.

But general prayers don't have as much power as specific prayers. When a Christian can tell other righteous Christians that he is struggling with pornography or addiction or envy or involvement with the wrong person or greed or pride or gossip or whatever else, the prayers of those righteous people will be powerful and effective in overcoming those sins.

I realize that confession of sins, hurts, weaknesses, and those other things we feel deeply carries a dimension of danger. If we confess to people who are unrighteous, they will use the information to help the evil ones, doing harm to the confessor. Gossip, slander, backbiting, and murmuring may result. I also know that some people find great power in knowing the sins or weaknesses of others. Some power-hungry Christians force others to confess their sins repeatedly, never letting them forget them, reinforcing the power and hold they have in their lives. Such abuse is absolutely evil.

Unfortunately, every blessing of God can be used in counterfeit form by evil beings pretending to be angels of light. That doesn't mean we abandon the blessing, just that we guard against misuse.

Righteous people hurt when they hear the pains, weaknesses, or sins of another. They pray for his healing. They don't explore his sin, asking morbidly curious questions, vicariously participating in the deed. They never bring it up again unless inquiry is needed to call a person to accountability until the spiritual crisis passes. When a sin is forgiven, they put it as far away as the east is from the west, not bringing it up again to anyone—not the sinner or anyone else.

When done in that godly manner, confession and prayer bring extraordinary freedom, power, and protection.

In our spiritual battle, confession and prayer bring both healing and strength. We need what they offer us. They are powerful tools to be used for helping each other in a ferocious battle.

As I accept invitations for weekend engagements with churches, I try to convince them to choose one of several seminars I offer rather than a weekend preaching service. Of course I'm willing to preach for their Sunday services, but a seminar spanning Friday night, all day Saturday, and all Sunday afternoon is much more effective. Why? Because we cover much more material in depth as I lead them through biblical models and spiritual exercises. More importantly, *it provides the opportunity to divide into small groups where people can begin to learn confession.* Yes, *confession.* I bring or train as many leaders as needed to have one for each small group, and we offer people opportunities to confess.

Since so many church folks haven't learned to confess or trust others, we ease into it slowly. No one is ever forced to confess, and no one is coerced into sharing anything they don't want to. We offer a warm, safe environment of Christian love and compassion. We offer prayer.

The results are phenomenal.

Several churches across America have participated in my seminars, and now regularly incorporate small groups into their Bible classes. These groups aren't typical care groups or zone meetings. They aren't like the small groups that focus on outreach. These groups meet during the Bible class hour—or other times during the week—and provide a place to share with immunity. The participants confess whatever they wish, never being forced to share anything at all. They share their dreams, their weaknesses, their hurts, and their sins.

It isn't as radical as it may sound. Conservative, traditional churches use the practice just as effectively as more innovative and progressive churches. It is simple, New Testament Christianity in practice.

I could fill a book telling you the spiritual success stories that have resulted. For now, let me encourage you to fight together in this spiritual war. You don't have to be alone. Many Christians want to help you—and want you to help them in the process.

To prove that true, find some righteous Christians you feel you can trust, and begin a confession group. Don't force anyone to share until he's ready. Just open up to each other, and then pray for each other.

But be careful of one thing: No one should share any weakness that directly involves another person. A few years ago a young minister asked me if he should share with a sister in his congregation the desires he felt for her. He thought that was the only way to find forgiveness and peace. I urged him not to tell her. Why? Several reasons: One is that if she were feeling the same desires toward him, he wouldn't find peace and forgiveness; he would open a door that would lead them both into sin. Another is that if she weren't feeling the same desire toward him, she'd become afraid of him. She would carefully observe his every action, often misreading him, probably seeing him as some kind of ogre. No good could come from that confession. Sharing with me was good; I could pray with him for the removal of that desire. Confessing to her would bring unwanted spiritual and moral consequences.

Avoid the dangers and pitfalls, but take advantage of the wonderful gift. Confession and prayer bring release and freedom. They remove guilt and take away desire. They give other Christians the responsibility of guiding you through any crisis.

Use them to win your spiritual battle.

Confrontation of Sin Prevents Defeat

Sometimes we help other believers in this spiritual war not by *waiting* for them to confess their sins, but by *confronting* them.

One reason God gave us the Bible is so we may use it to call Christians to correct behavior, rebuking when necessary. "All Scripture is God-breathed and is useful for teaching, *rebuking, correcting* and training in righteousness" (2 Timothy 3:16). Paul charged Titus with the responsibility: "These, then, are the things you should teach. Encourage and *rebuke* with all authority. Do not let anyone despise you" (Titus 2:15).

When Paul saw Peter acting hypocritically in Galatia, he confronted him in front of all (Galatians 2:11–14). Most times, a private rebuke is appropriate. But Peter's hypocrisy led others into hypocritical behavior; he even corrupted the loving encourager, Barnabas. He needed a public rebuke, and he got it.

We should confront others with sin they refuse to acknowledge or that affects the spiritual health of others. Waiting for that person to confess loses valuable time and sets up potential spiritual disaster. But as we use this weapon of spiritual war, there is a somber warning to be remembered. As with the other blessings God gives us through His people, this one, too, may be abused.

I dislike and avoid those misguided people who believe their mission on earth is to find fault in others and rebuke them. Those who rejoice in rebuking need to read what Jesus said about logs and splinters (Matthew 7:3–5). No one with a log in his eye need go looking for the splinter in mine. Although his own guilt drives him to find my weaknesses, *I* refuse to be tormented by *his* guilt. Torment boils inside him because of his guilt; I feel no need to allow him to shovel some of that torment onto me. You know people like that; they preach nasty sermons, write nasty articles, and say nasty things about people who aren't present. They seldom rebuke face to face, preferring the coward's way of pen and ink or distant verbal slander. They aren't focused on helping the other person; they're driven to calm the guilt in their own soul by striking out at someone else. It never removes their guilt, so they must keep striking. Like a wounded snake, they poison everything they can sink their dripping fangs into.

While acknowledging the abuse some make of confronting and rebuking, I also acknowledge that God designed those tools to be used for good. They are effective in helping us live spiritual lives. I can think of a few times when brothers or sisters have lovingly confronted me about my own spiritually inappropriate behaviors or attitudes. Each was a man or woman I respected. None lashed out at me because of his or her own guilt. I can say without reservation that each of those occasions were spiritual growth events for me. I can't say they were pleasant; it never feels good to be told you're wrong. But they brought me closer to God; they refocused me on the true enemy.

Sometimes we get so focused on the battle that we don't realize we have subtly shifted from fighting *for God* to fighting *for ourselves,* replacing His glory with our own. Like Peter in Galatia, our actions bring more harm to the church of God than good. When that happens, someone must bring us back to the truth—the truth of God, the truth about ourselves, and the truth about our behavior.

A good soldier needs others to sharpen him (Proverbs 27:17). We Christians need each other to be honest with us and to correct us. Sin hurting the believer or the church can't be tolerated. It must be confronted and corrected.

HOW THE DEAD HELP US

Some of God's people, who are active in this spiritual war, can't confront and rebuke us. Neither can they personally comfort us, though they sometimes do it indirectly as we study the stories of their lives. They are the people of God who have already gone home. They fight the war from heaven, helping us as best they can from there.

They Stand with Us

I must admit I didn't think much about this until I read Alexander Campbell's *Address on Demonology*. Toward the end of the lecture, he made a statement that riveted my attention.

> Be here we must pause; and, with this awful group of exasperated and malicious demons in our horizon, it is some relief to remember that there are many good spirits of our race, allied with ten thousand times ten thousand, and thousands of thousands, of angels of light, all of whom are angels of mercy and sentinels of defense around the dwelling of the righteous, the true *elite* of our race.

His phrasing almost sneaked past me, then called me back to alert attention. Did you notice? "There are many good spirits of *our race* allied with" angels ministering to us.

Campbell certainly isn't an authority to be equated with God, but his studious thinking makes anything he wrote worth examining. I read his statement to my bright young nephew, Dwight Lawson, a preacher of the Word. Dwight replied, "Sure, he's right. Think about it, and you'll agree. Can you think of a time when a righteous dead person mentioned in the Bible *didn't* know what was happening here? They always knew and were always concerned. They haven't left the war altogether just because they aren't here anymore. They can't be personally attacked in heaven, but they join the battle with us."

A casual tour of references to the righteous dead proves Dwight's contention about the knowledge the dead have. They always knew the events on earth, sometimes even bringing messages about the future. Three quick examples should be enough to prove the point.

The *first* comes from the Old Testament era. When King Saul urged the witch of Endor to bring Samuel from the dead, he thought Samuel could help him. When Samuel arrived, things didn't go quite as Saul planned.

> Samuel said to Saul, "Why have you disturbed me by bringing me up?"
>
> "I am in great distress," Saul said. "The Philistines are fighting

> against me, and God has turned away from me. He no longer answers me, either by prophets or by dreams. So I have called on you to tell me what to do."
>
> Samuel said, "Why do you consult me, now that the LORD has turned away from you and become your enemy? The LORD has done what he predicted through me. The LORD has torn the kingdom out of your hands and given it to one of your neighbors—to David. Because you did not obey the LORD or carry out his fierce wrath against the Amalekites, the LORD has done this to you today. The LORD will hand over both Israel and you to the Philistines, and tomorrow you and your sons will be with me. The LORD will also hand over the army of Israel to the Philistines." (1 Samuel 28:15–19)

Samuel knew Saul was fighting the Philistines. When Saul stated his purpose for wanting to talk with him, Samuel's reply showed thorough knowledge of the situation. He used words like "now" and "the Lord has torn the kingdom out of your hands and given it…to David." He knew everything that was happening and those things about to happen. He told Saul he would die the next day in battle with the Philistines.

Samuel lived in the world of the dead, not inhabiting earth any longer. But he knew what was happening on earth among the living.

The *next example* is found in the New Testament era. When Jesus tried discussing His impending death with Peter, James, and John, they gave Him no support. Peter urged Him not to go through with it, angering Jesus with his words (Matthew 16:21–23). Shortly after that, Moses and Elijah came to Him and spoke with Him about His death. "As he was praying, the appearance of his face changed, and his clothes became as bright as a flash of lightning. Two men, Moses and Elijah, appeared in glorious splendor, talking with Jesus. *They spoke about his departure, which he was about to bring to fulfillment at Jerusalem*" (Luke 9:29–31).

Both Moses and Elijah knew what was happening on earth; each knew that Jesus was about to bring the law and prophets to fulfillment in Jerusalem.

They lived in Paradise with God, with all the other righteous dead. Yet they knew what was happening on earth.

The *third example* comes from heaven itself. It doesn't give the story of a righteous dead person returning to earth. Instead, it tells of the righteous dead praying in heaven. John saw them there.

> When he opened the fifth seal, I saw under the altar the souls of those

> who had been slain because of the word of God and the testimony they had maintained. They called out in a loud voice, "How long, Sovereign Lord, holy and true, until you judge the inhabitants of the earth and avenge our blood?" Then each of them was given a white robe, and they were told to wait a little longer, until the number of their fellow servants and brothers who were to be killed as they had been was completed. (Revelation 6:9–11)

The martyrs knew they had not been avenged on earth. They were told to wait until the right time and that the vengeance would come.

They lived with Moses, Elijah, and Samuel in the presence of God. They weren't here on earth, but they knew what was happening on earth. Their blood hadn't been avenged, and they prayed for God to avenge it.

These three examples should be enough. Each shows that the righteous dead have knowledge of the happenings on earth. Can they see earth, or do they just know because the information is published in heaven? I don't know. But many Christians believe that Hebrews 12:1 teaches that the righteous dead have personal access to what occurs here. The verse says, "Therefore, since we are surrounded by such a great cloud of witnesses, let us throw off everything that hinders and the sin that so easily entangles, and let us run with perseverance the race marked out for us."

I'd like to think that the great cloud of witnesses do watch us and know what we do. Even if they can't see what is occurring, they have knowledge of earthly events. And they pray about them—effectively.

When the saints in Revelation 6 prayed to God that He avenge them on the earth, they made a specific request and were consoled as they were told to wait for the answer they desired. I'd like to think they pray for more than vengeance on those who killed them. Since they know what's happening on earth and since they still pray, I have no trouble believing they pray for us. If any of those Christians are praying for me, I know they receive just as quick and direct an answer as those praying in Revelation 6.

They Comfort Us

I believe there are people of God in heaven praying for us. Studying these passages led me to believe that my grandmother knows what happens here. She is part of that cloud of witnesses surrounding me as I run my race. I haven't any doubt that in heaven, whatever the level of her specific knowledge about me, she prays for me.

Earlier in this chapter I discussed the power of the prayers of the saints and the good they accomplish. How much more powerful must that prayer be when prayed without the filters of human doubt and struggle! Free from all vestiges of the flesh, there is nothing to inhibit or distort the purity of the faith behind the prayer. Petition prayed with belief, nothing doubting, works wonders the world can never understand.

> Jesus replied, "I tell you the truth, if you have faith and do not doubt, not only can you do what was done to the fig tree, but also you can say to this mountain, 'Go, throw yourself into the sea,' and it will be done. If you believe, you will receive whatever you ask for in prayer." (Matthew 21:21–22)

The dead have more focus than to pray about mountains swan-diving into oceans. They pray about the important things, worshiping God with all their hearts as they pray. God listened to the saints in Revelation 6. He listens to all His children, living or dead.

Yes, as novel as it may seem, I strongly believe that the dead know what is happening here. I believe that strongly enough that I'll ask you a favor. If for some reason I were to die soon, I want you to take a message to my children for me. At my funeral console my three daughters with this chapter. Read my words to them. Tell them I love them and I'll watch them throughout their lives. I'll hurt when they struggle. I'll rejoice in their triumphs.

I'll cry at their weddings.

Tell them that when they feel extra strength come from God, their daddy is praying for them. Just because he now lives in heaven doesn't mean he's forgotten them.

Tell them I'll hurt with them as they learn the tough side of life. I'll swell with pride at their successes. I'll gaze lovingly at any of my grandchildren they bear.

When you tell my retarded daughter, Angela, she'll have the toughest time understanding what you mean—and the easiest time believing it once she sorts it out in her way.

Her simplicity keeps her closer to heaven than the rest of us anyway.

THE POWER OF THE GROUP

We're all in this together—all of God's people—living or dead. When Christians act like Christians, we gain otherworldly strength from each other. We reach levels of peace beyond the world's comprehension.

When we stand together as brethren, the success of one is the success of all. The pain of any individual brings pain to the group. We participate with each other: we jointly share in a communion of lives.

We share in each person's sufferings, and we share in each person's comforts. "And our hope for you is firm, because we know that just as you *share in our sufferings,* so also you share in our comfort" (2 Corinthians 1:7).

We stand side by side with any believer being persecuted, never abandoning our brother or sister to those who attack them. "Sometimes you were publicly exposed to insult and persecution; at other times you *stood side by side* with those who were so treated" (Hebrews 10:33).

We share all of life because we share the most important thing in life—Jesus. "But if we walk in the light, as he is in the light, we *have fellowship with one another,* and the blood of Jesus, his Son, purifies us from all sin" (1 John 1:7).

Oh, Father, show us how much we need each other. Bring us close together, an army fighting victoriously for you. But, Father, even when no brother or sister stands with us, show us we still have you—and our elder brother Jesus, the best brother of all.

CHAPTER TWENTY-TWO

How Does Faith Give the Victory?

"The poor little thing just doesn't understand." She smiled one of those sweet little grandmotherly smiles as she uttered the words, oblivious to their effect. I wanted to shake her, to make her understand this was serious, not an exchange of pleasantries about the weather. Thinking back on it more than twenty-five years later, I find myself becoming as upset as if it happened this morning. How could any person rip a heart out while smiling so blithely, showing no sign of understanding or compassion?

She's dead now, surely. That was 1973, and she was old then. We put Angela in her program because people told us she had the best day school for three-year-olds. We got on the list early, waited for our call, and celebrated when Angel was accepted. I was a low-paid minister for a small church on the wrong side of the tracks. I had no social or political pull. We thanked God when our child got into her class, marveling at His goodness.

Angela did well for a child with so many physical problems. Her first surgery had come when she was only six weeks old. Two or three times a year we took her for intrusive, painful tests. Driving one hundred miles on two lane roads to spend all day waiting in one room and then another became a ritual of her early childhood.

Between waiting rooms were periods of screaming.

The tests they performed on Angel allowed no anesthesia. By the time she reached age three, Angel detested anyone in a white coat, even ice-cream salesmen.

Considering all she endured, she did well as an infant and toddler. She walked, talked, and learned her alphabet more quickly than the other kids her age at church. *Sesame Street* encouraged her to count in Spanish. We figured we had a genius on our hands, a regular chip off the old block.

Then she turned two.

She started to lag, hardly noticeable at first, but more pronounced as months rushed by. The other kids quickly passed her. We didn't panic; we just looked for the right resources to help our daughter reach her potential. That's how we found the day school.

She'd only been going there a couple of months when the sugary-sweet teacher brought her to the car. Acting as if she said this to every parent, she uttered those words through her practiced smile. No compassion, no sorrow, no support. Lightly, breezily—"The poor little thing just doesn't understand. I suggest you have her tested. She's not like the other children." Smiling, waving at other parents picking up their children, she headed back into her precious little day school. That's all she would say to us about our daughter—ever.

I hated her.

While I still resent the insensitivity and the total lack of understanding of how her words would knock us to our knees, I have long since forgiven her. I don't hate her now. Maybe she didn't know what to say or how to act. After all, how *do* you tell young parents their darling daughter is obviously retarded?

I didn't want her words to be true. Neither did Alice. We found a child psychologist and took Angel to him. I'll always remember Alice arguing with him, telling him how he couldn't be right. He said our child was retarded, IQ about 57, making her ability to learn doubtful. "She'll likely fall into the trainable category. But don't count on her getting into the EMR section of school."

"EMR?"

"Educably mentally retarded. People on that level learn specific skills that can help them live productive lives. Some of them learn well enough to live by themselves. That's not your daughter; she'll never reach that level."

Angel did fool him on that diagnosis. From the time she turned six until she turned twenty-one, she always attended the EMR classes. We moved around some, and different school systems called it different things, but it was always the higher level of education for the retarded. She never tested higher than a 57 IQ, but she always did the work on the higher level.

I know, it shouldn't be that important, but somehow it is.

Angel is twenty-nine now—a little girl in a woman's body. She's a loving, warm, happy child. God gave her wonderful teachers throughout her schooling. I praise Him for the dedicated men and women who work in special education, ministering to children the world forgets. They ministered to Angel, making her life richer, fuller. She functions very well, I think.

Alice and I love her in a special, deeply felt way. I wanted to tell you about Angel so I can explain the victory that believers have in this spiritual war. "This is the victory that has overcome the world, even our faith" (1 John 5:4).

Angel is an example of the victory that comes to us by faith. By faith, I don't see Angel as handicapped or unfortunate. By faith, both Alice and I see Angel as she shall someday be, freed from the prison of her malfunctioning body. We don't feel sad or persecuted because our daughter's brain doesn't work the same as yours. We know she's a spiritual being made in the image of God who will someday live in heaven. She won't be retarded there. And her retardation here has protected her from many of the miseries and hurts most of us face. As Solomon said, "For with much wisdom comes much sorrow; the more knowledge, the more grief" (Ecclesiastes 1:18).

Faith keeps us from pitying the "poor little thing" that others see. We see a beautiful person who will transform as she leaves this life.

That same intense faith sustains us through every part of our walk on this earth. It supports us through trials. It leads us from temptation.

It guides us to the ways of God.

WHAT IS THIS THING CALLED FAITH?

Defining faith is simple. "Now faith is being sure of what we hope for and certain of what we do not see" (Hebrews 11:1). That's simple enough, isn't it? Faith is being certain of something you can't see.

It's not defining faith that's difficult, it's living by it. Faith is more than just believing that God exists. "Without faith it is impossible to please God, because anyone who comes to him must believe that he exists and that he rewards those who earnestly seek him" (Hebrews 11:6).

Faith believes that God keeps His word, rewarding those who are His. Faith is trusting the promises you have no way to measure or authenticate until you receive. It's believing you have them when they aren't yet realities in the physical world.

Where does faith come from? In simplest terms, it comes from Scripture. You know the verse: "Faith comes from hearing the message, and the message is heard through the word of Christ" (Romans 10:17). The principle is that you believe in something you cannot see because you believe the message of the one who tells you it is there. The word of Jesus Christ is good testimony, believable and trustworthy. If He says something is true, you can be certain of it—even when you can't see it.

If you can see it, you don't need faith. Remember the definition in Hebrews 11:1? Faith is being sure of what we hope for, certain of what we don't see.

It's like a blind man led by a trained, trustworthy dog. When the dog gently pulls him into the street, he follows—even though he hears the rumble of traffic and smells the stifling perfume of exhaust. He knows danger is nearby, but he entirely trusts his life to the truthfulness of that dog.

That's what faith is.

Paul said if you live by those things you can see, you don't live by faith. "We live by faith, not by sight" (2 Corinthians 5:7). If you have to experience something with one or more of your five senses before you believe it, you don't have faith. You're walking by sight. Only when you can believe and trust something you can't experience do you live by real faith.

You can't see God with your eyes. You haven't touched Him with your hand, smelled Him in your nostrils, heard His voice rumble into your ear, or tasted Him with your tongue. Believing He's there without those physical proofs is an act of faith. You believe it because the testimony of those who have experienced Him is true. Their testimony is true because He who gave it to them is true.

When you trust God's testimony, you live by faith. When you know in your heart that all things work together for your good because He said so, that's faith. When you face death boldly, expecting the angels of God to escort you into heaven, that's faith.

When you look at your beloved handicapped child and know that someday she'll be free from that handicap, enjoying everything everyone else does, that's faith.

FAITH IN THE FUTURE

The Holy Spirit penned words through Paul to give us faith in the future, beyond this life.

> Therefore we do not lose heart. Though outwardly we are wasting away, yet inwardly we are being renewed day by day. For our light and momentary troubles are achieving for us an eternal glory that far outweighs them all. So we fix our eyes not on what is seen, but on what is unseen. For what is seen is temporary, but what is unseen is eternal.
>
> Now we know that if the earthly tent we live in is destroyed, we have a building from God, an eternal house in heaven, not built by human hands. Meanwhile we groan, longing to be clothed with our heavenly dwelling, because when we are clothed, we will not be found naked. For while we are in this tent, we groan and are burdened, because we do not wish to be unclothed but to be clothed with our heavenly dwelling, so that what is mortal may be swallowed up by life. (2 Corinthians 4:16–5:4)

By faith we believe what God said through Paul. The bodies we live in are meant for this realm—temporary tents meant for this world. These tents will fold. Our resurrection bodies will be vastly different. Paul told the Corinthians in his previous letter, "So will it be with the resurrection of the dead. The body that is sown is perishable, it is raised imperishable; it is sown in dishonor, it is raised in glory; it is sown in weakness, it is raised in power; it is sown a natural body, it is raised a spiritual body. If there is a natural body, there is also a spiritual body" (1 Corinthians 15:42–44).

Imperishable, glorious, powerful, spiritual: That's the resurrection body for all who choose to live with God in eternity.

That's the body Angel will have.

You see, there is no such thing as retardation in heaven—such handicaps exist in this realm only. Angel's brain doesn't work right because her body is perishable, weak, and natural. It is subject to decay (Romans 8:20–21). Her spirit is just as full and healthy as any other; it is simply trapped in a malfunctioning body.

When she dies—and as selfish parents we hope that doesn't happen for many, many years—she will be freed from the retardation that now affects her body. There isn't a special education section in heaven. There, at last, she can express all the things her mind can't get right now. She tries to tell us what she feels, how she thinks, but her brain works against her. She communicates on a simple, childish level. Someday, when Alice and I sit in heaven with her, we'll have all those conversations we wanted to have here—heart to heart, mind to mind.

Think about it and rejoice.

A baby isn't a baby after he dies; he's full-grown in heaven because being a baby is a function of flesh. There aren't any nurseries in heaven—no children's church; no monumental mountain of nondecaying plastic diapers; no angels preparing formula in the kitchen, squeezing drops onto their wrists to make sure the temperature is just right.

Children who die of starvation aren't fattened up at a giant banquet table in heaven. Whole, healthy people enter the gates of Paradise.

Older people suffering from memory loss because of Alzheimer's regain all those precious memories the moment they die. Paraplegics can run, jump, and dance before God. The deaf will cry joyously as they hear the harmony of the angelic chorus. The mute will join in, testing their new voices, still signing their words out of habit until they realize they need never sign again.

I can see all those things as I close my eyes and dream in faith.

I believe.

FAITH OVERCOMES TEMPTATION

Faith sustains us, making every temptation or trial lose its power over us. How? By faith we are transported beyond this world, giving us complete victory over it.

The devil can hurt me only while I live in his world. Although I walk the earth, my mind and heart live in heaven. While living in the world, I'm not part of it. For now, Jesus wants us here, representing Him; but He doesn't want us to be part of the world. His desire for us is the same as His prayer for the apostles: "My prayer is not that you take them out of the world but that you protect them from the evil one. They are not of the world, even as I am not of it" (John 17:15–16).

Our faith overcomes the world.

My friend Clay Humphries, a man who learned much about spiritual growth through his own sin, pointed out to me that faith answers every temptation. "Joe, have you ever thought about how pure faith takes the punch out of everything Satan tempts us with? A faith-filled man who is unhappy with his wife and falling in love with his secretary will end the wrong relationship and deepen the one with his wife. Why? Because he believes. His faith tells him God will bless him as he does right. God's power will change his wife or him or both of them to make that marriage be what it should be. As long as he believes that, he can never have an affair. He could never leave his wife for another. His faith in the power of God keeps him where he should be, doing what he should do.

"If we can just help people find greater faith, they'll sin less and serve more. It applies to every temptation, Joe. Who could steal anything if he believes deeply that God will supply every need? Who could seek vengeance if he believes God punishes those who deserve it and forgives those who need it? Faith, Joe. It's the answer to temptation."

When Clay first shared that thought, I doubted that its application was so widespread. I figured I could find a temptation it didn't apply to. He taught me the principle nearly a decade ago; I haven't found any exceptions yet.

The reason it makes so much sense is that temptations aim themselves at our emotions. Logic doesn't always give me the power to overcome emotion. Quoting Scripture doesn't make me have less desire for the sin facing me, though the practice may occasionally drive me to flee the opportunity. But faith goes beyond logic; it touches the emotions. Trust, belief, knowing that something is true even though I can't prove it—that's what faith is. It affects how I feel and what my heart focuses on.

The emotions evoked and increased through faith have more power than the emotions aroused by temptation.

FAITH TO GO ON

Everything I've written in this book I've written by faith. Will I always see everything just as I've phrased it here? Probably not. As I grow and learn, I continually modify my beliefs and opinions. Someone will likely show me a scripture that will lead me to change my view on some minor point I've made.

But I know that the basis of everything I've written will never change.

- I know with all my heart that God is.
- I know He rewards those who seek Him.
- I know that angels are on the earth—some good, some bad.
- I know the world belongs to Satan and that if I allow myself to love his world, I'll lose my love for God.

- I know that Jesus died to pay the debt required by the very nature of God.
- I know that through His sacrifice, I may be saved.
- I know the Holy Spirit lives in me, guiding me, protecting me.
- I know that God uses His angels to bless me.
- I know Satan uses his angels and demons to distress me in an effort to destroy me.
- I know that the spiritual battle fought around us is real, taking multiplied thousands of casualties.
- I know that God wants us to be active participants in that warfare, fighting for Him, delivering His people, finding His lost children.
- I know that angels will take me to heaven when I die (Luke 16:22).
- I know that in heaven neither I nor any other believer will ever be troubled or distressed by the limitations of flesh again—ever.

Do I ever doubt the things I know? Sure. I'm human, just like you. We all wake up some mornings wondering if any of the spiritual things we believe are true. Occasionally we doubt God Himself, questioning His existence. That's okay. God understands. He's not supersensitive. He doesn't abandon us just because we have periods of weakness. He doesn't forever view us through the capsule of a moment or an action, He looks into our hearts. He knows what we have in our hearts, even when we doubt we have anything there at all.

Hang on to His hand, even when you wonder if it's there. He never lets go of yours.

Your faith will revive, strengthen, and sustain you; and you will gain victory over the world.

FAITH TO DIE

Several years ago I ministered for a church in Montgomery, Alabama. As part of our ministry, we conducted a live, call-in radio program each Sunday evening. Sometimes the people who called to discuss the Scripture wanted to talk further. So it wasn't unusual that one of our calls led my associate minister, Doug Bush, and me to the hospital to visit a terminal patient. I'll call him Dan.

Dan had lived a most ungodly life. You name it; he had done it. For years, he had had no use for God or for anything that stood in the way of his pleasure. That arrangement had suited him as long as he had his health. Now he faced death. Dan's life had prepared him for many things, but it hadn't prepared him for the most important thing. It hadn't prepared him to die.

In our first visit, Doug set up a Bible study with Dan. Several times he returned to Dan's hospital room, Bible in hand, to teach this dying sinner about Jesus. As Dan learned the truth, he recognized his sinfulness and committed himself to God, asking Doug to baptize him. Too sick to leave the hospital, he couldn't be baptized at our church building. Doug arranged to baptize Dan in a whirlpool normally used for physical therapy. As Doug baptized the new believer into Jesus, doctors stood by, expecting Dan to die from the effort.

I wasn't there. Traveling across America on a preaching tour, I missed the new birth. I learned about it over the phone, celebrating with Doug over long-distance lines.

I didn't miss Dan's death.

The message waited for me as I stepped off the airplane—"Rush to the hospital." Tired, needing rest, I dragged myself to Dan's room to see what current crisis faced the family. They stood in the hall with Doug, talking quietly. The murmuring died as I approached, all eyes fastening on me.

After subdued greetings to the family, I turned to Doug.

"What's happening?"

"Dan's in a coma, Joe. He's clinging to life and has been for the last couple of days."

Turning to the family, I spoke words of sympathy and comfort, doing the proper ministerial thing. I figured I'd spend a few minutes with them to show my concern and then excuse myself and go home to bed. Obviously, Doug had everything under control, and I wasn't needed.

Doug's next words surprised me, shaking me.

"Joe, the doctor thinks Dan continues to fight for life because he's afraid to die. For the sake of his family and himself it would be better if he let go—went home. They want you to go in there and tell him it's okay to die."

"Wait a minute. I thought you said he's in a coma."

"Yeah. But they think he may still be able to hear. If he can, he'll listen to you. Go in there, and tell him he can die."

"Me? Doug, you taught him. You baptized him. If anyone should tell him, it should be you."

I felt guilty as I said it, glancing at the family whose eyes were glued to the pattern of the floor tile. I didn't mean to put a burden on Doug; I just didn't want one put on me either.

Doug plodded on, methodically, calmly. "Joe, you're the one he listened to on the radio. You're the preacher; I'm the associate. You're the authority figure, not me. Now, do what the family wants of you. Go in there and tell Dan he can die. He'll believe you, and that will put an end to this ordeal. He has no hope of life, and the longer he lingers, the harder it is for his family."

I looked at them again, catching the twelve-year-old daughter peeking at me before quickly looking away. Doug was right. The family needed the release, and so did Dan. My problem was I didn't know what to say or how to say it. How do you tell a man in a coma he should quit fighting and die?

I knew I couldn't turn down the request. I knew it should be me who did it, and I knew it should be done now. Pushing open the door, I entered the darkened room of the man who awaited my coming.

Standing next to his bed for a few moments, praying, I felt a tremendous spiritual burden to say the right words to this unconscious man, who appeared unable to hear. Because his doctor thought he *might* hear, I had to speak.

"Dan. This is Joe. Joe Beam from the church. I know you can't let me know whether or not you hear me, but I hope you can.

"Dan, I don't blame you for being afraid to die. If I'd lived the life you've lived, I'd be afraid too. You've lived for the devil ever since you can remember. But while you remember that, you need to remember something else—something very important, Dan. You studied the Scriptures with Doug and found the Savior. You put your trust in Him. Doug baptized you in His name.

"That means you're forgiven, Dan. Everything you did is gone, washed away by Jesus Himself. You're as clean as the newly driven snow, as pure as a newborn baby. You don't have to be afraid to meet God; you don't have a single sin on you to offend Him. He loves you, and He waits on you to come home. He paid a pretty hefty price to forgive you, Dan.

He's not going to punish you; He just wants to dry your tears and wrap you in His warmth.

"Angels are here. God sent them. They're waiting for you, Dan, and have been for a couple of days. Maybe you can sense them. They've come to take you to heaven, Dan. They'll protect you as they show you the way. They'll answer your questions and comfort you.

"Don't make them wait any longer, Dan. Go home with them. God's waiting to welcome you. It's okay to die."

Dan must have been listening. He died.

Within minutes.

He freed himself of this world and reached a new one.

He went home to Jesus, escorted by angels who rejoiced to deliver another precious soul from any further attack by satanic forces.

Discussion Questions

INTRODUCTION

1. How could "sensationalism" hinder a serious study of the unseen realm?
2. Joe writes, "The primary tool of Satan is not possession; it is deception." Do you agree with this statement? Why or why not?
3. Why would some want to completely deny the existence of the unseen realm in spite of scriptural teaching?
4. Why is it important to read this book and study Scripture on the subject of spiritual warfare?

CHAPTER 1. WHAT IS SPIRITUAL VISION?

1. Have you ever been "blinded" by a sinful situation? How did you get to that point? How did you finally see what was happening?
2. How does discerning good and evil + understanding God's Word = spiritual vision?
3. Joe writes, "You are the only barrier that cannot be overcome in opening your eyes to the unseen." Why is this statement true or untrue?
4. What do you think the unseen evil forces can and will do to hinder your spiritual vision?

CHAPTER 2. WHAT IS SATAN'S MASTER STRATEGY FOR DESTRUCTION?

1. In reference to 2 Thessalonians 2:10–12, Joe asserts, "If you really want to buy the lies that Satan sells, God will not stop you: He will even speed you on your way." Why would God do this and under what circumstances?
2. Why does Satan begin his strategy with a "darkening of understanding"? Tell about a time he darkened your understanding.
3. What is the connection between *confused thinking* and *twisted emotions,* as discussed under the heading "Hardening of the Heart"?
4. What would you tell "Jane" about her situation?
5. Why are Christians not immune to Satan's strategy?

CHAPTER 3. WHAT ARE ANGELS?

1. Were you skeptical when you read Dennis's story about his "encounter"? Why or why not? Do you believe Joe's assertion that "angels are among us"? Why or why not?
2. How do you think angels fit into the overall scheme of spiritual warfare?
3. What is the biggest difference between angels and humans?
4. What are some of the problems faced when trying to study or discuss angels with others? Is it important to do so? Why or why not?

CHAPTER 4. IS THERE REALLY A DEVIL?

1. Why do you think such a high percentage of evangelical Christians (47 percent), Catholics (69 percent), and Protestants (65 percent) doesn't believe that Satan is an actual being?
2. How would not believing in the devil make a person vulnerable?
3. Joe reasons that balancing the distinction between personal responsibility for sin and temptation from an evil being "gives us the dignity to go on." What are the usual "undignified" results of those who deny personal responsibility or deny Satan?
4. How do *you* know that Satan is real? How has he been real in *your* life?

CHAPTER 5. WHERE DID SATAN COME FROM, AND WHERE IS HE NOW?

1. What theories have you heard or entertained about Satan's origin?
2. What is the difference between God owning the world and Satan controlling the world?
3. What evidence do you see that Satan really does control the world?

CHAPTER 6. WHAT POWER DOES SATAN HAVE?

1. How does Satan seduce people? How does that differ from him forcing someone into an act of disobedience? Have you ever felt seduced by Satan? Share that experience, if you feel comfortable doing so.
2. How does the power of Satan figure in with personal responsibility for our own actions?
3. What are Satan's limitations in dealing with humanity?
4. Why should anyone "respect" Satan and his power? How would someone disrespect him?

CHAPTER 7. WHAT DO SATAN'S ANGELS DO?

1. Do you believe there are powerful evil angels at work under Satan's authority? If yes, what evidence have you seen that makes you believe it? If no, how has Satan accomplished what he has in the world without such assistance?
2. Joe asserts that "Satan [and his angels] works through nature, circumstances, and people." How are these effective tools?
3. In looking into the power of Satan's angels, why is it important to accept personal responsibility for our own sins?
4. Why does the idea of the world being regionalized under Satan's forces seem reasonable, or unreasonable, to you?

CHAPTER 8. WHAT ARE DEMONS?

1. Why is it important to understand what the word *demon* meant in Jesus' day? How is their understanding pertinent to ours?

2. What do we learn from the demoniac discussed in this chapter about demons' habitation of bodies?
3. On what basis does Joe claim that demons are not fallen angels?
4. What connection is there between *demons, gods,* and *idols?*
5. What can you do to avoid the power of evil spirits in your life?

CHAPTER 9. CAN DEMONS STILL POSSESS PEOPLE?

1. What are some possible reasons that Third World countries believe in demons and report demon possession more frequently than advanced nations?
2. What is *demonization* and how does it differ from demon possession?
3. What does it mean to give the devil a foothold? Does he have any footholds in your life now? If so, what are they?
4. Do people who are demonized have free will, or are they totally under the demon's control?

CHAPTER 10. HOW DO CHRISTIANS OVERCOME THE DEMONIC TODAY?

1. Why do many people deny demon possession today?
2. Do Christians today have the authority of Jesus to deal with demons?
3. How did Jesus' threefold ministry combat the evils that Satan brought to the human race?
4. What needs to be in place in our lives for us to overcome the demonic through the authority of Jesus?

CHAPTER 11. ARE SOME HUMANS EMPOWERED BY SATAN?

1. Have you ever encountered a situation in which you recognized someone's empowerment by Satan? Can you describe why you felt this?
2. How would it be to Satan's advantage to empower people for his purposes?
3. Joe points out three ways Satan empowers people: (1) by intensifying their personal traits, (2) by equipping them with evil angel escorts, and

(3) by deceiving them with false miracles and wonders. Which method do you think Satan uses most often? Which one is the most effective?

4. What can you do to keep from being a pawn of Satan and his evil forces?

CHAPTER 12. WHY DO CHRISTIANS SIN?

1. What did you learn from Joe's story about his experience at the fair?
2. Why do you think many Christians tend to blame themselves instead of Satan for the origination of sin in their lives?
3. How does not recognizing Satan's role in the Christian's sin cause further damage in his or her life?
4. How does James 2:13–15 actually point to Satan as the source of the Christian's sin?
5. In checking for the source of desire, Joe suggests you ask yourself some pointed questions concerning desire's focus, strength, and impending consequences. Discuss some specific evil and good desires you can identify from this "test." If you feel comfortable doing so, share a desire you identified in your life.

CHAPTER 13. HOW CAN PLEASURE BE BAD?

1. Joe writes, "Intellect guides us; emotions drive us." What might emotions drive one to do? What have you seen in your life and the lives of others that illustrates this principle?
2. How would you explain to someone how the "pleasure principle" works?
3. Why do the majority of people in the world seem to be driven by what pleases them rather than what pleases God?
4. Why are we so often unaware of the danger of evil seduction? Why do people so often "buy the lie"?
5. Joe asserts that once people reach the "craving" step in the pleasure process, they are unable to stop the sin on their own. Do you agree? Why or why not? What does Joe suggest is the only way out at this point?

CHAPTER 14. HOW DOES SATAN USE PAIN?

1. Why is pain such a powerful tool of Satan? Is it more effective than pleasure? Why or why not?

2. What lessons do you learn from Job in dealing with pain?
3. Have you ever been angry with God? How do you get past it?
4. How does Jesus respond to our anger?
5. How do you feel about Joe's statement: "No soldier is more important than the battle"? Do you agree or disagree? Why?

CHAPTER 15. HOW DOES SATAN USE RELIGION?

1. How does Satan use religion in his battle against God?
2. Why does hypocrisy turn off so many people, both Christians and non-Christians?
3. What dealings have you had with spiritual "fratricide?" How damaging has it been in the war with Satan? Can you see his hand at work? How?
4. Joe states, "Self-righteousness is arrogance—brash, snobbish, spiritual arrogance." If this attitude has been around for so long and is so unattractive, why is it still so effective?

CHAPTER 16. HOW DOES SATAN USE FAMILIES AGAINST THEMSELVES?

1. Why do you think families are so vulnerable to Satan's infiltration?
2. What methods of conflict does Satan seem to use most against families? Are they effective? Why or why not?
3. Why does abuse have such a long-term effect on a family?
4. How can doing *too much* good be bad for your family?
5. How has Satan attacked your family? What have you done or what are you doing to battle him?

CHAPTER 17. WHY DOES GOD LET SATAN HURT US?

1. Have you ever asked the question, "Why me?" or "Why them?" What circumstances led you to this thought?
2. How does God's "divine knowledge" make Him more trustworthy than ourselves in dealing with trials and difficult situations?

3. How do trials "burn away impurities?"
4. How does the "annealing" process make you more valuable for the kingdom of God?
5. Can you really be excited about suffering? Why?

CHAPTER 18. HOW DOES THE CROSS DEFEAT SATAN?

1. How does Joe's narrative of the events at the cross of Jesus make you feel? Why?
2. How do God's limitations actually help us?
3. Why does Jesus' substitutionary death on the cross bring about the opportunity of salvation for all humanity?
4. Why does Jesus' blood carry such a significance in forgiveness and salvation?
5. Why is the resurrection of Jesus so important to the Christian?

CHAPTER 19. WHY DOES THE HOLY SPIRIT LIVE IN ME?

1. Why would the protection of God's Spirit be more beneficial to a Christian than the protection of an angel?
2. How can we know God's Spirit lives *in* us?
3. How does the Holy Spirit lead us? Does this mean we are not in control of our own lives? Why or why not?
4. How does God's Word fit in with God's Spirit?
5. Have you ever felt strengthened by the Holy Spirit? Have you ever "lost" Him? Describe.

CHAPTER 20. ARE GOOD ANGELS ACTIVE IN MY LIFE?

1. Why are humans (especially Christians) so infatuated with angels? Can Satan use this infatuation to his advantage? How?
2. Do you think angels are still active today? If so, how? If not, why not?
3. Have you ever had an experience you attributed to angels?
4. What are some possible reasons that God does not answer our prayers as we desire or as quickly as we desire?

CHAPTER 21. HOW DO GOD'S PEOPLE—LIVING AND DEAD—HELP US?

1. Do you have someone you could call at 2 A.M. if you needed help? How important is it to have someone you can really trust to help you?
2. Why does the closed-off mentality that Joe mentioned exist so often in churches today?
3. How do God's people build up trust in one another to be able to be there when the need arises?
4. How does confession bring about spiritual healing in the life of a Christian? If you feel comfortable doing so, share a time when confession brought healing to your life.
5. Do you agree that the dead can help us? Why or why not?

CHAPTER 22. HOW DOES FAITH GIVE THE VICTORY?

1. How has faith in the *unseen* helped you live in the *seen* world?
2. How does faith in the resurrection affect how you live today?
3. What are some temptations that faith has answers for? Explain.
4. Are you afraid to die? Why or why not?

Notes

Chapter Three

1. Edward Myers, *A Study of Angels* (West Monroe, La.: Howard Publishing Co., 1999).

2. Gibbs, "Angels Among Us," *Time,* nd, np.

3. Kenneth L. Woodward, "Angels," *Newsweek* (27 December 1993), 52–7.

Chapter Four

1. George Barna, *What Americans Believe* (Ventura, Calif.: Regal Books, 1991), 204–6.

Chapter Six

1. Paul Bradley, *Richmond Times-Dispatch* (22 October 1993), np.

2. I don't know where Satan lives, but if I were him, I'd pick one of the two most powerful places on earth—Washington, D.C., or Hollywood.

Chapter Eight

1. In addition to being available in religious libraries, at the time of this writing, this article was also available on the Internet at http://www.mun.ca/rels/restmov/texts/acampbell/mh1841/DEMON1.HTM

2. Under the Old Testament law, a married man who had sex with a single woman was not considered an adulterer. Because he could have more than one wife, he didn't violate his covenant with a wife by having sex with another woman. Therefore, his sex with a single, unengaged woman was not a sin against his wife but against the single woman's father. Since a married woman did not have the right to any more husbands, anyone she slept with broke covenant with her husband.

By the time of the New Testament, it appears that the moors had gradually changed so that it was considered adultery if either mate had sex outside of the marriage covenant. Based on what Jesus says here, it appears that the common view of adultery was that it was a violation of the marriage covenant accomplished by having sex with another.

3. Unless otherwise noted, every statement in this chapter that logically requires a footnote will be validated by Campbell's lecture mentioned in the footnote above. To save time and to avoid interruptions in the reading, I will not list each footnote separately but simply refer you to Campbell's lecture as a whole. As to the meaning of this word, *Vine's Expository Dictionary of Biblical Words* (Nashville: Thomas Nelson, 1985) agrees substantially with Campbell.

4. International Standard Bible Encyclopaedia, Electronic Database (Biblesoft, 1996).

5. I believe the NIV misses the translation here when it uses "lifeless gods." The KJV, NKJV, and ASV all use "the dead."

6. William F. Arndt and F. Wilbur Gingrich, *A Greek-English Lexicon of the New Testament and Other Early Christian Literature* (a translation and adaptation of Walter Bauer's *Griechisch-Deutsches Worterbuch zu den Schriften des Neuen Testaments und der ubrigen urchristlichen Literatur*) (Chicago: The University of Chicago Press, 1957), 168.

7. Some commentators and Bible teachers believe that the pseudepigraphal book of Enoch implies that demons are fallen angels. Since I don't accept that Enoch is an inspired book, I doubt it makes much difference, but as I found in my research, Enoch doesn't actually argue that angels became demons but that the offspring of angels and human women became the evil spirits who roam the earth. "Now the giants, who have been born of spirit and of flesh, shall be called upon earth evil spirits, and on earth shall be their habitation. Evil spirits shall proceed from their flesh, because they were created from above; from the holy Watchers was their beginning and primary foundation. Evil spirits shall they be upon earth, and the spirits of the wicked shall they be called. The habitation of the spirits of heaven shall be in heaven; but upon earth shall be the habitation of terrestrial spirits, who are born on earth" (Enoch 15:8, Lawrence Translation).

8. Yes, there are passages where angels are referred to as spirits. (For example, see Ephesians 2:2 or Hebrews 1:14.) All angels are spirits, but not all spirits are angels!

Many passages refer to the spirit within us, our souls (e.g., James 2:26, 2 Timothy 4:22, Philemon 25, and many, many others). My argument is that the spirits of some humans stay on the earth as minions of Satan to bring misery to humans.

Chapter Nine

1. M. Scott Peck, *People of the Lie* (New York: Simon & Schuster, 1983), 182–211.

2. I personally have difficulty with religious titles, preferring the commonality of the priesthood of all believers. The religious titles used in this book are used accommodatively.

3. The Online Bible Thayer's Greek Lexicon and Brown Driver & Briggs Hebrew Lexicon (Ontario, Canada: Woodside Bible Fellowship, 1993). Licensed from the Institute for Creation Research.

4. When Paul writes that we give a place or foothold to the "devil," he must be using the word not to refer just to Satan himself but to all of Satan's hordes. Satan could not be everywhere to attack the unguarded weakness of every Christian. His minions, though, dwell throughout the nations.

5. All definitions in this paragraph are taken from Biblesoft's New Exhaustive Strong's Numbers and Concordance with Expanded Greek-Hebrew Dictionary (Biblesoft and International Bible Translators, Inc., 1994).

6. Brainwashing: Intensive, forcible indoctrination, usually political or religious, aimed at destroying a person's basic convictions and attitudes and replacing them with an alternative set of fixed beliefs (Microsoft Bookshelf 2000).

7. Interesting that the word translated "depravity" is *phthora* (fthor-ah′), which means "decay." What a chilling picture of the operation of the wicked dead. They want us to decay spiritually as their bodies decayed physically (Biblesoft's New Exhaustive Strong's Numbers and Concordance with Expanded Greek-Hebrew Dictionary).

8. The following quotes are from *Exorcism and MPD from a Catholic Perspective* by Fr. J. Mahoney. It may be found at http://207.238.20.223/exorcism.html. I strongly urge the reading of the entire article. Friar Mahoney writes:

> I have been told of Catholic priests and lay persons who under the concept of "deliverance ministry" have engaged in various forms of exorcism. At times a group of Catholics will engage in intense, prolonged, and repeated rites of exorcism. A popular culture has developed in which some Catholics, if confronted by phenomena that confuse or frighten them, will immediately diagnose the phenomena as demonic and begin a process of ordering an evil entity to leave the person. In these situations, the name of Christ and the authority of the Church is being invoked. I believe it to be a situation that is spiritually dangerous, psychologically dangerous and abusive, and scandalous. The motives of

those who engage in such activities can certainly vary. Some, with the best of intentions, may believe that they are doing good. Others may be motivated by grandiosity, a fascination with the dramatic, or the attraction of having psychological control over another human being.

There may be a tendency to view the situation as relatively benign, trusting that if indeed there is no possession present, the person will not be unduly harmed by the process. In fact that is not the case, but many who have been most severely harmed are not in a position to effectively protest.

There is substantial documentation that the victims of extreme abuse are especially susceptible to damage. Especially if the abuse involved some form of captivity and/or began during childhood, there is a process of psychological fragmentation and disruption of the person's sense of identity. There is frequently a high susceptibility to trance states and hypnosis, and a difficulty in resisting manipulation while in those states. The degree and symptoms of the fragmentation may vary, but the most severe and chronic form occurs in Multiple Personality Disorder (MPD). I will discuss the issue as it pertains to MPD, with the understanding that at least some elements may also be found in other trauma-related disorders.

The most prominent writers in the field of the treatment of MPD have noted that exorcism for MPD is therapeutically contraindicated, with various forms of harm described.

The only organized, retrospective review I am aware of was done by Dr. Fraser from the Royal Ottawa Hospital in Canada. He reviewed the experiences of a number of his patients who had undergone exorcism in various circumstances. The patients varied in religious background, as did the religion of those doing the exorcisms and the form and nature of the exorcism activity. Some exorcisms were supported by the Church or religious community of the exorcist. Some of the exorcisms had occurred before, as well as after, the diagnosis of MPD.

Based on his retrospective review of seven cases, he reached several conclusions:

- The exorcisms had an effect in that they produced a change and had an impact on the personality system.
- Alternate personalities can be, at least temporarily, "banished" and new personalities can be created in response to the sense of trauma.
- The effect in each case was severely destructive.

Chapter Ten

1. *Catholic Encyclopedia,* "Demonical Possession," http://www.newadvent.org/cathen/12315a.htm.

2. From existing Catholic liturgies and rituals, specifically *Exorcism: Chapter 1: General Rules Concerning Exorcism.* I have decided not to reveal how you may find this source. Why? For fear that the curious or impulsive will take this section of Catholic literature and try to use it to "confront demons." I can think of nothing more dangerous. If you wish to see the source, you will have to do the same research as I.

3. *Catholic Encyclopedia,* "Demonical Possession."

4. Though I have taught this for years, it was reassuring to find the same understanding in the writings of others. In his book *Deliverance from Evil Spirits,* Francis MacNutt writes:

> Charles H. Talbert, one of the foremost commentators on Luke among biblical scholars, states that Luke set forth the program for Jesus' total mission for His life during His inaugural sermon in the synagogue in Nazareth (Luke 4:16–27). It was a state-of-the-union address in which Jesus declared His three-fold mission: preaching, healing, and exorcism…
>
> Furthermore, the purpose of Luke in writing Acts was to show that the early Church continued Jesus' mission of preaching, healing, and casting out evil spirits.

5. Like Balaam, this exorcist defies all our rules, deductions, and doctrines. Balaam lived during the time of the Jews but had never heard of their God. Not only that, he worked sorcery! By all I ever learned as I received my degree in Bible, this man couldn't be one of God's. Yet he was God's prophet! Listen to the words that the Holy Spirit placed on his tongue: "The oracle of Balaam son of Beor, the oracle of one whose eye sees clearly, the oracle of one who hears the words of God, who sees a vision from the Almighty, who falls prostrate, and whose eyes are opened."

Quite a lesson to be learned in the story isn't there? Just when we figure we know whom God blesses and whom He doesn't, whom He gives power and authority to and whom He doesn't, what He will gift people to do and what He won't, we encounter someone casting out demons or hearing the words of God and receiving visions from Him. God makes it clear that we don't make His decisions.

6. Don't think that I have any problem with logic and deductions. I've done it in this book. All I want to point out is that human deductions base themselves on human skill and reasoning. And even NASA scientists have learned that there is no such thing as having perfect reasoning and skill when one is human. Even the most precise logic can contain flaws, and even the minutest flaw can so misdirect calculations and conclusions that it may result in a multimillion-dollar satellite going the wrong direction.

Souls too.

Therefore, in the realm of logic, reasoning, and deductions be careful how staunchly you stand and how jaundiced you judge. What you view as brilliance, the inhabitants of heaven may view as babbling. "For the foolishness of God is wiser than man's wisdom, and the weakness of God is stronger than man's strength" (1 Corinthians 1:25).

Chapter Eleven

1. Kenneth Barker, ed., *The New International Version Study Bible* (Grand Rapids, Mich.: Zondervan Bible Publishers, 1985), 461.

Chapter Thirteen

1. Arndt and Gingrich, *Greek-English Lexicon,* 751.
2. Ibid.

Chapter Fourteen

1. Joe Beam, *Forgiven Forever* (West Monroe, La.: Howard Publishing Co., 1998).

Chapter Seventeen

1. *Alabama Journal* (3 June 1991).

Chapter Twenty-One

1. Arndt and Gingrich, *Greek-English Lexicon,* 622–3.